*The Victorians and their Flowers*

ALREADY PUBLISHED

*Growing Fuchsias*
K. Jennings and V. Miller

*Growing Hardy Perennials*
Kenneth A. Beckett

*Growing Dahlias*
Philip Damp

*Growing Irises*
C.E. Cassidy and S. Linnegar

*Violets*
Roy E. Coombs

*1000 Decorative Plants*
J.L. Krempin

*Climbing Plants*
Kenneth A. Beckett

*Growing Lilies*
D.B. Fox

*Plant Hunting in Nepal*
Roy Lancaster

*The History of Gardens*
Christopher Thacker

*Better Gardening*
Robin Lane Fox

*Growing Cyclamen*
Gay Nightingale

*Slipper Orchids*
Robin Graham with Ronald Roy

*Growing Chrysanthemums*
Harry Randall and Alan Wren

*The Rock Gardener's Handbook*
Alan Titchmarsh

*Waterlilies*
Philip Swindells

*Country Enterprise*
Jonathan and Heather Ffrench

IN PREPARATION

*The Pelargonium Species*
William J. Webb

*Growing Roses*
Michael Gibson

*The Cottage Garden Year*
Roy Genders

*Growing Begonias*
E. Catterall

*Growing Bulbs*
Martyn Rix

*Wine Growing in England*
J.G. Barrett

# THE VICTORIANS AND THEIR FLOWERS

Nicolette Scourse

CROOM HELM
LONDON & CANBERRA

TIMBER PRESS
PORTLAND, OREGON

Text and illustrations © 1983 Nicolette Scourse
Croom Helm Ltd, Provident House, Burrell Row,
Beckenham, Kent BR3 1AT


British Library Cataloguing in Publication Data

Scourse, Nicolette
The Victorians and their flowers.
1. Plants — Public opinion 2. Public opinion —
Great Britain — History — 19th century
I. Title
581      QK46

ISBN 0-7099-2377-5


First published in the USA in 1983 by Timber Press,
PO Box 1632
Beaverton, OR 97075
USA
ISBN 0-917304-89-6

Printed and bound in Great Britain

# CONTENTS

List of Figures and Tables

Preface

Acknowledgements

1. Eighteenth-century Origins **1**

2. Mirrors of Victorian Society **9**

3. Sentiment **29**

4. Morality **47**

5. Botanical Fashion **67**

6. Foreign Exotics **95**

7. Realities **121**

8. The Passion for Detail **135**

9. Scientific Controversy **161**

Appendix: Biographical Notes **184**

Select Bibliography **189**

Glossary **192**

Indexes **193**

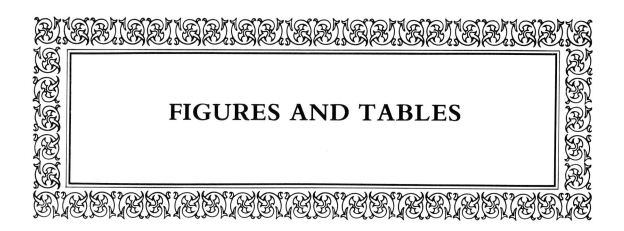

# FIGURES AND TABLES

## FIGURES

1.1 A romantic homage to Linnaeus **4**

1.2 'Group of Roses' painted by Robert John Thornton **7**

2.1 The romanticised garden **11**

2.2 and 2.3 Decorative glass and ironwork in the Conservatory, Coombe Cliff, Croydon **12**

2.4 The Conservatory, Broughton Hall, Yorkshire **13**

2.5 An example of the Italian-style garden **14**

2.6 Floral tile panels in a dairy **16**

2.7 Wardian cases **17**

2.8 An advertisement for rustic adornments **18**

2.9 A flower exhibition **19**

2.10 Cast-iron column decorated with horse chestnuts **20**

2.11 Hop-pickers **21**

2.12 Laced pinks **22**

2.13 Tulips from *The Temple of Flora* **24**

2.14 A self-portrait of Robert Dick **26**

2.15 A romanticised portrait of Robert Dick **27**

3.1 'Garden Flowers' by William Powell Frith **31**

3.2 Flower arrangement for the table **32**

3.3 Garlanded beauty **33**

3.4 'Shakespeare and his Flowers' by Clara Maria Pope **34**

3.5 'A Floral Fantasy in an Old English Garden' by Walter Crane **35**

3.6 'Hollyhock, Pink Beauty' from *Wood and Garden* by Gertrude Jekyll **36**

3.7 'Flora at play with Cupid' from *The Botanic Garden* by Erasmus Darwin **40**

3.8 The Temple of Flora at Stourhead **40**

3.9 Rustic garden reading room and tool-house **41**

3.10 'The Apiary' from *Rustic Adornments for Homes of Taste* by Shirley Hibberd **41**

4.1 'Trellis' designed by William Morris **48**

4.2 Thoughts of 'sacred meaning' over an infant's scattered bunch of flowers **50**

4.3 Miniature weeds from a cornfield **51**

4.4 The innocent infant gathering flowers **52**

4.5 Columbine or 'Folly's Flower' **55**

4.6 'Beech Hanger', Selborne **60**

4.7 Vegetable greed **61**

4.8 A bee on a globe thistle 'toils' for its 'just reward' **63**

4.9 The common twayblade orchid **64**

5.1 Hawkweed ox-tongue, a plant of Linnaeus's 'Horologe or Watch of Flora' **68**

5.2 Goat's-beard, a plant of Linnaeus's 'Horologe' **69**

5.3 Linnaeus's Table of Plant Classes **71**

5.4 The structure of the snowdrop **73**

5.5 *Bufonia tenuifolia*, named after Count Buffon **74**

5.6 A page from William Henry Fox Talbot's notebook **75**

5.7 Thereza Mary Dillwyn Llewelyn with her botanical press **78**

5.8 Bath Natural History and Antiquarian Field Club excursion **80**

5.9 A page from Robert Dick's herbarium **82**

5.10 Robert Dick's specimens of the small-flowered sweet-briar rose **83**

5.11 Robert Dick's specimen of wild angelica **84**

5.12 Robert Dick's specimen of sea spleenwort **85**

5.13 Robert Dick's specimen of hart's-tongue fern **86**

5.14 Robert Dick's specimen of royal fern **87**

5.15 The transplanting of wild plants into gardens and conservatories **88**

5.16 An advertisement for Wardian cases **90**

5.17 An indoor aquarium and fernery combined **92**

5.18 Mrs Hibberd's fernery **92**

6.1 Carpet bedding **95**

6.2 A parrot-house and vinery **96**

6.3 A small conservatory adjoining the drawing room **97**

6.4 Plants succumb to architectural embellishment **97**

6.5 Sublime mountain scenery and its attendant mishaps **100**

6.6 Vignette from *Orchidaceae of Mexico and Guatemala* by James Bateman **101**

6.7 Inside the Great Conservatory, Chatsworth **105**

6.8 The Palm House at Kew **108**

6.9 Water-lily glassware **110**

6.10 The royal water-lily **111**

6.11 Sir Joseph Paxton – architect of the Crystal Palace **113**

6.12 The elusive blue vanda orchid **116**

6.13 'Native Dinner Time' from *The Travels and Adventures of an Orchid Hunter* by Albert Millican **118**

7.1 The varnished acacia, discovered by Allan Cunningham **124**

7.2 The golden-rayed lily of Japan, introduced by Robert Fortune **126**

7.3 The cone of the sugar pine, that nearly cost David Douglas his life **127**

8.1 One of the early 'Sun Pictures' or 'Photogenic Drawings' made by William Henry Fox Talbot **136**

8.2 Pollen grain and poppy seed **137**

8.3 Anatomy of a leaf of the Venus' fly-trap **138**

8.4 Life in garden ponds and freshwater aquaria, as seen through a microscope **138**

8.5 Common mallow at different stages in the reproductive cycle **140**

8.6 The spring mechanism of broom **142**

8.7 A honeysuckle flower opened to show its nectary **144**

8.8 An elephant hawkmoth on a honeysuckle plant **144**

8.9 The butterfly orchid **149**

8.10 A spotted orchid hybrid **150**

8.11 A demonstration showing the extraction of *pollinia* from an orchid **150**

8.12 The man orchid **151**

8.13 The Madagascan orchid **152**

8.14 The 'tail-piece' of *Orchidaceae of Mexico and Guatemala* by James Bateman **154**

8.15 The sensitive plant **155**

8.16 The Venus' fly-trap **156**

8.17 The sundew **156**

8.18 A sundew leaf ready to clasp insects **157**

9.1 The pitcher plant **162**

9.2 Plants and their uses **163**

9.3 Common mullein **165**

9.4 The baobab tree, reputedly six thousand years old **167**

9.5 The fossil of a tree trunk, about 150 million years old **167**

9.6 William ('Strata') Smith's exposed cliff with sloping strata **168**

9.7 The leaf of a fern in a block of coal **170**

9.8 Horsetail growing today **171**

9.9 Robert Dick's specimen of horsetail **171**

9.10 Flower–insect co-operation: Design or selection pressure? **173**

9.11 Pansies, wild to cultivated **175**

9.12 The colour wheel **178**

**Table**

5.1 Botanical interests across families **76**

# PREFACE

The love of flowers kindles rapport across the centuries. Shared enthusiasms, wonder and enquiry render the separation in time irrelevant; something akin to companionship and understanding grows from the common ground of admiration, horticultural daydreams and even dislikes. Yet the appeal of flowers is not timeless – a wild rose from the nineteenth century is a different being from that portrayed in the seventeenth century. Each is a mirror of its time. In describing, eulogising, explaining and recommending the decorative use of flowers, Victorian flower writers left images of themselves and their time as well as of their flowers. The flowers, the people who wrote about them and the Victorian age were inseparable. This book is about flowers as the Victorians – with all their subjective views, prejudices and fantasies – saw them.

Gardeners, flower arrangers, amateur naturalists, botanists, artists and poets admire, create and understand flowers from a different viewpoint but unite in their overriding passion for their subject. My own enthusiasm pervades the description of the flowers in this book and is inevitably reflected in the interests and thoughts of the Victorians featured in the pages that follow. They are a varied circle of friends – with the occasional enemy – whose thoughts are sometimes beautiful and evocative, even philosophical and spiritual. Many have aspirations of grandeur or poetic inclination; some have travelled and survived against all odds in the most exotic of wildernesses while others have spent years in exploring far into the tiny world of fields and woodland bordering their own back

gardens; some have suffered for flowers, and a few are lonely, tragic figures, sacrificing themselves and their health in the quest for floral beauty and for the truth about the natural world. My introduction to this circle of friends was by chance but soon I found myself captivated by the era and the people who imbued the commonplace flowers of today with such living qualities of personality and romance. Looking at flowers will never be quite the same again: when lingering among hollyhocks or seeing the fanned leaves of a horsechestnut waving in the breeze, I shall hear the Victorian echoes of Louisa Anne Twamley and John Ellor Taylor.

So many Victorian ideals and roots of fashion were in evidence before 1837 that I have tended to equate the Victorian age with the nineteenth century. I have not limited myself to the angiosperms (strictly flowering plants) for ferns and pine cones were as much part of the Victorian house and garden as the gaudy-coloured flowers; the charisma of ferns and pines and their wild habitats held a spell over every Victorian for several decades. The quotations I have used come from their original sources (the editions are quoted in the bibliography), except in a very few cases. Where possible I have checked modern information sources, in several instances finding unexpected discrepancies between authors which accounts for an occasional lack of specific information where the reader might expect it.

Part of the nineteenth century falls within the 100-year span of the Golden Age of Flower Books and I have selected illustrations from some of the finest such as James Bateman's

*Orchidaceae of Mexico and Guatemala* and Sir Joseph Dalton Hooker's *The Rhododendrons of Sikkim-Himalaya*, and the best hand-coloured editions of the popular books of the middle classes such as Jane Loudon's *The Ladies' Flower-Garden of Ornamental Annuals*. In this book I have featured representative artists and the most talented botanical illustrators of the age: Mrs Withers, James Andrews (*Flora's Gems*), Walter Hood Fitch, Kate Greenaway, Walter Crane, William Morris, Clara Maria Pope, James Sowerby, William Powell Frith and Charles Collins. As well as being an era of excellence in the traditional means of portraying flowers, it was a time of exciting scientific discovery which introduced a new technique of accurate illustration – the photograph. Nothing captures the quintessence of the Victorian age so well: its atmosphere, its opinion of itself and its stance. As well as including records of people and events it seemed apt that the early photographic representation of plants should combine with the popular Victorian pastime of viewing flowers through the microscope in an early 'Sun Picture' of sections of plants by William Henry Fox Talbot.

I am much indebted to Robert Lassam, Curator of the Fox Talbot Museum, Lacock Abbey, who drew my attention to Fox Talbot's botanical interests, his early 'Sun Pictures' of plants and particularly to an unpublished botanical notebook of Talbot's which was photographed with Robert Lassam's kind assistance. I am extremely grateful to Richard Morris for the John Dillwyn Llewelyn photograph of Thereza Mary Llewelyn from a family album, which he printed from a negative made in contact with the original print, and then printed using silver chloride in the same way as the original. I am also indebted to Richard Morris for background information. My thanks go to Miss Anne Powell for lending the beautiful flower album of poems and watercolours by Thereza's parents, exquisite in itself but of particular interest in this book in its unique historical and botanical context. My sincere thanks go to Michael Pearman, the Librarian and Archivist, Chatsworth who was undaunted by my difficult request for a photograph to be taken of the Chinese wallpaper in the Wellington bedroom – of a detail I could not even define as I had never seen it. He directed photography with an unerring eye for composition and visual

interest suitable for my purpose for which I am most grateful. I am further indebted to him for background information and for seeking out the only list of plants which grew in Chatsworth's Great Conservatory: an obscure source in High German with old plant nomenclature dating from 1852. I have Elsbeth Symes to thank for translating this. For enabling me to trace and describe these plants my thanks are due to my mother, Margaret West, who searched and arduously transported books on tropical plants, and also to the untiring librarians at Bath Reference Library, who carried books in relays from the Strong Room. Without the willing efforts of these staff in tracing and obtaining books, much of my research and the lengthy searches for illustrations of very specific subjects would not have been possible. I was also allowed access to their fine collection of Valentine cards – my grateful thanks for all of this assistance.

I am indebted to Thurso Library and the museum staff of the early 1970s for allowing me to browse and take photographs of the Robert Dick Herbarium which seems to be so little known outside its home county. My thanks are also due to Professor R.G. West FRS of the Botany Department at Cambridge University for making available Charles Darwin's microscope and its instruction manual and to James Scourse of the same Department for viewing it on my behalf and for providing background information on geology, fossil specimens and pollen grains. I am also grateful to the staff of the Rare Books Room, Cambridge University, for their kind attentions between 1973 and 1977 and more recently the staff of the Anderson Room.

For generously allowing me a free hand to browse and photograph books in their libraries I am indebted to Rosemary Verey of Barnsley House, and Henry Tempest of Broughton Hall, who also kindly offered the opportunity to photograph the Nesfield gardens and Conservatory at Broughton. My thanks go to Jenny Rumens, Joyce Bull and Andrew Scourse for the loan of their books; John Presland who sought out and photographed specific plants and kindly assisted with identification; Westonbirt Arboretum for material for illustration; the Librarian of the Linnean Society of London; Paisley Museum and Art Galleries for providing information, and the Victorian Society for their assistance; Arthur Sanderson & Son, the London Borough of Croydon, Easton Farm Park and Dr J.B. Tucker, for their generosity in supplying photographs and factual background.

I am most grateful to Adam Tegetmeier for his endless patience on our various photographic expeditions and for his technical advice and skill in making the best of my own amateur efforts. It is a pleasure to thank Nola Edwards, the illustrator, who took immense trouble with her drawings regardless of some difficult subjects and problems encountered with living species.

Very sincere thanks go to Jackie Reeves who generously undertook typing from a rough, pencilled, patchwork draft in order to save me time, and other kind friends who helped with typing, Caroline Lawrence and Jean Allen. My thanks also go to other good friends who have helped in many different ways. With gratitude I would like to acknowledge a barrage of stimulating ideas, constructive criticism and above all encouragement and enthusiasm from the late Tony Adams, without whom this book would never have developed from its early awkward phases. Lastly, my thanks go to my husband for his patience while living with the several drafts of the manuscript, for checking and valued criticism, and for sharing the difficulties of field photography.

## Note on Sources

Where only one source for an author is cited in the Bibliography, the title is not given on every occasion in the main text in order not to detract from the flow of the book.

N.J.S.S.
Bradford-on-Avon

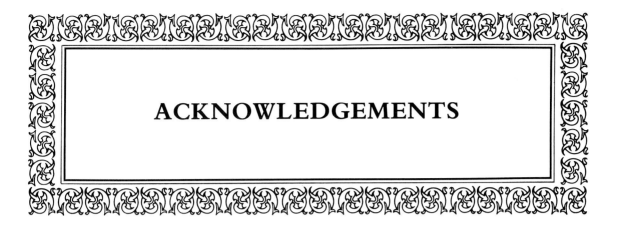

# ACKNOWLEDGEMENTS

Extract from John Dillwyn Llewelyn's letter to his father, 22 November 1843 by courtesy of Richard Morris.

Extract from William Henry Fox Talbot's letter to his mother, 16 September 1814 published in *William Henry Fox Talbot: Pioneer of photography and man of science* by H.J.P. Arnold, 1977 – by courtesy of Anthony Burnett-Brown, Lacock Abbey.

# Chapter 1

# EIGHTEENTH-CENTURY ORIGINS

Roses, pinks and hollyhocks make strange subjects for eulogies on filial duty, chastity and the mother image; stranger still as 'worthy advocates of morality and religion'. Yet these unexpected images were an everyday part of the nineteenth-century world of flowers. This world was essentially a pastiche of Victorian society: a garden of paradoxes where blushing flowers of romance flourished beside efficient floral machines with meticulous pistons and springs; virtuous flower-heads bowed true to ideals of humility and self-sacrifice while competitive scramblers strangled their fellows in a vegetable version of the industrial world; ruthless flowers killed feeble insects unable to pay for a floral favour and buds unfurled into paragons of christian perfection.

Such a bizarre collection of altruistic flowers, vegetable criminals and moral messengers seems more remote than a hundred years when one thinks of today's essentially useful flowers. Now they are beautiful potential for a garden vista, a flower arrangement or a colourful part of the workings of a living community. The more beguiling old-world flower with its sentiment, morality, snobbery and controversy disappeared with the Victorian attitudes and preoccupations which created it. Happily, period writings and illustrations can recreate these delightful images among today's flowers and bring to life a lost romantic world.

In drawing rooms and front parlours elegant matrons and their daughters dabbled away the hours with flower albums, genteel botanising and poetic thoughts on romance, morality and flower lore. Alternatively they turned their attentions to the room's fashionable adornments: glass tanks with underwater grottoes and wild newts, fish, duckweed and ferns. In extraordinarily ornamented greenhouses, gentlemen strove to collect and bring into flower the latest plant novelties from abroad, and read about their stranger structures as a prerequisite of respectability. Fanatical collectors had vast greenhouses (or 'stove houses' as they were called) in which they created escapist dreams of the Empire's tropical forests – entire landscapes complete with 'the damp and oppressive heat of Hindostan'. This Victorian love for flowers in all their aspects was not exclusive to the upper classes, but the many floral and botanical pastimes had their origins in the events and fashions associated with royalty and aristocrats of the eighteenth century. The passion for collecting rare and bizarre foreign flowers such as orchids during Victoria's reign was a natural continuation of the fashion originating in George III's time.

**Plant Collecting and Painting**

During the eighteenth century there was a great influx into Britain of extraordinary new plants from abroad as new accessions and overseas trade treaties opened up unknown and romantic areas of the world. Nearly 9,000 plants, many with the appeal of the weird and exotic, were introduced to Britain, as compared with less than 1,000 during the previous century (according to the calculations of John Claudius Loudon).

For the Hanoverians, as well as for the Victorians, a foreign flower was very much more

1

than a novelty for flower fanciers: it was tangible proof of Britain's expanding influence and wealth, and the glory of the monarchy. This imperialistic attitude persisted late into the nineteenth century. Appropriately, only the most splendid new plants were considered 'worthy of perpetuating the royal names', such as the vivid golden and blue bird of paradise flower from Africa (*Strelitzia reginae*), named after George's wife Queen Charlotte, daughter of the Duke of Mecklenburg-Strelitz, and the 'Queen of aquatics', the royal water-lily (*Victoria regia*, now *V. amazonica*), named after Queen Victoria (see Figure 6.10).

Queen Charlotte had a practical interest in flowers, as did George III, and their influence was very much present during the nineteenth century, most obviously in the magnificent gardens at Kew. George's father, Prince Frederick, had founded the gardens and thus the royal plant collection had begun. The Prince's wife continued collecting after his death (a true gardener's death: a chill caught through over-enthusiastic planting in the extreme cold), and in 1757 she appointed Sir William Chambers as architect–adviser for the garden, as well as tutor for the young George. This was the era of 'Capability' Brown's landscapes embellished with architecture, and Chambers was responsible for Kew's Pagoda, the Orangery, and the Roman triumphal arch, all of which still delight visitors of today as much as they did the Victorians. In 1760, nine acres were set aside for growing exotic plants. A young gardener called William Aiton was put in charge and the Botanic Garden formally came into being.

In 1772 the garden passed to George III who employed the passionate plant enthusiast, Sir Joseph Banks, who had just returned from his South Seas voyage with Captain Cook and was brimming over with rousing tales of strange Botany Bay flora. In the eyes of London society, the botanical excitement dwarfed all of the *Endeavour*'s other discoveries to the extent that the voyage was spoken of as 'Banks's voyage' rather than Cook's. Banks persuaded George to undertake serious collecting and to send out collectors to unknown areas. The first, like many who followed him, was a naïve and humble gardener, Francis Masson, who suffered terrible dangers in introducing 400 flower species alive from the Cape, including Queen Charlotte's *Strelitzia reginae* and the Victorian favourite, the

pelargonium. By 1789 the botanical collection had grown so much that William Aiton was able to list 5,500 species in his *Hortus Kewensis*. (By the second edition in 1814 his son had doubled that figure.)

Indirectly Banks's untiring energies helped to influence the fashion of flower-painting as well as that of flower-collecting. At his own expense he appointed one of the greatest botanical artists of the time, Francis Bauer, as Kew's first permanent draughtsman. Bauer took up residence at Kew in 1790 and remained there until he died in 1840. His work at Kew helped to make flower-painting a social necessity by Queen Victoria's time for he gave painting lessons to Queen Charlotte and the princesses and passed on to them his enthusiasm for the new foreign plants. Lessons from flower artists had become popular among the wealthy in the middle of the century; flowers presented a moral means of drawing-instruction for daughters seeking accomplishments while retaining their innocence and disposing of time before matrimony. There was an extraordinary selection of artist-teachers in the late eighteenth and early nineteenth centuries: after the death of the legendary Ehret in 1770, Francis Bauer and his brother Ferdinand were the greatest in England, while in France there was Pierre-Joseph Redouté and Pierre Jean François Turpin. It was no accident that the age of great flower-painting and the climax of magnificent flower books spanned the reigns of George III and Victoria – from about 1760 to 1860.

The social desirability of collecting and painting plant introductions was given yet more royal impetus by the Royal Family's habit of walking or driving round the Royal Botanical gardens, in which they had their family home, until George III died in 1820. The Royal Botanical Gardens inevitably became the venue of the fashionable.

The passion for flowers and the art of flower-painting was not exclusive to the aristocrats of eighteenth-century Britain. In France, the source of much of Victorian flower fashion, not even the Revolution stifled their appeal. In the days of Versailles, the fashionable ladies of Paris had taken lessons from the Draughtsman to the Cabinet of Marie-Antoinette, Pierre-Joseph Redouté, whose passion was the imported rarities in the Jardin du Rois. (He also illustrated a book on Kew's rarities, including some of Masson's introductions.) After the Revolution elegant young ladies were still idling away the hours alongside serious students at his classes until his death in 1840.

Extravagant plant-collecting did not die with the Revolution either and continued unhindered while Britain, Europe and the Mediterranean were in disarray at the hand of Napoleon. Ironically, the naval blockade of the Napoleonic wars was opened especially for ships carrying seeds, plants, or even a Hammersmith nursery-man (a 'Botanical Chargé d'Affaires') bound for Napoleon's wife, Josephine Beauharnais, who like George III was building up a famous collection of the rarest plants in the world. The priority given to plants extended to strict orders to the British troops in 1815 to protect Josephine's garden. In the style of Sir Joseph Banks, Josephine paid Pierre-Joseph Redouté a salary to paint her flowers, the most famous being her 260 roses which greatly encouraged the fashion for roses in mid-nineteenth-century Britain. It was in France in the 1830s that the sentimental flower book originated.

## Elegant Botany

Besides the novelty of exotic flowers and the zenith of great flower-painting, there were other less striking reasons for an obscure subject like botany becoming a focus of public attention. These were the seemingly dry topics of the identification of flowers and their *raison d'être*. Up until 1735 many complex and diverse methods of flower-identification were used, so that at the height of plant discovery there was no universal mode of description or cataloguing for 'the immense numbers of vegetables, which were daily augmenting the catalogue of Flora'. The words are those of Carl Linnaeus, the Swedish naturalist, whose supreme achievement was to dispel this escalating chaos. He created a single simple system that could be used by a child and as a result he was eulogised in his own lifetime and well into the Victorian era.

The Linnaean method of classification, with its tabulated flowers drawn by Ehret, allowed even the 'careless collectors of flowers . . . led to them through ostentation' to sort and name their treasured new plants. The ease of the system lent itself to the lady's occupations of painting flowers and pressing dried collections for her albums. Classifying plants was transformed to the level of a drawing-room game by the time

Princess Victoria was occupied with elegant pastimes. Combinations of Linnaean botany and the popular flower crafts even extended to cutting out 'pressed' flowers from coloured paper and classifying them.

Such occupations epitomised the graciousness of amateur natural history in the late eighteenth century. Linnaeus wrote:

> Among the luxuries therefore of the present age, the most pure and unmixed is that afforded by collections of natural productions. In them we behold offerings as it were from all the inhabitants of the earth . . . can any thing afford us a more innocent pleasure, a more noble or refined luxury, or one that charms us with greater variety?

Even the world itself was seen as a mighty collection:

> a vast globe of land and water . . . for it is altogether made up of wonders, and displays such a degree of contrivance and perfection, as mortals can neither describe nor comprehend. This globe may therefore be considered as a museum, furnished with the works of the Supreme Creator.

A notable group of amateurs indulging in such pastimes included the master of the 'paper mosaicks', Mrs Delaney (a close friend of Queen Charlotte), and the Duchess of Portland (who was also Ehret's patron). They filled cabinets with specimens ranging from bird's eggs to minerals, marvelled at living creatures in water-tanks and botanised and pressed flowers – all activities which later found their way into ordinary Victorian homes. The Duchess was rapidly building up the largest collection of natural history and art objects in Britain and was also making a botanic garden. She actually engaged naturalists to collect plant specimens for her.

The Duchess and Mrs Delaney were regular guests at *conversazioni* held by some London and Bath society hostesses. These soirées were events at which men and women held intelligent conversations in preference to playing cards. Another regular guest was Linnaeus's pupil, Solander, and Linnaeus's great English publicist and translator, Benjamin Stillingfleet, a constant friend and guest of these ladies. It was from his

**Figure 1.1** A romantic homage to Linnaeus. Flora (goddess of flowers), Æsculapius (god of medicine and healing [via herbs]), Ceres (Mother of Earth) and Cupid (god of love) honour the bust of Linnaeus. (From *The Temple of Flora* by Robert John Thornton)

eccentric taste for wearing blue stockings at the soirées (possibly recalling an old Venetian clique and passed on from French society), that the expression 'bluestocking' became . commonly used. (Fashionable attire, or possibly social decorum, presumably overshadowed mention of the badge's consistent display on one of the ladies.) The last of the bluestocking group died in 1840. Meanwhile, Paris society – dictator of fashion, obsessed with flowers and natural history – offered an equivalent image: aristocratic hostesses were similarly lionising Comte de Buffon, an ardent opponent of Linnaeus (see figure 5.5), who sat in full Court costume writing in fine dramatic prose a description of the entire natural world, eight hours a day, year after

4

year, for fifty-five years (44 volumes, 1749-1804).

Lesser ladies of fashion had little choice but to follow Paris, the Duchess and the Queen. Queen Charlotte received some instruction from the Duchess's botanically inclined chaplain as well as from William Aiton. The Duchess of Portland had then brought Linnaean botany to the Queen's notice by introducing her to her own tutor of botany and zoology, Sir James Edward Smith. In 1791, shortly after Banks's appointment of Bauer to Kew, Queen Charlotte employed Smith to arrange her herbarium of dried flowers and to teach her and her daughter some elegant botany. He was the English champion of Linnaeus's classification and had in his possession Linnaeus's entire collection of manuscripts and a 19,000-page herbarium (in spite of the King of Sweden's opposition), making him at the age of only 24 a person of influence in aristocratic and botanical circles. He founded the Linnaean Society, a natural history society, in 1788. Pupils at his house included many titled notables of the time. He was knighted in 1814; the fashionable future of botany was assured.

Most aspiring botanists of fashion were not so fortunate, especially those in the country who had to gain their 'useful and elegant studies' from books in the form of contrived conversations, as in natural history's first bestseller, translated from French into English in 1736, *Nature Display'd*. 'Such particulars of natural history as were thought most proper to excite the curiosity, and form the minds of youth' were presented in this book via a grandiose intellectual discourse including an enquiring aristocrat, with whom the reader could identify.

Later books consisted of lengthy polite dialogues between aspiring model-mothers and studious infants. The children gave prompts of unlikely and grammatically impeccable enquiries such as: 'This is very entertaining: pray, ma'am, tell us how nature has provided . . .' and the intricacies of flower structure and Latin names were laid before them.

## Botanical Euphoria – and Snobbery

Most endearing of all, the eighteenth century introduced an extravagantly grandiose attitude to plants and botany which was continued, and often unbelievably exceeded, by the Victorians.

In the golden ages of books and botany, a book 'to induce the ingenious to cultivate the knowledge of botany' and to encourage readers in the use of the Linnaean classification would extend much further: it would boast royal assent and would seek to 'enlist Imagination under the banner of science', intermingling the Georgian dream of the classical idyll with temples, garlands and the goddess, Flora. Isolated thoughts on esoteric topics and current affairs were often included in such books. New plants were displayed with a splendour characteristic of the time and its aspirations rather than of the plants.

The passion and eccentricity of the broad view of botany was captured by Erasmus Darwin (Charles Darwin's grandfather), who portrayed the wonders of Linnaean classification in part of an incredible science poem entitled *The Botanic Garden* which was full of melodrama and innocence, vegetable swains and shepherdesses. In the manner of the time, Darwin digressed frequently and delightfully far. Beneath their romance and politics, Darwin's poem and notes were very far ahead of their time, bursting with new ideas such as bypassing the natural process of plant photosynthesis by synthetic means, thus allowing more creatures on the earth – a theory fit to delight the Victorian, as well as the modern love of progress. Erasmus Darwin was a man of both the past and the future. At the turn of the century, botany was not simply a matter of flowers and stamens but part of the great change of viewpoint which . was to escalate into the excitement of the Victorian future. Traditionalists of the nineteenth century continued in the idiom of Greek as a necessary vocabulary for gentlemen, and as part of culture and the naming of plants. Hence, even the self-taught humble botanists of Victoria's reign felt it necessary to acquire proficiency in the classics. Sir James Edward Smith, Queen Charlotte's botanist, gives a clear picture of the old style of botany among traditional gentlemen in his correspondence of 1808 with the Bishop of Carlisle (another person of influence instrumental in introducing Smith at Court). They were concerned with the naming of a Greek water-lily, which 'an indifferent person' was about to name *Castalia*, from 'casta' (chaste), because the petals 'chastely fold over and cover the organs of impregnation'. Smith felt it should allude to the Castalian fountain, whose waters inspired the gift of poetry in those who drank them. The

Bishop commenced his outraged reply in Greek:

> for I must talk to you as a Graecian . . . To make the name of the nymph of the fountain where Apollo and all the Muses drank the purest lymph, serve for the denomination of a plant inhabiting foul, stagnating, foetid water, and that too in a *Flora Graeca*, which is to preserve the memorial of all Graecian excellence in the natural world, will be an offence of the grossest sort . . . Really if such things, so very gross, are to be allowed, natural history Latin must soon come to be a language fit for barbarians.

Enquiries into 'the commonest things' of natural history such as 'the Cock Sparrow and the Common Snail' were regarded with similar condescension and published 'quite to the nausea of purchasers'.

The great writer, critic and nature lover, John Ruskin, was incensed about the 'Latinising' of plant names. In 1874 he held *Curtis's Botanical Magazine* to ridicule over the necessity to include no less than seven alternative botanical names for his favourite lily. 'Nobody', he wrote, 'loves Latin more dearly than I; but, precisely because I do love it . . . I have always insisted that books, whether scientific or not, ought to be written either in Latin, or English; and not in a doggish mixture of the refuse of both.' As a somewhat quaint alternative he proffered his own system of poetic classification and nomenclature, which was one of 'pretty mists and mysteries . . . as opposed to the vulgar and ugly mysteries of the so-called science of botany'.

The extremes of traditional snobbery, classical purism and optimistic progress continued to mingle far into the nineteenth century as did the preoccupation for naming new species and the highest aspiration of finding one. This was another target for Ruskin: 'There are generally from three or four, up to two dozen Latin names current for every flower; and every new botanist thinks his eminence only to be properly asserted by adding another.'

Perhaps the most extravagant celebration of botany and flowers ever produced, which also reflected the country's state at the turn of the century, was one whose appeal to imperialistic aspirations was such that it precipitated an 1811 Act of Parliament authorising a lottery to assist its ailing finances. It was no ordinary lottery, but the Royal Botanic Lottery, under the patronage of the Prince Regent. Robert John Thornton had taken it upon himself to produce the most sumptuous botanical book ever seen – on the Linnaean plant classification. Part of the work first appeared in 1799 as *The Temple of Flora* with later, smaller editions appearing in the first decades of the nineteenth century, including the 'lottery edition' in 1812. It boasted the best artists and engravers to depict the 'ravishing beauties of the vegetable world' (see pages 7 and 24), and fashionable poets to eulogise them, making it a work of which England and her monarchy could be proud.

Like Erasmus Darwin and the rest, Thornton interleaved his botanical thoughts with his particular grievances, the greatest of which was the war in Europe against Napoleon, which England had entered in 1793. Heavy taxation for the war effort, he maintained, exhausted the resources of the book-buying public. Although he blamed the slump caused by the war, in fact the public were temporarily sated by an excess of botanical publications. In spite of 20,000 tickets being issued at the large sum of two guineas each, the lottery was not a success and Thornton died almost penniless in 1837.

The recession which so impoverished the 'moderately rich' book-buyers was relatively short-lived and the war ended in 1815 at Waterloo. The cause of flowers and flower-collecting suffered a further decline with the loss of George III and Sir Joseph Banks, both of whom died in 1820, after which the great achievement of Kew Gardens began to deteriorate. However, the accomplishments of botany and flower-painting were still increasing in popularity and the sentimental flower book from France was reaching high fashion.

Flowers became a preoccupation of the Victorian age and the fashions associated with flowers assumed the most extravagant and bizarre proportions. Thus it was public opinion and later the influence of the Prince Regent and the Linnean Society (see page 77) which saved Kew from being abandoned in the 1830s. It was taken over by the State and the post of Director went to William Jackson Hooker, assisted by the backing of some aristocrats, the other main candidate being John Lindley. The garden was enlarged from 11 to 600 acres and entered a renaissance, with fine new ironwork gates, vast greenhouses and a Museum of Economic Botany,

**Figure 1.2** 'Group of Roses' painted by Robert John Thornton himself, from one of the earlier editions of *The Temple of Flora*. Included in the group are three types of Cabbage or Provence Rose (*Rosa centifolia*): double pink, white and striped.

the first of its kind. In its first year, the public were allowed to walk freely and admire the garden.

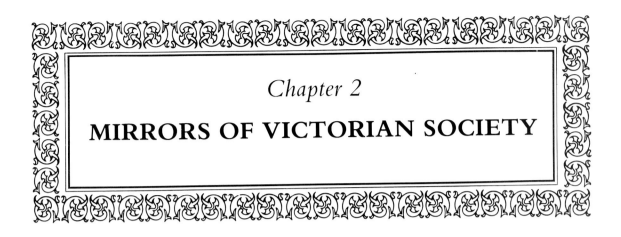

# MIRRORS OF VICTORIAN SOCIETY

## The Flourishing of Sentiment

### A Young Queen

After the young Princess Victoria assumed the throne in 1837, floral pastimes reached a peak, Kew seemed to be at the height of its popularity and the era of flower sentiment was just beginning. Adulation of the young, female monarch appeared in every possible context, going beyond the traditional adoration and deference due to a monarch at that time. Her youth fitted the mood of the new flower books filled with romantic daydreams and nostalgia of flowers: here the maiden's cheek and the blush of the rose were inseparable and Her Royal Highness received the full treatment from Louisa Anne Twamley in *Flora's Gems*:

ROSEBUD of ENGLAND! young and
cherished Flower,
    To thee a sisterhood of Flowers we bring,
    And pray thee to receive the offering
Which simple Song, and Art's most gentle
    power,
Have blent to form for thee.

Flowers of the 'garden bower' would fade with the coming of winter but in the book's verses and painted flowers they would bloom once more:

With smiles and blushes lighting each bright
    face,
In joy, that they thy notice shall obtain,
    And gaining from thine eyes a gentler grace
While thou to gaze on them dost kindly deign.

Miss Twamley's complimentary verses were not excessive for the time. Authors managed to introduce reverential eulogies on royalty into the remotest topics, as was demonstrated by the young Queen being even more extravagantly featured in 1838 in the unexpected natural history setting of hive-bees. Bee-keeping had become a popular hobby: the hives were part of fashionable garden ornamentation, while observation of the bees themselves was part of the socially desirable interest in nature. Their rigid society was a popular topic at a time when people were preoccupied with the glory of sovereignty and the divisions of class, whether of bees or men. Thus the author of *The Honey Bee* hoped that 'the beautiful analogies afforded by the oeconomy of the insects' would 'sanction' the book in Her Majesty's estimation and he proceeded to draw analogies between Queen and queen-bee. Both destined to royalty from an early age, they were 'sedulously guarded from those hazards, to which it is the lot of bees, more humbly born and educated, to be exposed' while both queens enjoyed 'the devoted attachment of her people'. The devious comparison considered the 'fervent and sincere' mourning at the death of a 'sovereign bee', concluding: 'Whenever it shall please the Almighty Disposer of events to call Your Majesty from this present state of existence, may the beneficence of your reign, while living, render the comparison after death, no less complete . . .'

In the eighteenth-century tradition there was a flower painter connected with Queen Adelaide and Victoria's mother, the Duchess of Kent, called the 'Flower Painter in Ordinary'. Like

9

Queen Charlotte before her, Queen Victoria pressed flowers but her motivation was not academic flower classification; for her it was a collection of memories in the sentimental vogue. Flowers were customarily pressed as 'mementos of friendship', souvenirs from lovers' bouquets and wreaths from graves.

A detailed knowledge of flower identification was an integral part of love and life for fashionable ladies, even without the social necessity of botanising, for a new cult had just begun – the Language of Flowers. Each flower had a meaning and in carefully chosen posies there was the opportunity for coy secret communication between boy and girl, which provided ideal material for the new sentimental flower books. Dreamy thoughts of the heart speaking through the beauty of flowers were not far from amateur musings in verse, of which there was a profusion in personal albums, diaries and published books. Lavish hand-coloured prints of paintings by good botanical artists accompanied the ridiculous and the sublime: *Flora's Gems* by Miss Twamley (see Plate 2) and *Floral Gleanings*, chosen from Shakespeare and Sir Walter Scott.

*The Origins of Sentiment*

The sentimental fashion, and the books associated with it, originated in France, the most notable being *Le Language des fleures* of 1833 by Charlotte de Latour which was translated into English and continually imitated. The kindred spirits, Rebecca Hey and Louisa Anne Twamley, were encouraged into print and were heavily indebted to William Wordsworth and his imitators. Wordsworth was consistently a favourite poet alongside the 'peasant poet', John Clare, who received a more transient adulation. Landscape, flowers, traditional country pursuits, floral history, associations and novelties became part of Victorian life and culture.

This fashion for flower sentiment was an inferior nineteenth-century version of the Romanticism which had emerged in the mid-eighteenth century. The early industrial changes occurring at that time had coincided with the appearance of a real fascination with nature in the arts. Painters and poets had pictured serene pastoral scenes which spoke of their belief in the beauty and innocence of nature: it was the time of the Romantic poets, Wordsworth and Coleridge, and of Constable. The true Romantic

inspiration had been the total loss of self, and mental suffering, in an almost mystical absorption in natural beauty, something in the manner of yoga contemplation. It was a feeling of being completely at one with nature, be it the tumbling of a stream, the repetitive lap of waves, the spectacle of a landscape, or the shadows of bright sunlight through petals. This sensitive sense of being led to Rousseau's famous philosophy: 'I feel therefore I am.' From the quiet enchantment of Wordsworth's hills and daffodils, the emotion intensified to Byron's torrid fascination with nature's harsher forces – bare mountain crags, immense torrents and storm thrashed seas – the sublime emotion beloved of Blake and Turner, which also appeared in garden designs. (Sir Joseph Paxton moved huge boulders in order to create an apparently natural rugged wilderness of towering rocky pinnacles and rushing water – a romantic corner of Chatsworth which can still be seen.)

As the Romantic response to nature was beginning in the mid-eighteenth century in England, religion was on the decline, and the one fulfilled the need for the other – for a time. Love of nature was elevated to worship. Rousseau believed in the innocence of nature, Wordsworth felt its moralising balm, Ruskin preached nature as moral law, while for Goethe it was the source of truth. From such passionate heights of religious commitment to the Romantic ideal came the facile moralising and simpering flower adoration of the nineteenth century.

Of course, there were still romantic idealists and great artists in the Victorian age, but for the new middle class lacking tradition and values, this inherited preoccupation with nature was an imposter. The very existence of the sentimental ladies of the new wealthy classes relied on the reality of the expanding industrial era which had come of age in about 1810. In its early days, machinery had promised total domination of nature and the excitement of a new and very different world. In the words of one Victorian: 'No previous era in the world has exhibited so glorious a spectacle of man conquering brute matter.' Unfortunately, the eventual reality was just the reverse, with industrialisation assuming the role of the conquering brute stripped of its early optimism, a stark embodiment of disillusionment and of man's inhumanity to man, woman and child. It could be argued that the only path open to the majority was hypocritical,

When the sun of life more feebly shines,
Becoming thoughts, I trust, of solemn gloom
Or of high gladness you shall hither bring;
And these perennial bowers and murmuring pines
Be gracious as the music and the bloom
And all the mighty ravishment of spring.—WORDSWORTH.

**Figure 2.1** The romanticised garden, with 'green bowers', 'mossy seats', 'arches of umbrage' – and inevitably a verse from Wordsworth.

rose-tinted and nostalgic, and with nature having become remote from many people's daily experiences, its absence and contrast made it a preoccupation.

## Flower Fashions of the Upper Classes

With the advent of industrial wealth and the emergence of the *nouveau riche*, fine flower paintings, extravagantly illustrated books and living exotic plant collections were no longer the exclusive domain of royalty, fashionable aristocrats and enthusiastic botanists and collectors. However, the upper classes still set a fashionable example in the first half of the nineteenth century. Following in the eighteenth-century footsteps of the Duchess of Portland and her

circle of amateur naturalists, the wealthy brought their preoccupation indoors, surrounding themselves with flora and fauna, alive and dead.

The Industrial Revolution brought exciting improvements in the display of the living plant and animal collections. The new expertise with glass, cast-iron (see Figures 2.2 and 2.3) and hot-water piping combined in the creation of an irresistible green oasis of light within the mansion – the conservatory (see Plate 8). With only a slender framework to throw shadows, tender plants could flourish and even flower in as much light as if they were outside. Where status was more important than species, conservatories sometimes became Victorian extravaganzas akin to jungle ballrooms, in which maximum size, number of embellishments, fountains and details of decoration were all-important. Others were

**Figures 2.2 and 2.3** Decorative glass and ironwork in the Conservatory at Coombe Cliff, Croydon (now demolished). (By courtesy of the Council of London Borough of Croydon)

architectual delights, blending with the existing house and adding their own character and proportion as at Broughton Hall, Yorkshire (see Figure 2.4). The ability to make a vast artificial environment for plants provided a great potential both for status-seekers and for serious collectors. There was serious contention for the 'first' and the 'most'. Commercial availability entered the picture, for in the 1820s tropical plants and orchids had begun to be housed by nurserymen in the new heated greenhouses, thus enabling orchid-collecting to become a widespread cult.

That brashly Victorian flower, the dahlia, was another novelty of the time. In 1818 at Lee's nursery at Hammersmith the first ball type was seen; the first cactus dahlia appeared later in 1864. Following France's dahlia craze in the 1830s (when one plant was recorded as being traded for an unusual diamond), it became England's fashion flower of 1841 and 'the glory of our gardens in the Autumn . . .'. It became an accepted standard: 'the cottage has its pink, its

rose, its polyanthus; the villa, its geranium, its dahlia, and its clematis.'

The passion aroused by a new exotic was enough to move gentlemen to remove their hats publicly to a fine flower (the species (see Figure 7.2) receiving such deferential treatment was from Japan – a country newly opened to the West and still an extremely dangerous place for foreigners). Like Robert John Thornton (author of *The Temple of Flora*) at the turn of the century, plant enthusiasts thrilled at the romantic and often dangerous origins of the new flowers. Industrial progress brought less inhospitable places within the reach of the wealthy and in 1835 fashionable collectors were answering the call of the mountains and seeking alpine flowers for the latest cult. With new mobility and speed enthusiasts could retrace the steps of earlier plant explorers in the relative safety of a Grand Tour, glorying in some of the real landscapes of their plants. Meanwhile there were still the serious plant hunters, oblivious of transient cults; the

**Figure 2.4** The Conservatory in William Nesfield's Italian garden at Broughton Hall, Yorkshire.

improvements of travel between continents and plant transportation in sealed glass (Wardian) cases brought the numbers of their plant introductions far beyond the eighteenth-century level. These imports sometimes had the backing of Kew or syndicates of wealthy plant enthusiasts. Another financer of collectors was the London Horticultural Society which had been formed in 1804 in a Piccadilly bookshop at the suggestion of John Wedgwood, son of Josiah Wedgwood; other founder members included Sir Joseph Banks and William Forsyth, after whom the forsythia was named. In 1861 the Society became the Royal Horticultural Society.

Flowers had re-entered the grand garden towards the end of the eighteenth century. Humphry Repton, 'Capability' Brown's successor, had introduced terraces of flowers around the mansion to bridge the gap between building and landscape. The fashionable garden became an inaccurate copy of the early Renaissance style, with parterres of intricately shaped compart-

ments made with clipped evergreen plants such as box, filled or 'embroidered' with flowers. Parterres, and the knot-gardens from which they derived, had frequently been filled with coloured pebbles, but with the heated greenhouses in their grounds as well as a conservatory, wealthy Victorians could fill them in grandiose manner with bright and tender exotics, changing the planting with the season and creating a patterned carpet of flowers. Statuary and fountains added to the overall effect of the Italianate garden which was superimposed on the eighteenth-century landscape style (see Figure 2.5). At the turn of the century picturesque and sublime landscapes had also been fashionable: these were meant to be romantic and awe-inspiring and demanded rock precipices, skyline groups of stark pines, grottoes and castle ruins. All of these elements, including their emotional appeal, entered the smaller Victorian garden, often in combination.

At a more mundane level the wonders of machinery helped to maintain the clipped appeal

**Figure 2.5** William Nesfield's design at Broughton Hall, Yorkshire: a fine example of the Victorian fashion for Italian-style gardens with parterres, statuary and terraces. It has been described as Nesfield's 'finest memorial' and is the best preserved example of his work.

of the new garden style: the first lawnmower made its appearance in 1831 and was regarded as a healthy and amusing item. 'The Improved Mowing or Grass Cutting and Rolling Machines' which followed were advertised with all the snobbery typical of the time: the maker 'earnestly solicits the attention of the Nobility, Gentry, Professional Gardeners and Amateurs to the Above machine'. Its desirability and status was further emphasised by a suitably stratified list of persons already in possession of the strange array of drums, levers, pulleys and scoops at the price of £6. 0s. (in 1858).

## Floral Pursuits and Middle-class Respectability

As well as contributing material benefits to elegant floriculture and collecting, the Industrial Revolution created a new section of society in the towns and cities: a reasonably well-to-do middle class eager to better themselves. They lacked the culture, traditional tastes and wealth of the Georgian-style gentleman but believed that adoption of upper-class interests and attainments held the key to respectability. Floral pursuits had a long and royal lineage and became a social necessity for the *nouveau riche* and the comfortable bourgeoisie.

There was an increase in the demand for teachers of flower-painting and many daughters of nurserymen took up the art and its instruction. The charges were substantial: half-a-guinea for a lesson in the early years of the nineteenth century. For those unable to afford the services of an artist, there were botanical drawing manuals with shading and colouring shown stage by stage, together with some floricultural instruction. These reached a peak of popularity in the first half of the nineteenth century when there was the lure of the social incentive in the books' unashamed announcements of their titled subscribers. Besides painting, a personal album of sentimental flower pressings enlivened with flower eulogies was a social necessity for middle-class ladies. There was also practical flower-spotting and classifying with the help of a little light Linnaean botany, while children were reared on relentless *Conversations on Botany* and similar books. Botany was ideally suited to children, ladies and clergymen as, unlike some other branches of natural history, no cruelty was involved. Gardening was also considered an instructive activity suitable for children; all of the royal children had their own gardens with tools scaled down to an appropriate size. In the true Victorian spirit of thoroughness and just reward, their gardening projects were professionally criticised and they were remunerated by the hour.

The ideal home interior also followed the traditional example: flora and fauna, natural or artificial, were very much part of the drawing room and front parlour. In fact, the middle-class Victorian house aspired to be a cocoon of nature with echoes of eighteenth-century visions of nymphs and sylvan glades, albeit embellished with nineteenth-century baubles. After 1840 aristocratic taste and its mimicry were becoming submerged in yet heavier decoration and in greater quantity: confident Victorian taste was taking over.

In the 1850s flowers embellished everything: wallpaper (see Figure 4.1), carpets, windows, ceiling ornaments, fireplaces, picture frames, mirrors, cabinets, silverware, inkstands, pistol handles, lace, textiles, painted blinds, pottery and, on show at the Great Exhibition of 1851, an essential to real gentility, 'The Fairy Summoner' which was a silver bell. 'The natural productions' were the focal points of the room: making collections was a total preoccupation of the Victorians. As well as cabinets and cases of shells, butterflies and stuffed birds, there were bouquets of grasses and peacock feathers, flower-stands and potted plants in profusion. In the 1860s the centrepiece of the circular sofa or the front parlour window was a palm; in the absence of the real thing there were artificial ones. But often the *pièce de résistance* was living nature study in the form of realistic or fairy-tale classical settings. Ferns were one of the favourite plants of indoor habitats, with all their echoes of the beautiful classical world of nymphs in enchanted caverns. The ethereal nymph's world was mimicked with 'delicate "ferns, flowers, and ivy" round her mossy fountain, which bubbles and splashes under lace curtains, behind windows of stained glass . . .' The enclosure for such scenes was a glass dome or cabinet, the Wardian case (see Figure 2.7), named after its inventor, Dr Nathaniel Bagshaw Ward; in effect, it was the Victorian equivalent of the modern bottle-garden. Authorities on taste were adamant as to its importance: 'Who would live contentedly, or consider a sitting-room furnished, without a Ward's Case, or an Aquarium?' There were unlikely combinations incorporating Wardian case, aquarium, and even a bird cage. They sometimes featured unexpected wild plants and creatures but typically included the fern and a fountain. Sometimes carnivorous plants (see Figure 8.17) presented a somewhat macabre spectator-sport behind glass. Such ostentatious displays showed the owner's interest in natural history which was considered socially superior even to gardening. Charles Kingsley wrote: 'Nay, the study is now more than honourable; it is (what to many readers would be a far higher recommendation) even fashionable.'

A horticultural writer of the time conveyed the new industrial context of plant and natural-history collections in the home when he explained how Dr Ward's realisation of '*rus in urbe*' (nature in the town) enabled:

> the citizen living in a smoke-charged atmosphere, and surrounded by walls and houses . . . to enjoy living reminders of the freshness and beauty of the country. . . . Yet though we cannot have the mountain dells, and creeping thorns, and purple knolls of wild thyme, we may have the emblems of them in our little mural paradise.

Affluence and novelty were important aspects of the respectable man's image and the home of 'good taste' had the most extravagant developments of Wardian cases, revolving and fitted with prisms to concentrate sunbeams on the miniature paradise.

In addition to escapism and status, there was another desirable aspect of indoor nature. Watching the antics of the encapsulated living world was a hallmark of Victorian progress, as portrayed by Mr Shirley Hibberd:

> The mark of our progress is seen in our love for toys, plant-cases . . . fish-tanks, and garden ornaments, – they are the beads in our Rosary of homage to the Spirit of Beauty. Happily in this country the Home of Taste is

**Figure 2.6** Floral tile panels in a dairy. This was one of Maw & Co.'s standard designs of the 1870s. (By courtesy of Easton Farm Park, Suffolk and by permission of the National Monuments Record)

not a merely ideal creation; our domestic life is a guarantee of our national greatness, and as long as we shall continue to surround that life with emblems and suggestions of higher things, so long will the highest teachings of knowledge, elegance, and virtue be attainable at the fireside. . . . Our rooms sparkle with the products of art, and our gardens with the curiosities of nature. Our conversation shapes itself to ennobling themes.

Thus knowledge was essential to the man of

**16**

benefits of exercise while seeking specimens in the fresh air. Botanising became a social as well as a healthy pursuit with membership of a local natural history field club or society, some of which tended to be more social than botanical.

The age of machinery brought the microscope within reach and there were popular guides to its use 'as a means of amusement and instruction', plants offering most of the subjects to be observed.

These 'simple toys' of recreation and education were also seen as 'worthy advocates of morality and religion'. Visible morality was another attribute of Victorian respectability, underlying most aspects of life, and the understanding of nature was no exception. In the transition from botany to enlightenment, the flowers and their lives often became unbelievably transformed: niceties of structure and habit as well as their *raison d'être* were subject to strict judgement. Natural history for the amateur appeared under such unlikely titles as *Rays from the Realms of Nature: or Parables of Plant Life* and *The Sagacity and Morality of Plants, a Sketch of Life and Conduct of the Vegetable Kingdom.*

*Greenhouses and Gardens*

The greenhouse was as much of a social necessity outside as the Wardian cases were indoors. With the great 200-feet (61-m) stove-houses of the aristocratic rich to which to aspire, the more expensive and ornate the suburban greenhouse the more respectable was its proud owner. Designs were exotic, ranging from grossly decorated Grecian-style temples to Moroccan arcades (see Figure 6.2), for the point of a garden was not the overall effect. The suburban garden was acknowledged as a means by which a person could obtain social credit via his obvious wealth and his 'correct taste'.

The instructor on gardening taste and stratified classes of gardens was John Claudius Loudon. Villa gardens were divided into three classes:

*First-rate Gardens* we shall consider as including all those which have a lawn and pleasure-ground, and also a park or farm. In residences of this class, the house stands at some distance from the entrance gate; and the extent of the grounds may be from 10 acres upwards. . . . *Third-rate Gardens* may be such as have the house at some distance from the entrance gate,

**Figure 2.7** Wardian cases or 'parlour pets' as Shirley Hibberd called them.

progress and respectability, and to this end the 'charming and suggestive results of modern botanical investigation' lent themselves admirably. The science of his drawing-room toys was an asset readily to hand in books aimed at painless instructions in the delights of natural history suitably diluted with illustrations, educational poetry and literary asides. Tax reductions on paper in the 1830s assisted the blossoming of vast numbers of natural history journals and instructive books such as *Wandering Among the Wild Flowers* by Spencer Thomson and the Rev. J.G. Wood's *Common Objects of the Country* (to modern eyes a fairly ordinary book for the time but it sold 100,000 copies within a week of publication in 1858). In addition to improving the mind, natural history was purported to improve the character, encouraging cheerfulness and patience as well as bringing the physical

**17**

but in which the lawn, pleasure-ground, and kitchen-garden are combined; and they may be an acre or more in extent.

Lastly, there were the gardens of street houses and cottages which were included as Fourth-rate, extending from one perch to an acre. (The houses themselves were stratified on a separate scale.) Exact plans for the type of garden expected in each status could be found in books such as John Claudius Loudon's *The Suburban Gardener and Villa Companion* of 1838 and subsequent editions. The most desirable was a miniaturised version of the great gardens, squeezing in all the fashionable features such as statues and parterres, rockwork and fountains (see Figure 2.8), regardless of space and effect. John Claudius Loudon's wife, Jane Loudon, wrote similar guides on horticultural good taste: for middle-class ladies there was *The Ladies' Flower-Garden of Ornamental Bulbous Plants* and *The Ladies' Flower-Garden of Ornamental Annuals*, for example. Status in foreign garden plants was achieved with monkey puzzles, pampas and bamboo groves, rhododendron collections and North American conifers, all of which can still be seen, somewhat overgrowing their period villas. Today's commonplace Japanese anemones, mahonia, flowering currant, winter jasmine and forsythia were at that time exciting eastern treasures in the fashionable garden.

Side by side with the craze for foreign exotics and a grand garden there was always a fascination with the British countryside as it had been. The dream of the crude innocence of a 'back-to-nature' past was painstakingly reproduced in rustic summer-houses, thatched beehives, log seats (see Figure 3.1), and fern-filled tree stumps; as complete self-contradictions there were even seats of entwined ivy, heavily cast in iron (see Figure 2.4). The juxtaposition of tastes in combinations of the grand and the rustic, the traditional and the new, the exotic and the natural, may have been partly a reflection of the varying backgrounds of the new gardening townsfolk, seen by Shirley Hibberd as 'children of the manor-house, the farm, the cottage, and the way-side smithy'. Some, very much in the eighteenth-century style, were those 'whose minds are stored with the rich honey of classic love . . . who know the fourth Georgic by heart in the original', and who, at the buzzing of bees, would 'recall the green youth of the world . . .

**Figure 2.8** Advertisement for rustic adornments of 1870. A fountain was essential indoors as well as outdoors. Garden fountains and waterfalls made romantic settings for items such as an Aeolian harp – instructions on how to create and site one appeared in *Cassell's Household Guide* of 1875.

the hum of Pan's great festival'. The others perhaps remembered 'but not too fondly – the scenes of early youth, the rustic home . . .'. All were now hurriedly pacing the dry pavements of crowded towns but still they 'retain the elastic step with which they brushed the cool dew from heather bells, or threaded the maze of mossy woodland, under the patterning of beech-nuts or the flutter of cooing doves'. At heart these somewhat florid thoughts were possibly true, for many new townspeople must have felt a deep-seated psychological need for contact with the nature – its peace, space and beauty – they had so recently lost. The quiet country scene was already gilded by sentiment.

Having taken people from the country to the towns and cities, the Industrial Revolution also provided the means of escape. In the 1840s railways revolutionised mobility and to a large

**Figure 2.9** A flower exhibition illustrated in *The Florist* in 1848. New introductions from abroad and new varieties of flowers, such as pinks (see Figure 2.12), were exhibited at flower shows all over the country.

extent, society. Middle-class people could visit a great garden, such as Stourhead (Figure 3.8) or Chatsworth (Figure 6.7) or indulge in a day in the real countryside – as it was – but most important of all, so could the poorer working man.

## Botany and the Lower Orders

'For a penny a mile, the poor man may be winged by the Pegasus of iron into the green fields, and join with nature in her carnival of beauty.' This delightful vision of industrial progress at its most benevolent was not just another wealthy philanthropist's dream of flower-spotting excursions for the working man. For in Manchester, 'even within the very atmosphere of its smoke', there was a club making weekly botanical expeditions. It was a group of 'working naturalists' – by which the Victorian writer, Mrs Phoebe Lankester, meant all were: 'artisans in some one of the great factories of the district'. She wrote in one of her light but informative flower-spotting books, *Wild Flowers Worth Notice*, in 1861:

An account of their weekly botanical excursions, their field-days, and the healthful and exhilarating effect on the minds and bodies of the members of this club, is most encouraging and delightful. The actual longevity of these humble naturalists is very remarkable . . . There is evidently something in natural history wonderfully promotive of length of days.

In fact, there were many such clubs in the textile manufacturing areas.

The weekly escape from an industrial city's 'thousands of furnaces belching out smoke and poisonous gases' must indeed have been health-giving, for these were the days when the young suffered from consumption and the mortality rate was high. References to waning health and the smoke of towns were frequent, even in sentimental flower books. Anne Pratt, a more serious writer on wild flowers, gives an irresistible pastel picture of hop-pickers, but it is touched with reality. They worked:

beneath the blue sky at their employment, while the cradled infant sleeps the sounder from the soothing influence of the hops which hang over its head . . . while often among those pickers may be found someone who has come hither from the distant town to seek the long-lost health, and has found it here. (See Figure 2.11)

Kew Gardens, opened to the public early in Victoria's reign by its new Director, Sir William Jackson Hooker, also offered fresh air, flowers and a weekly escape for the poorer people of London's East End, as well as the well-to-do. 'As to conveyance, there are the railroads for those who have little time, the omnibus for those who have more, and the steam boat, taking the chances of the tide, for those who have most.' Kew promised total escape from the rigours of factory existence: '. . . the odours and fantastic beauties of the tropics, the fairy-like vegetation of a clime more favoured in this respect than our own, and such a bewitching sight of exotic loveliness as may no-where else be obtained'.

**Figure 2.10** Cast-iron column extravagantly decorated with horse chestnuts at Great Malvern railway station in Worcestershire.

EXHIBITION OF THE NEW SOCIETY OF PAINTERS IN WATER-COLOURS.—"HOPPERS."—PAINTED BY WILLIAM LEE.

**Figure 2.11** A scene of a charming nature: 'The artist could scarcely have chosen a happier phase of truly English rustic life: the occupation is so winning, as to afford amusement to children, who love to gambol amid the luxuriance of the hop-ground. The business of the picking is, however, not forgotten here . . . the wood-framed bins and the pickers at the sides, with the placing of the poles, are correctly given; and the whole scene reminds how superior is the picturesqueness of the English hop-garden to the boasted vineyards of the Continent.' *The Illustrated London News*, June 21, 1851. (By permission of Avon County Library (Bath Reference Library))

The marvels of the newly imported plants of the Empire were great attractions and special displays were put on show. Visitors were thrilled by the grand enclosure of the tropic paradise, the Great Palm House, completed in 1848, 'truly . . . a magnificent work, worthy of this great nation'. The Palm House demanded another master plan to unite the old eighteenth-century Kew of Sir William Chambers with the new structures and their awe-inspiring technology and size. The garden designer, William Nesfield, based the new plan on the Palm House, his design remains in broad outline today, with the wide vista to Syon House, the Broadwalk and the Pagoda vista. Erasmus Darwin's eighteenth-century verses on Kew were still quoted as late as 1857 and were appropriate to the Garden's new magnificence and universal appeal:

So sits, enthroned in vegetable pride
Imperial Kew by Thames' glittering side.

It was especially appropriate that Kew should have provided pleasure, pride and wonder for the poor Victorians, for some of the famous who worked there were themselves of humble origin – such as Walter Hood Fitch who was Kew's draughtsman for 50 years of Victoria's reign. Although its origins were royal, much of its creation, even in the time of George III and Sir Joseph Banks, was due to the dedicated efforts of ordinary working men who were in love with plants. Its first humble collector, Francis Masson, like many nineteenth-century gardeners who followed him, became so enthusiastic about his plant finds that he forgot the financial embarrassments and dangers of his journeys and could not rest until he was on unknown territory seeking more. In a dedication to George III in 1797 he wrote: 'To extend the Science of Botany, to enrich the Royal Gardens at Kew, and to obey your Majesty's gracious commands, are the only objects of ambition that actuate the breast of . . . Francis Masson.' On his next mission he died.

The Victorian champion of floriculture and glass-building design (exceeding even Kew) was Sir Joseph Paxton (see Figure 6.11), who worked his way up from an under-gardener at 15 through apprenticeship, gardener and foreman before becoming the Duke of Devonshire's superintendent of gardens, land agent and business adviser. The Duke was an eccentric plant collector on a vast scale (see page 104), but fanatical cultivation of flowers was as much a working man's prerogative as that of an aristocrat and had a similarly long lineage.

Beautiful varieties of pinks had been developed by textile workers for well over a century. Towards the end of the sixteenth and seventeenth centuries, particularly the seventeenth, Huguenots fleeing religious persecution had settled in the British centres of the cloth trade where they remained in discrete communities for generations. They brought with them seeds, bulbs and corms of their favourite flowers, the cultivation of which was their hobby. The silk weavers of Paisley brought the breeding and cultivation of pinks to a peak which has never been repeated, their goal of perfection being smooth-edged petals in place of the old serrated ones and a symmetrical round bloom edged or 'laced' in a dark colour (see Figure 2.12). Their flowers were almost stylised, having patterns as intricate as their fabrics. The laced pink which brought first hopes of new varieties appeared in 1772, and in the 1830s the Paisley weavers were carried away by an enthusiasm akin to the 'tulipomania' of the seventeenth century and grew over 300 varieties. John Claudius Loudon commented:

> Their ingenuity is continually in exertion for new and pleasing elegancies to diversify their fabrics and where such habits obtain, the

1. Young's Double X      2. Mr. Edwards

**Figure 2.12** Laced pinks illustrated in *The Florist* of 1848. Young's Double X was raised by P. Young Esq.: 'a staunch florist . . . and, though arrived at a good age, his Floricultural ardour is unabated, and he perseveres with his favourite flower, the Pink, with the fondness and enthusiasm of youth.' 'Mr Edwards' was named after a 'very successful amateur'.

rearing of beautiful flowers will easily be adopted. On the other hand, the rearing of flowers must tend to improve the genius for invention in elegant fancy muslins.

It has been said that the laced pinks found their way on to the Paisley shawls, so fashionable in the 1840s. However, charming though the idea is, the evidence is that this was pure fancy.

Flowers like the pink were only to be found in humble gardens during the eighteenth century, for those of the rich were fashionable landscapes where flowers had no place, except hidden behind kitchen-garden walls. The ordinary flowers – including pinks and carnations, auriculas, anemones, ranunculi, polyanthuses, hyacinths, and flamed and feathered tulips – were grown exclusively by labourers. They were the so-called florists' flowers, and they were shown, competed and developed into new varieties by their enthusiastic growers. Joseph Gutteridge, a Coventry ribbon weaver working at a home loom in the old tradition, mentioned how he had 'oft times produced hybrids of a favourite flower by inoculating it with pollen of an allied species'. His nonchalance about such dedicated gardening is indicative of it having been commonplace in the early and mid-nineteenth century. Working men tended to specialise in one species: auriculas were the window-sill favourites of the Lancashire and Yorkshire cotton workers. Since the early years of the Industrial Revolution working men had formed Florists' Clubs and Floricultural Societies in the villages and towns. In accordance with the snobbery of the period, flowers as well as gardeners thus had a tradition of class. Thus the old 'florists' flowers' were referred to as 'mechanics' flowers' while there were others more fit for the rich man's parterre.

The Florists' Clubs, with their sixpenny journal, brought immense impetus to flower-breeding, as well as pleasure to their members. The mere cultivation of fine flowers, regardless of breeding new varieties, must have been a solace as well as a hobby for workers in poor conditions such as the Lancashire textile workers, among whom women and children worked a sixteen-hour day. Solace and hope were scant: the intense demands of work with inadequate wages were far preferable to the horrors of sickness or unemployment with their accompanying poverty and hunger.

It was observed that in the 1850s the Lancashire textile workers grew better specimens of flowers than anyone anywhere. By then, the Florists' Clubs were dwindling, because after the 1840s industrial villages declined, while small gardens in towns became fewer under the pressure of new developments as the hand-looms of cottage industry gave way to the factory system. And factory smoke affected some flowers badly, particularly pinks; by the mid-nineteenth century pinks had disappeared from Paisley.

Interest in flowers as well as the hobby of growing them was potentially a great social leveller. Louisa Anne Twamley wrote in her book *Flora's Gems*: 'I love flowers, as forming one of the sweetest lines in the GOD-WRITTEN Poetry of Nature; as one of the universal blessings accessible to all nations, climes and classes.' Mrs Phoebe Lankester, admirer of the 'humble naturalists', wrote with similar joy: 'The poorest inhabitant of a cottage has within her reach the same delight from flower-spotting as the lady of the mansion.' These were advanced ideas to coexist with the concept of 'mechanics' flowers'. In spite of Miss Twamley's image of a girl of delicate disposition indulging in embroidery in between visitations from the poetic muse, she well understood the pressures of house and family and the great commitment to flowers needed to write and paint as well. After marrying she spent some rugged years of Australian pioneering life, sewing all the clothes for a family of three sons while continuing to eulogise flowers. The sensitive 'nature' poetry of John Clare, so fashionable in the early decades of the nineteenth century, was written in the face of poverty beyond the imagination of most of his readers, yet he sacrificed a better livelihood in order to continue writing some of the most evocative verses on the nineteenth-century landscape and its flora.

For the lower levels of society and the 'shabby genteel' who had come down in the world, dedication and a certain amount of self-sacrifice was the only path to the study of natural history, which therefore had to be a passion: without the nineteenth-century virtues of tenacity and thoroughness, the era would have lost many popular books and sizeable contributions of new knowledge and interpretations. The discoveries of the self-taught men were often infinitely painstaking and personally demanding, a state to which they were already long accustomed in their quests to become naturalists, and a price the more fortunate might have been less willing to pay. Several of the writers quoted in the chapters that follow were educated partly or wholly through their own efforts while working the long day of an artisan. Some sacrificed everything for the understanding of flowers and their insects.

The Coventry weaver, Joseph Gutteridge, was apprenticed at the age of 13 after an elementary education. Always fond of nature, he found difficulty as a child in teaching himself plant and animal identification because of Latin and Greek terminology. While apprenticed in a factory, nature study in the field was of necessity

**Figure 2.13** Tulips from *The Temple of Flora*. The uppermost, opened tulip, 'Louis XVI', was black-edged portraying his sorrow: an offer of one hundred guineas for a bulb was refused in 1827. Striped tulips later became workers' favourites; in 1847 a worker covered tulips with his blankets and died of cold and in the 1850s beautiful varieties were bred by a Derby engine driver.

confined to the early hours of the morning and to Sundays. Access to books was extremely limited, so that although he artificially cross-pollinated his favourite flowers, pollination itself remained a mystery until he witnessed it under a microscope that he made himself. Not only did he learn microscope (and telescope) design, how to grind lenses and work metal with home-made tools, but with the help of old books and museum exhibits he also taught himself herbal treatment, medicine and anatomy under the severe motivation of family illness and doctor's bills, while self-taught cabinet-making and violin repair saved his family from starving on several occasions. He read mythology, early bible history and the philosophy of Voltaire: religious doubts and questions on the transition from inorganic to living matter led him into an intensive study of science. His level of self-teaching was such that he was familiar with the difficult and controversial publications of Charles Darwin, Alfred Russel Wallace, Robert Chambers, the stonemason–geologist Hugh Miller and Sir Roderick Murchison. His plant, fossil and shell collections and his knowledge were recognised at a local level, and his sacrifices and extraordinary labours under the continual threat of poverty were to some extent rewarded by the publication of his diary and an anonymous annuity when he was seventy-five.

Also born into the weaving trade was Thomas Edward, whose father was a hand-loom linen weaver in Fife. Thomas started work at the age of six at a tobacco factory at 14d. (just less than 6p) a week before being apprenticed to a shoemaker at eleven. His source of 'book-learning' at 18 was the *Penny Magazine* published by the Society for the Diffusion of Useful Knowledge. Behind a droll cartoon frontispiece featuring working characters using such information, magazine in hand and oblivious of imminent crazy catastrophes, there was some natural history information and he absorbed it all. Less formally, he learnt from stuffed animals in shop-windows and pictures on bookstalls. His later vast knowledge of Scottish plants and animals was acquired from studying the organisms in the wild and preserving them in his collections. It was not until his late twenties that a benevolent vicar lent him some books; nevertheless he provided science with many new facts and species acquired by dedicated collecting at night, regardless of weather and illness, and in circumstances of poverty. His sacrifices were finally recognised in his election to learned societies and his material well-being in his latter days.

John Ellor Taylor, writer of several delightful botanical books for the amateur and twelve research papers on geology, started work as a 13-year-old store boy in a locomotive works. He graduated to an apprenticeship as a fitter and turner while teaching himself Latin, Greek and natural sciences. It was not until he was 17 that he attended evening classes but by 21 he was a popular lecturer on science. He toured Australia and ultimately attained recognition and the honour of election to two learned scientific societies.

Henry Walter Bates received an elementary education up to the age of 13 when he became apprenticed in a local hosiery factory. In spite of labouring 13 hours a day, he attended night classes where he excelled in the classics, French, composition and drawing. He read in the awe-inspiring idiom of the traditional gentleman – Homer in the original and one of his favourites was Gibbon's *Decline and Fall of the Roman Empire*. He became an amateur insect collector and left a prospect of security to spend eleven years of physical and social deprivation in the Amazon forests, where he collected 8,000 species new to science and made observations for his classic book, *The Naturalist on the Amazons*. As an incidental activity he taught himself German and Portuguese. His deprivation and impaired health were rewarded with recognition and encouragement by Charles Darwin, and much later by many academic honours for the discovery of 'Batesian Mimicry', the phenomenon of an innocuous insect mimicking the often conspicuous markings of a distasteful or poisonous species.

There were others, less dazzling in their attainments, but perhaps the most vivid picture of the dreadful pressure of Victorian poverty on the self-taught is that of the geologist and botanist, Robert Dick, who received no rewards, only increased hardships and slow dwindling to his death. He attended a small village school in Scotland until he was ten and at 13 left an unhappy home to become a baker's apprentice. In return for board and lodging his working day began at three in the morning, when he kindled the bakery fire, and ended at about seven or eight at night. His childhood occupation was observing plants and his introduction to science and plant-collecting was through an old borrowed encyclopaedia. From such inauspicious beginnings he became, through practical observation, an authority on the geology and botany of a hitherto unknown area of North Scotland, instructing, with mounds of flour as models, the Director-General of the Geological Society, Sir Roderick Murchison, and contradicting established scholars who tended to study plants while 'driving along the public road and viewing the country from gigs!' His immense and largely unacknowledged geological collections and interpretations of past landscapes were particularly relevant, as it was the time of new theories about the age of rocks and fossils, and the means of evolution. In order to collect fossils and plants for others and to pass on his interpretations, he baked bread in the small hours of the morning and walked 30 or more miles by day to observe and collect, returning at night to sort his specimens and sleep a few hours before baking once more. He was ill clad for such expeditions in northern weather and could sustain himself only on the broken and stale biscuits which he could not sell. His bakery trade was always small (in those days baker's bread was a luxury, usually reserved for the Sabbath), and began to decline because of criticism from the pulpit of his scientific activities.

His treatment by his fellow-townsfolk mirrored the religious bigotry of the time, which regarded plant-collecting on Sunday as a sin in spite of it being the only available time for working-men naturalists, and also reflected Establishment suspicion of the natural sciences and new discoveries. When, after 14 years of scratching a living from his shrinking trade, Robert Dick was alone, ill and hobbling about the countryside in search of specimens, the religious gossips were in their element, saying he was prematurely old and bent as a Divine Punishment for his Sunday activities. (The dilemma of being a good Establishment churchman and a true scientist faced with evolutionary evidence contributed to the suicide of Dick's famous correspondent, Hugh Miller.) From his pittance Dick accumulated a library of 389 books, large even by wealthy standards, and being a religious and cultured man by his own reading, he had seven Bibles, biblical maps and commentary, and books on distant countries as well as the standard scientific works. An application by some geologist friends to Queen Victoria for a pension for his geological discoveries came too late and after months of desperate illness during which he still continued baking, corresponding and classifying his herbarium, he died in debt.

At the lowest levels of society plants were the lifeblood of many of the poor of the city streets and country hovels. Tinkers supplied the ferneries and Wardian cases of rich townsfolk with fresh country plants. Plant tinkers, or 'Botany Bens' as they were called, carried baskets of wild ferns from door to door, having gathered them from among the 'creeping thorns' of the wild 'paradise' which the well-to-do were trying to recapture indoors.

Lower down the poverty scale, plants were a utilitarian part of traditional survival from the distant past: for example, beech leaves and reedmace ('bulrush') heads were used for

**Figure 2.14** A self-portrait of the baker Robert Dick on 27 September 1864 during his worst troubles: diminishing trade, deteriorating health, sudden financial loss, the recent death of his sister and his one friend and fellow geologist being moved far distant. With crippling rheumatism in the feet, he still scoured the countryside and cliffs for mosses and ferns by moonlight and, with failing eyesight, tended his herbarium and correspondence by candlelight. He died two years later. (By permission of Thurso Museum)

mattress-filling and ground beech-nuts were used as a flour substitute. Street beggars also had a good working knowledge of plant potential. John Ellor Taylor, himself of humble origins, wrote of the 'semi-humorous aspect' of the poisonous foliage of the common meadow buttercup (*Ranunculus acris*): tramps used the leaves of this plant and the celery-leaved species (*Ranunculus sceleratus*) to produce blisters on their arms in order to excite compassion in the hearts of the gullible.

**Figure 2.15** A romanticised portrait of Robert Dick, executed posthumously, with Dunnet Cliffs in the background. Dick's poverty-striken death and the lack of attention from fellow-townsmen for a man of his calibre was immediately prominent in a rival town's newspaper. Local uproar followed. The ensuing massive public funeral accompanied by the biggest band the town had ever produced and the conspicuous granite obelisk paid for by a memorial fund would have appalled Dick. (By permission of Thurso Museum)

*Chapter 3*

# SENTIMENT

## Floral Crafts and Pastimes

Charles Kingsley scathingly described the traditional occupation of Victorian girls as 'novels and gossip, crochet and Berlin-wool . . . [and] the abomination of "Fancy-work" – that standing cloak for dreamy idleness (not to mention the injury which it does to poor starving needle-women)'. Dreaminess aside, proficiency in the arts and crafts was a vital accessory to a Victorian lady's social standing.

Floral arts and crafts were part of life in the Victorian drawing room which was itself almost a homage to flowers. At one end of the summer drawing room was a lady's masterpiece: the dressed fireplace. The fresh moss stuck with 'orpin flowers, and Sweet Bryer flowers . . . as if they grew' from previous centuries was transformed into a Victorian concoction of a material mound on which there might be 'a slight wreath of myrtle' or a few 'well-made' muslin flowers. *Cassell's Household Guide* advised that:

> Nothing can be prettier than the palest shade of pink tarlatan [open-weave muslin], un-ravelled in the grate, with a few moss roses carelessly arranged about it, and the lace window curtains lined with pink tarlatan throughout, a couple of shades deeper in tone.

There was a profusion of house plants, artificial flowers and a whatnot covered in ornaments in imitation of, or made from, real flowers, leaves and cones.

Roses, carnations, fuchsias, poppies and daisies were taken apart, petal by petal, and used as templates for the 'elegant' art of making paper flowers. Shells were painstakingly pieced together to make flowers in baskets, alongside less convincing floral contrivances of seeds, leather, hair and seaweed. These were set on red velvet and covered by a glass shade or framed like a picture. The sudden influx of North American pines in the 1820s and 1830s led to the introduction of the American art of pinework into Britain. This involved cutting off the scales of large pine cones and arranging them like fish scales to make items like baskets and even pincushions. Doilies were decorated with spatter-work using fern and leaf stencils. Furniture embellishments included chintz cut-outs and leafwork mimicking Japan Decoration by means of a coat of 'fine black paint' with pressed yellow leaves stuck on top, the whole thing being varnished. There were samplers, tapestries, embroideries, crocheted antimacassars, too, as well as flower paintings, drawings and the prolific products of collecting – pictures and albums of pressed flowers.

Then as now flower-arranging was part of home-making. For the winter there were 'wonderful realisations' of flowers in cambric – 'Roses, lilies, hot-house plants, ivies . . . occasionally represented, with most truthful effect, in their day of declining and withering, with the canker-worm at the core, and blight upon the face.' A popular style of arrangement was a tight nosegay bunch of a mass of flower-heads fringed by a filmy foliage frill in a highly decorated vase. The making and giving of fresh nosegays was an everyday part of Victorian childhood. Later on in life, the ability to make them for wearing at social gatherings was an attribute which was subjected to severe judgement – a nosegay badly chosen or executed was not considered appropriate to anyone of 'high breeding'. For the drawing room *Cassell's Household Guide* described a wonderful variation on an orthodox flower arrangement – frosted flowers, owing their 'peculiar beauty to the sparkling . . . appearance which vegetable forms assume under . . . [water] and to the illusive and fairy-like effect caused by the refraction of light, and the magnifying power of . . . glass and water.' Fresh flowers were skilfully submerged under an inverted glass full of water. Flower arrangements on dinner tables were no less ambitious. In the 1890s a miniature palm tree made a popular centrepiece, rising out of a round island of flower-heads fringed with leaves – not so inappropriate considering the frequent inclusion of a leafy pineapple standing on end on its own island of leaves further down the table. At a circular or oval table a centrepiece might be encircled with strewn flowers and foliage out of which rose six or eight tall flared vases of tightly packed flowers and ferns, each with its own echoing miniature. Particularly charming was the habit of individual tiny glasses of flowers at each guest's place. Also not to be found on modern tables, there were ferns in rustic slatted boxes and nautilus shells, and vases trailing foliage and flowers into finger bowls and across the tablecloth. According to the 1899 edition of Mrs Beeton's *Cookery Book and Household Guide*: 'for the dinners that are served *à la Russe*, it is absolutely necessary that the table should be covered by artistic and pretty decorations'. According to the same book, the fashion changed so rapidly that only a weekly journal could keep pace: 'fashionable dinner-givers vie with each other'.

Away from the dinner tables of the wealthy, the embellishment of vases was often floral. Glass pickle jars were transformed with wire worsted work and vases of plain glass were rendered bright and hideous by pasting picture cut-outs inside, varnishing, then pouring in paint to create a background. Ornamental jardinières were made in the manner of Sèvres and Wedgwood. 'The most elegant of flowerpot covers' were made with 'materials furnished by the hand of nature.' The cover was woven, using long stems of lavender, corn or barley as the warp and 'new bright-green satin ribbon' as the weft,

leaving a fringe of heads at the top and finishing with a bow on each side as handles. The Berlin wools so dreaded by Kingsley found their way into bizarre mats for vases and flowerpots rather than carpet slippers.

Such decorative items reached a nadir of sensitivity, positively assaulting the eye. It was Gertude Jekyll who introduced a note of restraint, simple colour sense and sense of composition in one of the first books on flower arranging to be published. William Morris (see Figure 4.1) and the Pre-Raphaelites were also trying to promote a new understanding of fine art and design.

## Pretty Paintings and Poetry

The whimsical appeal of flowers was mirrored in some of the most popular varieties of the time: the graceful fuchsia (see Plate 2), the fragrant pinks (see Figure 2.12), the white lilac and the plush pansies or heart's-ease, the fashion-flower of 1870 (see Figure 9.11):

> What empress in all her splendour ever found purple to compare with the richness of a heart's-ease? . . . for the most part they are of purple and yellow mixed, and sometimes put us in mind . . . of a man, with a purple cap on his head, and a beard on his chin. It is probably to the very smiling face of this purple-capped gentleman, that the flower owes its name of heart's ease.
>
> (Charlotte M. Yonge)

One of the most consistent favourites was the rose. In the Romantic era early in the nineteenth century, roses climbed artificial ruins and classical columns (Figure 1.2), while high Victorian taste preferred strongly scented, full-faced flowers straddling gothic trellises and arbours:

> Gem of the bower, sweet rose! the fairest, brightest
> Of the gay tribes which drink the summer beam.
> (From *The Moral of Flowers* by Rebecca Hey)

The quiet moss roses, with intricate frilled calyces, climbed the social ladder from cottage garden favourite at the beginning of the century to become a national craze from 1850 to 1860. Delicate and subtle, the moss roses epitomised

**Figure 3.1** 'Garden Flowers' by William Powell Frith. (By permission of Birmingham Museums and Art Gallery)

the fashionable ideal of the shy and bashful maiden. These paragons of feminine virtue were everywhere. A whimsical watercolour of a girl picking a flower would be judged as much for its subject as for its merit: 'a sweet impersonation of the female character' was one such judgement. Louisa Anne Twamley (later Mrs Meredith), eulogised the girl Queen in this vein (see page 9) and the timid complexion of the moss rose was shared by the wild rose, whose colour she described as:

> not positive enough to seem the colour of a flower, but like a blush or reflected glow, and redolent of an odour as appropriate to their own fragile beauty, as is a soft voice to the

lovely and fairy-like form of a young and gentle maiden.

The virtuous maiden also appeared in other floral disguises. Charlotte M. Yonge, writing in the *Magazine for the Young* in 1853, thought that 'the wood anemone may put us in mind of some quiet, shy, modest girl, who makes all sunny and happy round her in her own safe, shaded home'. (See Figure 5.15.) In a modern world such interpretations are a caricature of the Victorian age. The sentimental flower writers mirrored maidenly virtues and duties long since passed but they have the magnetism of a romantic lost era. Through their delightful contrived verses and prose, one can still enter the flower-strewn world

**Figure 3.2** Flower arrangement for the table from Mrs Beeton's *Cookery Book and Household Guide*.

responsible was a pupil of Peter de Windt. Kew's great botanical draughtsman, Walter Hood Fitch (Plates 11 and 13), produced a series of illustrated articles in the *Gardener's Chronicle*, a publication which crossed all frontiers and which presented practical gardening advice, observations on plant breeding and natural history (with contributions from Charles Darwin), and advertisements for wheelbarrows and greenhouse boilers.

Victorian ladies read such titles as *Butterflying with the Poets*, *Flora Poetica*, *The Queen of Flowers; or the Memoirs of the Rose*, *Plant Lore and Garden Craft of Shakespeare* and *The Naturalist's Poetical Companion*. In the 1830s, 40s and 50s much time was spent in writing eulogies and rhymes in the manner of these sentimental flower books, for these were 'rhyming days, when almost everyone lays claim to some acquaintance with the muse'. Such activities continued as late as 1899, beautifully depicted in *A Floral Fantasy in an Old English Garden* (see Figure 3.5). On another page a dreamy young lady was drifting through the garden with 'an old English book' in one hand, considering 'A jonquil will serve for a pen', before embarking on noting 'from the green arbour's nook, Flowers masking like women and men'. The rhymes which followed were contrived of flower names, typical of their type and little changed through fifty years:

> First in *Venus's Looking Glass*,
> You may see where *Love Lies Bleeding*
> While *Pretty Maids* all of them pass
> With careless hearts quite unheeding.

Other verses were more solemn and were pervaded with the nineteenth-century sense of filial duty and love, complete with such clichés as chastity personified by the lily. Louisa Anne Twamley strangely illustrated the mother image with the hollyhock. The hollyhock moved her to tell of a disillusioned traveller who returned to his birthplace and his 'childhood's home'. In keeping with the ideals of the time, this 'shrine of pilgrimage' was where his mother had revealed the marvels of botany. He wanders through the old garden, remembering:

> I sought the terrace –'twas my mother's walk,
> Where I so oft had staidly paced along,
> My childish hand in her's so fondly clasped,
> And my eyes fixed upon her pale, fair face,
> While, with a gentle yet impressive voice,

of the elegant gentlewoman of the nineteenth century.

One of a lady's occupations was filling her album with watercolour paintings of her favourite flowers (see Plate 5). Ladies unable to have personal lessons from artists could learn to draw and paint flowers from copy books such as *A New Treatise on Flower Painting; or Every lady her own drawing master* of 1816. Instruction by this means came from the relatively unknown as well as the famous artists, such as Pierre Jean François Turpin, James Sowerby (Figures 5.1 and 5.5), James Andrews (Plate 2) and Peter Henderson who painted some of the illustrations for *The Temple of Flora*. Plate 5 could have been executed by either of two ladies; the one probably

**Figure 3.3** ' "Flowers" is a very May Queen, who is garlanded with floral beauties, and wears a crown, or turban, most fantastically wrought. Her path is strewn with flowers. . . . The flaunting gaiety of the maiden is delightful.' *The Illustrated London News*, 1851. (By permission of Avon County Library (Bath Reference Library))

She told me, couched in simplest phrase, of all Nature's most glorious works. . .

All from the past seemed gone until the traveller came upon that most evocative of old-fashioned flowers:

. . . HOLLYHOCKS – those tall majestic Flowers,
              . . . The first seeds
My mother planted there; and, till we left
.   .   .   .   .   .   .   .   .   .
They seemed a Fairy-city of tall spires,
Wreathed, as for some high festival, with
   Flowers . . . [see Figure 3.6]

The forget-me-not (see Plate 4) was a particular favourite. The derivation of its name appealed to the Victorian taste for melodrama and chaste blind devotion. The story, here recounted by Phoebe Lankester in *Wild Flowers Worth Notice*, was set, predictably, in 'the days of chivalry' by the Rhine:

. . . a knight and his lady-love were wandering on the banks of a stream where grew clusters of these gem-like flowers. In those days the wish of a loved one was law to the lord . . . [a strangely wistful thought for a Victorian authoress] . . . the lady, desiring to possess some of the bright blue blossoms caused her faithful knight to rush into the stream. . .

Here the gallant noble was overcome by the current's strength but true to his dearest's whim to the last, he 'cast, with dying hand, the flowers she wished for towards her, exclaiming: "Forget-me-not." '

On account of this romantic christening and

**Figure 3.4** 'Shakespeare and his Flowers' by Clara
Maria Pope. (By permission of the Trustees of Sir
John Soane's Museum, London)

**Figure 3.5** 'A Floral Fantasy in an Old English Garden' by Walter Crane, 1899. (By courtesy of Avon County Library (Bath Reference Library))

sentiment, the forget-me-not was a constant feature of Valentines and communications between lovers (see Plate 4), as well as amateur paintings and flower albums. The drama also set lady verse writers ablaze. The dewy-eyed Miss Twamley, with unaccustomed realism, wrote what can only be described as one of the few anti-heroic verses on the floundering knight who had named the over-exposed flower:

That silly Lover, tumbling down
    And drowning in the Rhine,
First set the jingle-makers on. . .
(From 'The Complaint of the Forget-me-not, showing the pains and penalties of popularity')

Presumably she considered herself outside this category! Miss Twamley's poem portrays the archetypal lady of that era, dabbling in the fashionable pursuit of flower-spotting. Miss

Twamley's fair damsel picks up the forget-me-not and with splendid period aplomb kisses away the river spray which 'like tears of regret on her azure eyes hung' (the forget-me-not's, that is). The lady commences a portrait of the flower in her album and the 'fair sitter' (the forget-me-not) then 'sighed forth this touching lament':

And misses, in those curious books
    Called 'albums', and so forth,
Paint a blue marigold, whose looks
    Proclaim her none of earth;
On which the parson, if he's young,
    Or doctor, if he's handsome,
Must perpetrate a doleful song:
    Oh! will no fairy ransom

My face from such a libel vile?
    And clear my reputation,
So slurred by treachery and guile,

**Figure 3.6** 'Hollyhock, Pink Beauty' from *Wood and Garden* by Gertrude Jekyll, 1899.

From such an imputation.
As that *I* set the twaddlers on
 To so be-rhyme and saint me?
As I'm a flower, they know no more
 Of me, – than those who paint me.

Once started, there is no stopping Miss Twamley, who extended her criticism even to botanists who have the misfortune to erroneously identify flowers:

E'en 'Botanists' mistake my form,
 That's seen by brook and fountain, [*Myosotis palustris*]
For my rough cousin's, who's clad warm
 [*Myosotis alpestris*]

To dwell on moor and mountain,
But this I'd pardon, if the Bards'
 And Poetasters' chorus
Were silenced once – we'll give rewards
 To all who'll no more bore us.

The paradox of criticising romantic doggerel in the same vein could be seen as a window on Miss Twamley's own character which was an unexpected coexistence of opposites: on the one hand publishing newspaper articles in support of the Chartists in the early 1830s and astute (and controversial) comment on colonial life in New South Wales, and on the other hand writing endearingly dreadful verses on flowers and flower lore.

## The Language of Flowers

For many drawing-room muses, flower-spotting was a purely nostalgic pastime rather than an artistic or poetic one: albums of pressed flowers were treasure hoards of memories – another face of fashionable sentiment – recalling country rambles, picnics and holidays. The importance of time, place and circumstances far outweighed the flower names: 'little bouquets of the blossoms and foliage . . . help to carry away the thoughts to some pleasant spot whence the flower was gathered'. These musings from Anne Pratt are particularly touching in their personal escapism, for she was a flower spotter cut off from first-hand enjoyment of the natural world she so obviously loved. Delicate health allowed her no active pursuit; her elder sister gathered wild flowers from meadows and hedgerows for her to draw and press for her extensive herbarium and to provide the material for her books. Images of wide landscapes seem to have floated through her mind as she worked.

Most treasured of all were the flowers of love, saved from lovers' posies or morbidly kept from deathbeds and wreaths – Queen Victoria preserved floral tokens of her beloved Albert.

. . . Have ye n'er prized
Some token flower? an early rose . . . culled
And given into yours by hands so dear,
That all flowers seemed grown holier from
   that time?

.   .   .   .   .   .   .   .   .

For very fondness could not fling away
Those dim and faded records of the past,
But laid the frail things in their wonted place,
To gaze – and dream – and weep upon again?
(Louisa Anne Twamley, *The Romance
   of Nature*)

Far from being just souvenirs, each flower carried a meaning, carefully selected by the sender. A bouquet could thus be a complete letter via an intricate Language of Flowers. Through the centuries 'the fair maidens of the East had lent a mute speech to flowers', the niceties of which had been introduced to European ladies by Lady Mary Wortley Montague in her Turkish Letters, published in 1763. She sent a friend a Turkish loveletter, the contents of which demanded a box:

| Pearl | Fairest of the young |
| a clove | You are as slender as this clove; You are an unblown Rose; I have long lov'd you, and you have not known it. |
| a Jonquil | Have pity on my passion |
| paper | I faint every hour |
| pear | Give me some hope |
| soap | I am sick with Love. |
| coal | May I die, and all my years be yours! |
| a Rose | May you be pleas'd, and all your sorrows mine! . . . |

and by way of a postscript:

| pepper | Send me an Answer. |

You see this letter is all verses . . . there being (I beleive [sic]) a million of verses design'd for this use. There is no colour, no flower, no weed, no fruit, herb, pebble, or feather that has not a verse belonging to it.

The 'verses' rhymed with the Turkish name of the object, providing codes for those who knew them.

Translated into a Victorian setting (see Plate 3), the emphasis was less on 'bits of Charcoal, Scarlet Cloth . . . and such like Trash' (another traveller), but altogether more floral and without associated verses or rhymes. For flowers had 'an oratory that speaks in perfumed silence . . . no spoken word can approach to the delicacy of sentiment to be inferred from a flower'. Floral associations, often vague, denoted their meaning: cloves now stood for dignity, the jonquil: 'I desire a return of affection', and a rose meant love. Plants like laurel retained their ancient Greek symbolism of glory, while many floral meanings were contained in the name, such as love-in-a-mist – perplexity. The 'variegated beauty' of the flower vocabulary also included the obscure, whose size and shape made unlikely inclusions in a pretty bouquet – lettuce meant cold-heartedness and the lichen, dejection or solitude.

The Language of Flowers became almost a cult. For the reticent it provided a ready vehicle: 'the softest impressions may be thus conveyed without offence.' For secret lovers it provided that all-important ingredient, opportunity. Chaperons and parents could be outwitted or a lady could retain her dignity while happily concocting a risqué and embarrassing message which would be a social impossibility verbally. Even Christmas cards, decorated somewhat inappropriately with summer flowers, were in fact a frequent means of a surreptitious message (see Plate 4). Valentine cards were, of course, the foremost means of coy communication. Garlands or bunches of roses, violets, forget-me-nots, lily-of-the-valley, pansies, daisies and love-lies-bleeding were among the most frequent orators. Paintings, cut-outs and cloth flowers were mounted, often layer upon layer, on embossed paper lace cards – sometimes they were seen through a gauze window, or the flowers were hand-painted on silk cushions or tiny feather fans. Some incorporated nearly everything – silk frills, ribbons, gold paint, flags, drapes, anchors, harps and cherubs.

For those suffering from ennui the Language of Flowers was a splendidly time-consuming interest, as a large floral vocabulary was involved in which even subtle distinctions of colour and variety held immense significance. Something like thirty types of roses conveyed emotions far removed from each other, ranging from bashful shame to pride. Many 'dictionaries' were necessary. Subtle nuances of floral communication extended accurate flower identification far beyond those with botanical leanings: it had become a prerequisite for the survival and progress of love.

Opportunities for misunderstanding abounded, as Louisa Anne Twamley revealed in a cautionary tale to all inattentive young ladies entitled 'Carnations and Cavaliers'. All the suitable accessories of the 'moon in June' Victorian style were present when:

> A Ladye and her Lover once,
>   In a Summer evening-tide,
> Within a stately garden walked,
>   And whispered, side by side.

The subtleties of 'Love's ambassadors' were imparted to the Lady Edith by Sir Rupert, but in vain:

> . . . Edith (as dames mostly do),
>   Liked Learning less than Love
> .   .   .   .   .   .   .   .
> And sometimes gave, in careless mood,
>   Flowers for the time unmeet.

> The eve I tell of 'gan to close,
>   Fast fell the soft twilight;
> And the young moon amid the leaves
>   Peeped forth, all chaste and bright.

The time comes to say goodnight and Edith is presented with a pink. Inadvertently she gives him 'a bright, fitter one', namely a carnation, forgetting that:

> The Pink, by Knight to Ladye given,
>   Prays her to be his Bride –
> The proud Carnation answering tells
>   That fervent prayer's denied.

The knight, Sir Rupert, takes the flower seriously and traditionally sinks his sorrow on the battlefield in France, where, once more in Miss Twamley's irresistible 'eventide', the saga continues with melodrama. The knight is struck down by the arrow of a slight young archer, who rushes to kneel by him and turns out to be the lady in disguise. The carnation 'crushed long-faded' falls from Rupert's vest and explains all.

With a warning word on the 'frail emblems' of pinks and carnations, their mid-battle conversation turns to orange blossom in the best tradition. The floral ballad ends with the verse 'ARGUMENT' which is about good Victorian values:

> Now, Ladye – when a Cavalier
>   Presents a chequered PINK,
> 'Tis time to ascertain, my dear,
>   His rent-roll, you may think;

> And then – provided his estate
>   Don't meet your approbation,
> It cannot, surely, be too late
>   To cut – with a CARNATION.

### Romance of Days Gone By – Rustic Bliss

Nostalgia was an essential part of floral musings, as in the sagas of knights and chivalry and the carnations and forget-me-nots of 'yesteryear'. 'How well I remember the days when . . .' and the rose-tinted days of childhood were also favourites, standing somewhat inappropriately beside Elysian fields of ancient Greece. This had been an eighteenth-century ideal, splendidly portrayed in *The Botanic Garden* by Erasmus

Darwin and *The Temple of Flora* by Robert John Thornton. Nearly a century later, there were still classical echoes from Erasmus Darwin in quotations from his verses and his scientific views. The Goddess Flora, her 'court of flowers', Ceres (the goddess of the earth's fruits), Cupid (the god of love) and Pan (the god of pastures, forests and flocks) remained prominent persona with some mid-Victorians such as Philip Henry Gosse and Shirley Hibberd. Such images had changed little since the days of *The Temple of Flora* (see Figures 1.1 and 1.2). Gardens continued to feature temples of vaguely Greek inspiration (see Figure 3.8), and dreams of them, including every classical illusion, were crowded on to Valentine cards. Against a background of paper lace trees, exotic palms and cordylines, stood silver pavilions: graceful goddesses led suitors to their spreading steps while ferns, fawns and recumbent poets draped themselves around limpid pools and cherubs drifted in clouds above.

At the other extreme, there was a longing for the country rustic and his floral delights. Here again the dream appeared in Valentine card design. Instead of love birds, two sparrows built a nest among the foliage. Forget-me-nots bedecked the cottage porch and above, a tiny diamond leaded window nestled under the thatch. Two classical maidens held aloft a drape on which were the words: 'Can you tell me how to build a happy home'. Even serious flower books included wistful thoughts on peasant life.

Idealising the simple life and the worthy rustic was part of the creed of nature worship of the Romantics: natural man was virtuous, the savage was noble. Actual memories may well have played a part, too, particularly for those who had recently moved to the new towns – described inimitably by Shirley Hibberd (see page 18). Well mellowed by time, such recollections of the past stood like a treasured memorial of lost youth, lost innocence and lost opportunity – the antithesis of all the ill of industrial town life which had promised so much. Cottages and their flowers stood for all that was wholesome and happy, as in *The Herb of the Field* by Charlotte M. Yonge: 'the dark red China [roses] cluster round the cottage window, almost a sure token that content and cleanliness are within.'

The mythical peasant paradise was not exclusive to flower books: it kept reappearing at intervals in the nineteenth-century garden. Rustic-styled embellishments and feature flowers co-existed in the garden and competed with Italianate geometry and tender exotic plants. In the 1820s the great landscape style was still an aspiration but the reality was becoming a debased imitation peppered with Victorian versions of the picturesque. Nestling in the landscape there were rustic cottages predictably pictured by garden planners with a homely curl of smoke creeping out of the chimney. In 1838 John Claudius Loudon advised that 'nothing gives more general satisfaction than a neat and comfortable picturesque cottage – even in the grounds of small villas'. The wealthy expressed their 'good taste' in a complete collection of such extraordinary cottages, from Greenland, Norway and Switzerland, while at Alton Towers in Staffordshire a Welsh harpist was installed in the Swiss cottage to enhance the general ambience. More usually the ornamental cottage housed 'a working mechanic, a shoemaker or weaver' and spouse. A basic square dwelling for two, described by Loudon in 1842, could be altered to suit the sentimental mood: it could be transformed to castellated Gothic, monastic Gothic, Elizabethan style, Italian style with a campanile-type watch tower, or Indian Gothic. The types of trees suited to various cottage designs were stipulated, as were its garden beds for flowers, herbs and appropriate vegetables and fruit. There was a hermitage design complete with crosses which was in keeping either with a landscape that was seeking to be sublime or the sentimentalist's penchant for religious overtones such as holy wells and monks' gardens.

In the 1850s and 60s Shirley Hibberd advised on garden embellishments for the less affluent: the new industrial middle classes moving in to Loudon's 'fourth-rate' houses (terraces), 'third-rate' houses (semi-detached), and detached 'second-rate villas' (but still in a row). He wrote a book entitled *Rustic Adornments for Homes of Taste, and Recreations for Town Folk in the Study and Imitation of Nature*. Rustic bliss was to be recreated on a small scale – with beehives. Hibberd was a great advocate of the Victorian bee-keeping hobby both in its own right and as an adjunct to flowers and gardens, somewhat in the vein of Louisa Anne Twamley: 'the golden belts upon the body of the bee, and the fairy song he chants among the flowers'. As to the romanticised dwellings of the bees, Hibberd wrote: 'Every form of bee-hive is graceful, from the humble dome of straw perched among the

◄**Figure 3.7** 'Flora at play with Cupid' from *The Botanic Garden* by Erasmus Darwin, 1799 (4th edition). (By permission of Avon County Library (Bath Reference Library)).

▼**Figure 3.8** Ingredients of the classical dream at Stourhead: the Temple of Flora, c. 1745. A visit to this magnificent garden with its architectural embellishments was a popular outing in the Victorian era. (At the other end of the romantic scale, there is also a Gothic cottage, c. 1806, in the garden.)

►**Figure 3.9** Rustic garden reading room and toolhouse from *Rustic Adornments for Homes of Taste* by Shirley Hibberd (1870 edition).

►**Figure 3.10** 'The Apiary' from *Rustic Adornments for Homes of Taste* by Shirley Hibberd. The buzzing of bees recalled 'the green youth of the world . . . the hum of Pan's great festival'.

THE APIARY

hollyhocks . . . to the dignified pavilion which . . . [is entitled] the Temple of Nature.' (See Figure 3.10.)

Thatch was essential for a country effect and hives ('bee-canopies'), and anything with peasant potential such as croquet seats and dovecots had roofs of bark, thatch, reeds, moss or heather. In such delectable settings suited to ladies' ambles, painting and poetic musing there was the joy of John Clare's *The Shepherd's Calendar*, without so much as a hint of the harsh realities of typical Victorian peasant life (or Clare's tragic later years). In this poem Clare described the flowers of the traditional, uncontrived cottage garden:

> Fine cabbage-roses, painted like her face,
> The shiny pansy, trimm'd with golden lace,
> The tall-topp'd larkheels, feather'd thick with
> flowers,
> The woodbine, climbing o'er the door in
> bowers,
> The London tufts, of many a mottled hue,
> The pale pink pea, and monkshood darkly
> blue,
> The white and purple gilliflowers, that stay
> Ling'ring, in blossom, summer half away,
> The single blood-walls, of a luscious smell,
> [wallflowers]
> Old-fashion'd flowers which housewives love
> so well,
> The columbines, stone-blue, or deep night-
> brown
> Their honeycomb-like blossoms hanging
> down,
> Each cottage-garden's fond adopted child
> .   .   .   .   .   .   .   .   .
> With marjoram knots, sweetbrier, and ribbon-
> grass,
> And lavender, the choice of ev'ry lass,
> And sprigs of lad's-love – all familiar names,
> [traveller's joy]
> Which every garden through the village
> claims.

It was unplanned simplicity such as this which in the 1870s inspired rustic styles which were real and lasting: the woodland garden with natural-ised bulbs and herbaceous borders. The steering forces were William Robinson and Gertrude Jekyll, both of whom were captivated by the wild countryside and cottage gardens as they really were. Country cottage gardens had also been lovingly described by Wordsworth in his *Guide to the Lakes*. Theirs were the old-fashioned flowers lacking flamboyance: hollyhocks (see figure 3.6), foxgloves, love-in-a-mist and lavenders.

The charm of the cottage garden was its lack of contrived design and this was the springboard of Robinson's garden-making. Flowers were not a pigment to colour a geometric bed, nor were they planted to create a feigned echo of thatched rusticity; the colour, scent, texture and shape all went to make up the particular quality of each flower and all these things were combined in the creation of Robinson's herbaceous borders of hardy perennial plants. He brought the wild flowers of the countryside into his gardens where they were planted in a natural setting.

Ruskin was of a similar inclination: he 'took more pleasure in the wood anemone – Silvia, he called it' than anything a nurseryman could offer. At Brantwood in the Lake District his land-scaping of paths, steps and bridges was dictated by the local features and natural advantages, and he pointed out the wild mosses and ivy of an old stone wall with the same loving pride as an orchid fancier showing off an odontoglossom. Here was a real love of the simple and the rustic: 'just the refinement of feeling which made a flight of steps into a rock-garden and a tennis-ground into a Purist painter's glade'. He planted his field with narcissuses.

These were practical and beautiful ideas, but woodland settings of drifts of snowdrops, daffodils, wild bluebells, foxgloves and colum-bines held a certain charisma for ladies of Sentiment – the nostalgia of childhood. The wild carpets of flowers were rendered as irresistible as the Rhine forget-me-not. Bluebells had been barely mentioned in literature prior to the Vic-torian era but then blossomed in eulogies and childhood musings. Tennyson aptly described them as 'blue sky breaking up through the earth'; the drawing-room muses were transported to a fairyland. The childhood fantasy of pendant flowers, with their delicate petals so reminiscent of bells, was too much for Louisa Anne Twamley and Charlotte M. Yonge. In *Flora's Gems* the former wrote her verse to the bluebell along bedtime story lines:

> We gaily sing, will Bluebells ring
>   Their peals, so soft and fine;
> Our banquet's spread on a mushroom's head,
>   While the laughing stars do shine.

Thus sang the 'Chorus of Fairies' in the poem 'The Fairy Couch', written for adults. Charlotte M. Yonge was ostensibly writing natural history for a young audience when she wrote:

> the foxglove peals of bells have in general ceased to ring before the 1st of August . . . but surely if we could but hear them, the sweetest and softest tones of all must be rung out by the single bells of the dear little delicate harebell, nodding on its slim tender stalk, looking so frail. . . . Other bells are ringing round it on the common, especially the heather bells, which I could fancy would make a sharp, quick, tinkling sound, just fit for a fairy's dinner bell.

Leaving aside the fairy bells of woodland, meadow and heath, the whole countryside lent itself to daydreams. Anne Pratt gave irresistible pictures of the countryside and its traditional occupations, with every ingredient of the idyllic life away from it all. She wrote, for example, about the hop gardens of Kent, Sussex and Hereford (see Figure 2.11):

> We have in our summer walk many sweet scents wafted to us by the breeze from honeysuckle hedges and flowering bean-fields, from the hay lying outspread on the meadow, from blossoming broom and briar roses, or stronger still, from fields of lavender, which spring up to reward the grower's toil; but not one of the summer odours can equal that which, in September, and October, fills the hop-garden with incense, and may be enjoyed long ere we approach its bounds.

Common country scenes like water-lilies in village ponds and streams brought similar effusive outpourings, with a touch of jingoistic patriotism:

> The waters which run their silvery course through our meadows, or lie in quiet lakes amid their greenness, bear some of the loveliest of our native flowers. Those who have marked the rich vegetation of tropical countries, tell us that nowhere are they so much reminded of their luxuriance as when they gaze on a stream with its margin decked with tall blossoms, and its little islets of emerald grass and glowing wild flowers. . . . [The

water-] lily with its rose-like sculptured cup of alabaster lying among its glossy bright-green leaves, is without gainsay queen of the waters.

## New Discoveries of Botany and Science

Fairytale glades and alabaster water-lilies seem to be daydreams far removed from scientific instruction. In fact, the two were inseparable for the Victorian writer with sentimental inclinations and for the romantic writer with botanical leanings. Part of Louisa Anne Twamley's verse on hollyhocks illustrates the botanical muse. She focused not on the bright petals but on the insignificant green cup, the calyx, which holds them invisible in the open flower until one twists it round. The calyx is most noticeable in the tightly closed bud. This most unpromising feature of the hollyhock came in for Miss Twamley's brand of transformation bound to suit nineteenth-century ideals:

> Lessening to the top,
> The yet unopened buds, enfolded close
> Within their paly calyces, all seemed
> Liked veilèd nuns beside the gorgeous show
> Of their gay rainbow-relatives.

Wallowing in her quasi-religious vein, Miss Twamley forgot the botanical detail that the hollyhocks so demurely 'veilèd' held both sexes – hardly suited to the life of botanical nuns.

In ostensibly serious books botany lent iself to sentiment in connection with the sort of places where one sought the subject under investigation. Also, the beauty and the undoubted marvel of mechanism of the subject were a source of wonder.

In 1879 Arabella Buckley rendered the science of life palatable to children along these lines before handing on all the queries to convenient fairies in *The Fairy-land of Science*. After the bare winter, 'the whole wood is carpeted with delicate green leaves, with nodding bluebells, and pale-yellow primroses, as if a fairy had touched the ground and covered it with fresh young life'. One of her dazzling (and ever extending) cast of real fairies then enters the enchanted glade. The real 'wonder-working fairies' of science:

> have been at work here; the fairy 'Life', of whom we know so little, though we love her

so well and rejoice in the beautiful forms she can produce; the fairy sunbeams with their invisible influence kissing the tiny shoots and warming them into vigour and activity; the gentle rain-drops, the balmy air, all these have been working, while you or I passed heedlessly by.

The invisible fairies then busied themselves to materialise a third fairy, 'the force of "chemical attraction" ', which mysteriously explained how things like the little snowdrop plant grew and blossomed 'without any help from you or me'. Up in the clouds there was another of 'our invisible fairies, which, for want of a better name, we call the "force of crystallization" '. 'I promise you', wrote Arabella Buckley:

> they shall be true fairies, whom you will love just as much when you are old and greyheaded as when you are young; for you will be able to call them up wherever you wander by land or by sea, through meadow or through wood, through water or through air; and though they themselves will always remain invisible, yet you will see their wonderful power at work every where around you.

This promise followed the opening page of the book which had featured a vignette of Sleeping Beauty's palace encrusted with icicles (hanging decoratively from the first letter of the text), with a medieval Prince Charming rousing the princess. Throughout the book, the first page of each chapter was similarly embellished, regardless of the unpromising subject-matter, 'W's lending themselves to leafy twiggery and 'I's to a coal face axe.

Other writers were striving to clothe naked science in 'the more attractive garb of fairy tale', such as J.C. Brough in *The Fairy Tales of Science*, published in 1859. Most writers avoided fairies but still managed to impart a certain smugness to honey bees and a nebulous imagery to lichens. Pollinating bees were transformed into 'clever little gatherers of honey' while lichens were rendered fascinating (by Charlotte M. Yonge) via a devious look at the human occupants, squalid or wholesome, behind the windows of a brick terrace of houses. This led eventually from the moral lessons therein to the equally varied life of the lichen inhabitants of the bricks:

> First is a cloudy sort of splotch of grey, shaded off into edges of silvery white . . . then comes another cloud, but this is yellow instead of white, and what a funny shape it is, something like China and Hindostan in the map, with two or three little yellow islands round it. . . This strange painting on bricks and stones is one of the least understood and most curious things in creation, for when I have told you that these grey and yellow clouds are lichens, you know nothing more than their name, and I have very little more to tell you. Great microscopes, and minds which are microscopes in comparison with ours, have been set to work on these little things, and can only make out enough to be sure that there are still greater wonders yet to be discovered.

Shirley Hibberd's portrayal of scientific discoveries with *Brambles and Bay Leaves: Essays on the Homely and the Beautiful* was similarly awestruck. He was confident (like so many) that Victorian science was uncovering respectable truths in accordance with religious tradition which were suitable for translation into a popular guise:

> In one direction the earnest workers are probing the secrets of nature, and unravelling one by one the mystic threads that run through all her fabrications; and in another, poet minds are arranging and diffusing the facts . . . that all the world may become inheritors of the new possession. . .

'Diffusing the facts' was certainly apt but the 'new possession' complete with its woolly veil which Hibberd's 'poet mind' conveyed to the world of flower lovers is nonetheless irresistible. Few authors could make whimsy out of the cycle of death and decay and the circulation of carbon through the air, plant, earth and back to air. 'Nature', said Hibberd, 'is like a great laboratory, a necromantic palace of mutation . . .':

> The atom of charcoal which floated in the corrupt atmosphere of the old volcanic ages, was absorbed into the leaf of a fern when the valleys became green and luxuriant; and there, in its proper place, it received the sunlight and the dew, aiding to fling back to heaven a reflection of heaven's gold; and at the same time to build the tough fibre of the plant. That

same atom was consigned to the tomb when the waters submerged the jungled valleys. It had lain there thousands of years, and a month since was brought into the light again, imbedded in a block of coal. [See Figure 9.7] It shall be consumed to warm our dwelling, cook our food, and make more ruddy and cheerful the hearth whereon our children play: it shall combine with a portion of the invisible atmosphere, ascend upward as a curling wreath to revel in a mazy dance high up in the blue ether; shall reach earth again, and be entrapped in the embrace of a flower: shall live in the velvet beauty on the cheek of the apricot; shall pass into t' .e human body, giving enjoyment to the palate, and health to the blood; shall circulate in the delicate tissues of the brain; and aid, by entering into some new combination, in enducing the thoughts which are now being uttered by the pen. Yet out of all this passing and repassing . . . she still . . . looks upon us with the same sweet mother's smile which gladdened the hearts of the old thinkers, and cheered the builders of the ancient temples. Nature has but a few simple materials . . . and yet with this poverty of means does she trick out all the world in scenes of delicious beauty.

One can smile at his verbal excesses but such fanciful thoughts are the more endearing as in essence they are true and as breathtaking today as they were then. The antiquity of coal and its combustion was a source of continuous fascination and Arabella Buckley's style of explanation in *The Fairy-land of Science* makes an interesting comparison with Hibberd's picture:

Have you not read of gnomes buried down deep in the earth, in mines, and held fast there till some fairy wand has released them, and allowed them to come to earth again? Well, thousands and millions of years ago, those coals were plants; and, like the snowdrop in the garden of to-day, they caught the sun-beams and worked them into their leaves. Then the plants died and were buried deep in the earth and the sunbeams with them; and like the gnomes they lay imprisoned till the coals were dug out by the miners, and brought to your grate; and just now you yourself took hold of the fairy wand which was to release them. You struck a match, and its atoms clashing with atoms of oxygen in the air, set the invisible fairies 'heat' and 'chemical attrac-tion' to work, and they were soon busy within the wood and the coals causing their atoms too to clash; and the sunbeams, so long imprisoned, leapt into flame.

Later on she led the young readers on an imaginary journey underground through coal galleries to see the fossil ferns in the coal.

An equally improbable rendering of scientific discovery involved Halley's comet, which appeared on a Valentine card of 1835. In the distance stands the church; a pair of lovers sit under a splotlight emanating from the great star, while cherubs attend them, draping garlands which are being scattered from the clouds by Hymen in a dove-drawn chariot. A banner proclaims 'The COMET changed to a VALENTINE for the 14th of February' while the verse beneath has the necessary scientific content:

Cupid by the Comet's blaze
Sets Lovers hearts on fire. . .

*Chapter 4*

# MORALITY

## Morals from Eden

The Victorians inherited a tradition of floral morality originating from the Book of Genesis. In the eighteenth century the expanding interest in horticulture and botany had been lent a certain desirability as an 'Innocent and Healthful occupation', in view of horticulture 'being by the All-wise Creator appointed to be the Employment of our first Parents in their Innocent State'. The same phrases appeared unchanged through much of the nineteenth century.

The Old Testament was seen to endorse the investigation of plants as well as their culture; Linnaeus named Adam as 'the first, and most intelligent Botanist' who spent most of his hours 'in this garden or museum of delights' examining 'the admirable works of his Creator'. Nearly a century later the Victorians had elevated these enquiries to the highest moral standing.

The other side of the coin was the presence of thorns and prickles as punishing reminders of the fall of Adam and his expulsion from the innocent garden. The presence of weeds and other difficulties of cultivation were directly attributable to Man's disobedience rather than any natural cause favouring weed dispersal. Philip Miller in *The Gardener's Dictionary* 1731 described gardening thus:

It is true, since the Fall of our Progenitors, the Work is not so easy as before it was; the Curse having covered the Ground with *Thorns* and *Briars*, and caused unprofitable Weeds to spring up among the useful Plants, to rob them of their proper Nourishment; so that the Ground which before, without Cultivation, would have been spontaneously obedient to vegetative Nature, must now, by the Sweat of the Brow, and no little labour, be brought under Subjection.

Again the nineteenth century merely reiterated the view of its predecessors. Punishment appealed to the Victorians and members of the family *Rosaceae* were frequently cited as reminders of 'the curse of Adam', since they were 'the thorn-bearers'. Rebecca Hey was moved to verse in 1833 in *The Moral of Flowers*:

Ere yet the primal curse had traced
Ruin and blight on all, and placed
Thorns on the rose's stem.

Charlotte M. Yonge extracted one of her several moral reminders on the subject along the more circuitous route of one plant flourishing from another's demise – 'beauty and vigour out of rottenness and decay' – which, she decided, was not punished with the same degree of unwholesomeness as the degenerating animal corpse:

Nay, perhaps to speak more truly, it is flesh alone that really corrupts; in the vegetable world, which partakes not equally of our doom of sin, decay is not so much real decay as a change of life.

Literal interpretations of the Bible's account of the creation made it essential that every plant had a use benefiting man. If a practical purpose was not immediately apparent, there were the infinite

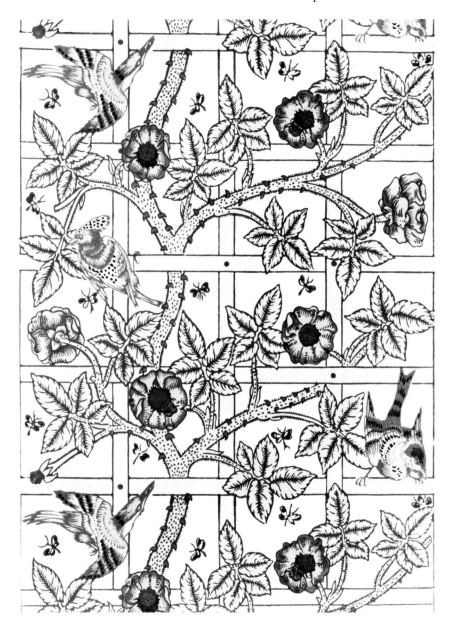

**Figure 4.1** 'Trellis', designed in 1864, was one of William Morris's earliest designs. It is thought to be based upon the rose garden and trellises which bordered the well court at Red House, Morris's home from 1860 to 1865. The superimposed birds were designed by Phillip Webb. (By courtesy of Arthur Sanderson and Sons Ltd)

possibilities of moral enlightenment. If necessary the botanical reality was corrected to fit the moral, as in the columbine (see Figure 4.5), depicted by early Flemish painters as having seven petal and sepals to accord with the seven gifts of the Holy Spirit (appropriate to the flower's supposed resemblance to fluttering doves). In fact there are five. The sweet violet (*Viola odorata*) was another portraying a message via its form and habit. It was ascribed and explained anthropomorphically in *De Proprietatibus Rerum*, a medieval treatise on nature, translated into English in 1397: 'The more vertuous the floure thereof is, the more it bendyth the head thereof downward' (quoted here from the 1535 version). The delightful idea of the humble flower, eyes downcast, was easily transferred to the Sentimental mode of the Victorian age.

A further heritage lay in the symbols of Christianity: ears of corn signifying the Holy Communion, ivy the Resurrection, orange-blossom virginity, and the lily (*Lilium candidum*), as in Roman times, the emblem of purity (see Plate 1). For Rebecca Hey the charisma of the lily extended to all white flowers. Their peculiar attraction was that they seemed 'to embody the very idea of purity and innocence'. Louisa Anne Twamley even extended the lily's features to the girl's name, in a melodramatic account of a child finding her sister Lily dead in bed one morning (having failed to appear for the healthful occupation of flower-spotting). The symbolism associated with the passionflower (see Plate 1) dated from the early Spanish missionaries in South America. They saw in it all the signs of the Passion: the five anthers signifying the five wounds when Christ was nailed to the cross by the three nails, which were depicted by the three-branch style. The long slender 'filaments' represented the crown of thorns and the calyx depicted the glory surrounding Christ's head.

## In the Eye of the Beholder

The Victorians also inherited the eighteenth-century Romantic view of natural beauty and natural theology. Nature's soothing effect on the troubled mind was frequently echoed as a reason for taking up the study of natural history. Nature's contemplative balm, expounded by the Wordsworths and Coleridge and Rousseau, became sentimental and intensely moral, even religious. For even more important than the beauty of nature was the reason *why* it was beautiful. J.S. Duncan, author of a compilation of *Botano-theology* in 1825, explains:

A man in the midst of the ocean sees . . . only the wide surface of waters, a continual sameness, which wearies the eye and sickens the heart. On a hill, amidst a fertile country abounding in produce beneficial to man, what principally meets the eye under the cope of heaven? Vegetation. It presents . . . a vast diversity of form and colour; the eye and heart are delighted. . . The eye of man is adapted, harmonized to the perception of [this] beauty. The forms and colours of external objects are adapted and harmonized to the excitement of such perception.

Thus natural beauty, indeed all beauty, was designed 'to affect the eye of man, and the eye to move the soul'. The argument was continued by J.L. Knapp in *The Journal of a Naturalist* (1829):

[for the] mind that is delighted with such admiration, must be almost insensibly led to an attendant pleasure, the contemplation, the perception of infinite wisdom and power, manifested in the adornment, splendour, and formation, of even the simplest flower of the field. [see figure 4.3]

The intricate design of flowers was part of this Grand Design for man's edification and, as ornaments of house and garden, flowers were the most immediate subjects for wonder and contemplation. They were, in the words of 'that elegant poetess, Miss Twamley':

the sweetest lines in the *God-written* poetry of nature . . . [that] seem to form the easiest and pleasantest path-way to further love and knowledge of Nature's glories . . . [each being] so wonderfully and so beautifully adapted to its appointed portion in the vast whole.

(The Romance of Nature)

John Lindley in *Ladies' Botany* used the same allusion:

We must learn to understand the mysterious language in which we are addressed; and we find its symbols in the curious structure, and the wondrous fitness of all the minute parts of which a plant consists, for the several uses they are destined for. This, and this only, is the 'language of flowers' . . .

The Design of each living thing 'for a wise and worthy end' with nothing 'made in vain' formed the backbone of natural history study throughout most of the nineteenth century. The

**Figure 4.2** Thoughts of 'sacred meaning' over an infant's scattered bunch of flowers: 'Was not this beautiful green dell His Court, and had not His angels led little King Pepito here to worship him?' (From *The Royal Progress of King Pepito* by Beatrice Cresswell, illustrated by Kate Greenaway)

authority to whom all referred (or mostly just alluded, by means of the key words, Design and Providence), was William Paley's 1802 rendering of *Natural Theology*, which harked back to eighteenth-century philosophy. (Paley's misunderstandings of floral mechanisms and insect metamorphosis dated from about the same time.) Natural theology's overriding message of looking 'through Nature up to Nature's God' was a quote from Alexander Pope's *An Essay on Man* of 1733. To understand the 'divine

œconomy' was to gain a closer knowlege of God, thus natural history gained a pious aura; a massive collection of pressed plants implied immense dedication and virtue, while writings were heavily punctuated with appropriate thoughts. 'Good moral lessons' were everywhere: John Ruskin found them in the city gutter: 'Even in the heart of the foul city it is not altogether base; down in that, if you will look deep, you may see the dark serious blue of far off sky, and the passing pure clouds.' Charlotte M.

**Figure 4.3**
And simple small 'forget-me-not',
Eyed with a pin's-head yellow spot
I'the middle of its tender blue,
That gains from poets notice due

.    .    .    .    .    .    .    .    .    .    .

And oft the dame will feel inclined,
As childhood's memory comes to mind,
To turn her hook away, and spare
The blooms it loved to gather there.

(From *The Shepherd's Calendar* by John Clare)

The picture shows miniature weeds from a cornfield: the field pansy (*Viola arvensis*), common forget-me-not (*Myosotis arvensis*), scarlet pimpernel (*Anagallis arvensis*), and common persicaria (*Polygonum persicaria*). (Photograph: Hampshire, July)

Yonge saw 'how in every plant, God has set lessons of His Name and Nature for those who will look for them'.

Notice of the simple flowers and 'minor productions' growing wild by cornfields (see Figure 4.3) and hedgerows or 'twinkling' through the grass (see Plate 1) seemed to carry extra virtue. Botanists of the calibre of John Lindley wrote:

The power and wisdom of the Deity are proclaimed by no part of the Creation in more impressive language than by the humblest weed that we tread beneath our feet . . . The love for flowers is a holy feeling, inseparable from our very nature . . . it grows up and flourishes with our innocence.

The simpler the flower (and the more beloved of

children), the more piety surrounded its minute study. The innocence and simplicity of 'the infant sporting in the sunny field' and the simplicity of the common daisy habitually merged into an intoxicatingly potent mixture of sentiment and morality. Canon H.N. Ellacombe, a popular writer of sentimental flower books, began a lecture in 1874 thus:

> I almost feel that I ought to apologise to the Field Club for asking them to listen to a paper on so little a subject as the Daisy. But indeed, I have selected that subject because I think it is one especially suited to a Naturalists' Field Club. The members of such a club, as I think, should take notice of everything. Nothing should be beneath their notice. It should be their province to note a multitude of little facts unnoticed by others; they should be 'minute philosophers'.

After twelve pages of poetic associations and less than two on botany, he concluded with the thought that the daisy was:

> the special flower of childhood, but we cannot entirely give it up to our children. And I have tried to show you that the humble Daisy has

**Figure 4.4** The appeal of the innocent infant gathering wild flowers: 'Pepito has smelt something sweet, it comes from a pale greeny-white flower, and eagerly he gathers it in his chubby hand. Ah, those butterfly orchids, how they lead one on!' (From *The Royal Progress of King Pepito* by Beatrice Cresswell, illustrated by Kate Greenaway)

been the delight of many noble minds, and may be a fit subject of study even for those children of a larger growth who form the Bath Field Club.

Thus a naturalist did much more than identify and collect: it was his (or her) occupation 'to note and proclaim such manifestations of wisdom or goodness as may be perceived by him', learn 'the poetical images' connected with flowers and accord with Rousseau's thought that flowers 'seem to grow beneath our feet as if to invite us to their contemplation'. J.L. Knapp, and many others, wrote eloquently on this elevated aspect of botanising:

> Perhaps none of the amusements of human life are more satisfactory and dignified, than the investigation and survey of the workings and ways of Providence in this created world of wonders . . . it occupies and elevates the mind, is inexhaustible in supply, and, while it furnishes meditation for the closet of the studious, gives to the reflections of the moralizing rambler admiration and delight, and is an engaging companion, that will communicate an interest to every rural walk.

### The Moral and the Useful

True to their time, most Victorian naturalists considered the more tangible advantages of their subject – in terms of personal and social gain. One recommendation they gave was that 'the examination of the plants . . . collected tends much to quicken the faculties, improve the memory, induce habits of order and neatness'. It was particularly recommended for the young, for once having seen 'the wonders that nature has in store . . . a field of research is ever open that well compensates for the loss of those venial pleasures in which the young of both sexes in this age of sensational enjoyment too often indulge to the injury of both mind and body'. Surprisingly these thoughts did not stem from a comfortable middle-class villa but from the spartan rooms of a working man, Joseph Gutteridge. The Rev. Mr Boyd, who was the patron of the humble Thomas Edward, proffered similar advice to all through *The Fraserburgh Advertiser*:

> Happy would it be, if our tradesmen were to take a leaf out of Mr Edward's book, and

instead of wasting their time, squandering their means, and embittering their existence in the haunts of dissipation, they would sally forth in these calm summer evenings to rural scenes and sylvan solitudes, to woo Nature in her mildest aspect.

Considering the physical suffering Edward suffered in order to make his natural history collections and to learn his subject, the Reverend gentleman's images were ludicrously misplaced.

There was also the promise of a happier, more patient disposition, a more interesting character and a longer life of increased virtue. For 'men never step into the presence of nature with appreciation and reverence, but they come back blessed and strengthened with a reward', said Phoebe Lankester, a mill owner's daughter. There were many like her, brimming with approval and good advice for the working classes based on their personal experience of 'the superior tone and manners' of 'humble admirers of nature'. Horticulture was an equally beneficial occupation for the 'working man . . . and for those who might cast a glance at his home', according to 'a novice' who wrote to *The Floricultural Cabinet and Florists' Magazine*. He suggested it would be 'most desirable' for horticultural exhibitions to offer cottagers' prizes for flowers as well as produce, as:

> What is more refreshing to the eye when walking, than to see the nicely kept and prettily stocked garden of the cottager, with its various flowers! How it raises one's opinion of the inmates! How desirable to induce the working-man to attend to his little plot, and desert the beer-shop and skittle-ground . . . The cultivation of flowers is not sufficiently attended to by some cottagers near our large towns.

Health of body and mind was a recurrent theme: 'Rambling over the fields, in the necessary search for the little gems that grow there, tranquilizes the feelings, and invigorates the health both of body and mind' – a stirring call to botanise by G.W. Francis in *The Little English Flora* of 1849, while Anne Pratt even cited a priest who had said 'that, in all his extensive practice in insanity, he never met with an insane naturalist'. Joseph Gutteridge, one of the few writers in a position to truly judge nature's healing properties, attributed his fortitude in bearing up against his 'difficulties and trials' to his 'love of natural products' which brought him 'plenty of fresh air'. The middle classes were more in need of fortitude to survive boredom – and natural history lent itself admirably as an 'innocent amusement', comparable even to a theatre play. The traditional view shaped by natural theology was that such entertaining occupation was by Divine appointment for otherwise 'it would have been sufficient for that wisdom . . . to have produced an undigested chaos, in which, like worms in cheese, we might have indulged in eating and sleeping' – sage thoughts from Carl Linnaeus. Fortunately the 'great and bountiful Author of nature' seemed to have had the foresight to provide stimulating botanical hobbies for those who were tempted to follow the example of the worms. For, as Linnaeus said, the world was formed such:

> that the earth should afford an endless variety, seemingly with intent that the novelty of the objects should excite his curiosity, and hinder him from being disgusted by two [sic] much uniformity, as it has happened to some wretches, whose station in life placed them above labour, and who wanted curiosity to look into these things.

By the nineteenth century the entertainment value of floral study had extended beyond those in the idler stations of life reading *Botanical Dialogues* (1797) for whom 'philosophical experiments' would provide an interest at home, so that no more time than was absolutely necessary would be given in 'the civility of social life to idle and profitless company'. With botany behind him, any young man would be 'eager to return to [his] . . . seeds and roots'. Alphonse Karr's *A Tour Round my Garden*, translated by the Rev. J.G. Wood in the 1850s, showed:

> what compensations the Creator provides for persons in different stations. Its first object is to solace those who cannot travel, by showing that in the small compass of a Paris garden all the advantages of travel are to be obtained, without its expense and inconveniences. On the other hand, it consoles those who have not a yard of ground of their own by showing that they are free of the whole earth. (From *Blackwood's Magazine*, October 1855)

## Fanciful Morality

Where there were no biblical and traditional morals or poetic associations with a flower, the Victorians created fanciful ones of their own in an attempt to display the moral and the useful. Rebecca Hey was a devotee of the art in view of 'the frequent allusion to flowers in the holy writ' which seemed 'to invest them with a sacred character'. She said that God 'referred us to them for instruction.' Her musings had an unmistakeable Victorian message, conveyed in her poems gathered together under the title *The Moral of Flowers*. To her, flowers spread the world not with sweetness and light but with moral messages heavy with overtones of mortality and gloom. She was ever mindful of 'emblems and suggestions of higher things' and managed to create moral symbols out of the most unlikely raw materials, such as night flowering species. To her, an evening primrose drooping by day was not a night flower off duty but an emblem of christian humility and just reward. Asked to explain its lone night vigil by a genteel lady, the 'pale flower' replied:

> Eve is my noon – at this still hour,
> When softly sleeps each sister flower,
> Sole watcher of the dusky bower
>     I joy to be,
> And conscious feel the pale moon shower
>     Her light on me.
>
> Say thou who thus dost question me,
> Wouldst thou from earth's dull cares be free
> O listen and I'll counsel thee
>     Wisely to shun
> Tumult and glare and vanity,
>     As I have done.

The enjoyment and beauty of even a brightly coloured flower was always checked by dark clouds and nowhere more appropriately than in the scarlet pimpernel (*Anagallis arvensis*). Traditionally the flower was a look-out for oncoming rain, hence its alternative name, 'Poor-man's-weather-glass' (the flower opens in the morning depending on temperature and humidity). Mrs Hey drew suitable conclusions from the flower's forecasting abilities 'warning the swain to sheltering bower'. She challenges the flower for being shut on a bright sunny day:

Despite my taunt, the prescient flower,
　　Still closed its petals bright,
And soon the storm, with voice of power,
　　Shew'd its forebodings right.
'Tis ever thus – some sudden blight,
　　When most we dream of joy,
Does on the shining prospect light
　　To mar it and destroy.
Oh! when like this poor flower shall I
Discern aright life's changing sky?

Louisa Anne Twamley found a moral message in an unexpected source. She aspired to the ideals of the time with an intensity that belongs only to that age and in the columbine (see Figure 4.5), saw the flower's moral inclinations hinted in its shape. On account of the five tubular petals, containing nectar, the columbine was also known as 'Folly's flower'; Miss Twamley explains that it was given the name: 'in allusion to the form of its nectary, which turns over like the caps of the old jesters, and those which the painters give to Folly'. Here was a golden opportunity which an aspiring moralist could not pass by and she urged the reader to pick columbine as an appropriate flower for all:

Examine well each flow'ret's form –
　　Read ye not something more
Than curl of petal – depth of tint?

　　.　　　.　　　.　　　.　　　.

Know ye the cap which Folly wears
　　In ancient masques and plays?
Doth not the Columbine recall
　　That toy of olden days?
And is not folly reigning now
O'er many a wisdom-written brow?

'Tis Folly's Flower, that homely one;
　　That universal guest
Makes every garden but a type
　　Of every human breast;
For though ye tend both mind and bower,
There's still a nook for Folly's Flower.
　　　　　　　　(From 'Folly's Flower')

The beauty of the rose was akin to folly, for when it was not 'upon the virgin thorn' destined to 'grow, live, and die in single blessedness', it was the embodiment of vanity: a mere reminder of its own transience. Louisa Anne Twamley

**Figure 4.5** Columbine (*Aquilegia*) was given the alternative name of 'Folly's flower' because of the resemblance of its five long nectary petals to a jester's cap.

rendered the lesson in a verse in *Flora's Gems* describing the pride of the rose the day it burst from the bud:

And how delighted with the praise
　　Of a bright butterfly.

But other roses opened soon,
　　And he to them did hie –
The rude winds ruffled my fair leaves –
　　Alack! how sad was I!

The theme of beauty's transience and its inevitable demise was popular with Rebecca Hey who introduced it into her musings on the woody nightshade (*Solanum dulcamara*):

　　. . . let thy graceful wreath
For one moment be lightly flung
Round the mirror of beauty, to show her
　　beneath

What is lovely and bright lurk the seeds of
    death;
    And despite bland flattery's tongue,
She might learn this lesson for after-hour,
That beauty alone is a worthless dower.

Surprisingly she did not even approve of the
woody nightshade's beauty as a fitting guise of
poison. She vehemently denounced its purple
and yellow flower and berries, glinting green,
yellow, orange and red (see Plate 15):

Away, away with thy tempting bloom –
    Go seek thee a fitting bower –
In the church-yard drear by the haunted tomb,
Or the falling shrine make thy cheerless home,
    Thou fair but treacherous flower. . .

Love, where it dared to raise its head in these
moral verses, was long-suffering and wholesome.
In contrast to the transiently gorgeous rose as the
quintessence of true love in *The Language of
Flowers*, Rebecca Hey chose the dark evergreen
ivy in its most gloomy and sublime setting of
crumbling ruins. Before launching into the
moral of its 'thousand tendrils' – unfaltering love
in old age – she gave a brief acknowledgement
of:

the picturesque beauty it throws around every
object to which it attaches itself . . . we doubt
whether Adam, to whom his fair consort . . .
assigned the task of directing 'the clasping ivy
where to climb', could have twined it more
tastefully. . .

Have you e'er seen the moon's soft splendour
    Sleep peaceful on some ruined pile,
Gliding, with radiance mild and tender, o'er
    Each broken arch and mouldering aisle?

Have you e'er seen the ivy clinging,
    Round fragments broken and decayed,
As if its mantling wreaths 'twere flinging,
    To hide the breaches time had made?

.   .   .   .   .   .   .   .

And when, at last, each youthful token
    Shall yield to wasting and decay,
And thou, like arch or column broken,
    Shalt feel proud manhood's stength give
        way;

Oh! then may love, by time unshaken,
    Around its earliest prop still cling,
(For when was mouldering arch forsaken
    By the fond wreath it caused to spring?)

The poisonous berries of the ivy did carry a
warning but not the one which one might
expect. Traditionally ivy was companion to the
vine, and formed the crown of Bacchus. Regardless of this mythology and of druidic associations, Mrs Hey steered it sternly down the
straight and narrow path of christian morals
away from 'such unhallowed purposes'. She
managed to be consistent in her approval of the
ivy's morality and to twist the ancient traditions
to hidden virtue:

Besides the consideration of its usual haunts [in
graveyards], there is something so sombre in
its appearance as makes it seem but little akin
to revelry. One might almost imagine that in
wreathing the goblet with its graceful
branches, garnished with bright but poisonous
berries, it was designed to point a moral by
alluding to 'the sweet poison of misused wine'.

Other plants associated with ecstatic revelry
were not so fortunately judged. The tulip was
initially a wild Turkish and Middle Eastern
flower (see Plate 14), possibly named after a
turban, and the flower's unfortunate association
was the tulip fête of eighteenth-century Turkey.
Among garlanded trellises, candles and singing
birds, the harem was ceremoniously let loose
into a tulip-decked courtyard as a prelude to the
ruler choosing one privileged woman. Apparently some of the women, in a state of near-
hysteria, tore at the tulips to destroy their
beauty, in a spasm of passionate jealousy. To
nineteenth-century Britons tales of such debau-
chery were utterly scandalous and the tulip
became, for some, a marked flower:

Thou art honoured there,
Where Sultans hold the 'Tulip Feast', mid all
That lavish luxury's fantastic dreams
Or royal sensuality can ask.
There, amid turbaned courtiers like thyself,
And Harem-beauties, charming but the eye,
Thy garish, scentless flowers are in place. . .
                                    (*Flora's Gems*)

The horrified Louisa Anne Twamley could
barely find insults enough for the flower:

I have less love for thee, thou gorgeous
    Flower,
Than many a hedge-row weed: for thou dost
    seem
So haughty and unbending, so elate,
Rising alone upon thy pillar-stem,
And looking ever upward, as if nought
Beneath thy turbaned head were worth a
    glance.
Oh, thou'rt a courtier, Tulip! and thine eye
Looks ever to the fount whence favours come,
With greedy avarice. Thou would'st
    methinks,
Be a fit emblem for some beings here,
Who proudly flaunt it in a gay attire,
And lift themselves disdainfully as thou:
Like thee, their gaudy show is all their wealth;
In both alike we find a blackened core.

              (From *Flora's Gems*)

Like Louisa Anne Twamley, Rebecca Hey disapproved of flowers tainted by association with non-christian living, particularly the oriental variety. The beautiful scented summer jasmine, for example, bordered on the suspect as its blooms decorated the shining black tresses of oriental women, while from its stems were fashioned 'the highly ornamented pipes so needful to the enjoyment of their idle and luxurious lords'.

There were less elegant, more direct ways of delivering the morals to be drawn from flowers. One of these was the sudden and unashamed sermon – appearing like an oasis – in the middle of botanical detail. In describing the tiny heather flowers tinting purple moorlands and distant mountains, Charlotte M. Yonge drew this parallel: 'The whole Church, and the whole nation, take their colour more from the multitude of the lowly and humble numbers, than from the great and noted.' The daily turning of the sunflower head to follow the sun's course was, for her:

one of the brightest, clearest lessons written in God's great book of nature; for is it not thus that the Christian, through the morning, noon-day, and even-tide of his life, earnestly looks up to the Sun of Righteousness in heaven . . . and when at length night comes upon him, is he not laid down to sleep, with his face towards the east, watching for the dawning of the brightest day?

The good fruit of the grafted peach or apricot tree (versus that 'sprung from seed') drew predictable thoughts, for example, in the middle of explaining the Linnaean classification and flower structure from Charlotte Yonge: 'should not the grafting of a tree put us in mind to pray that God will graft in our hearts the love of His name, increase in us true religion, and nourish us with all goodness?'

The polypody fern – or maybe its lesson – was one of Charlotte M. Yonge's unashamed favourites:

I like the polypody . . . it is one of those cheerful, humble things, that seems to have a kindness for what is venerable and excellent, even in decay. It . . . feathers up the broken arch of the ruined chapel, through autumn and winter, just as we should cheerfully, though soberly, hold fast to the old bulwarks of our faith, and of our law, and do our best to adorn them by our adherence.

Margaret Gatty went the whole way and wrote sometimes charming, sometimes morbid, moral tales for children in the vein of Aesop's fables, featuring animals, plants and the elements with characters appropriate to their habits. A villa garden was the setting for one entitled 'Training and Restraining': the Wicked Wind chides Convolvulus Major, Honeysuckle, Carnations and Rose-tree for meekly accepting their loss of freedom at the gardener's hand. Dazzled with images of the good life of their wild counterparts they beg him to tear away their canes and fastenings. He obliges and heavy rain dashes them to the ground where the errant flowers must remain bruised and untended in their remorse until the lady of the house and her daughter return. The child weeps at the sight of her 'once orderly' garden:

'This is a sad sight, indeed, my darling,' said her mother's voice.
'I am not thinking about the garden, mamma,' replied the young girl, without lifting up her face; 'we can plant new flowers, and tie up even some of these afresh. I am thinking that now, at last, I understand what you say about the necessity of training, and restraint, and culture, for us as well as for flowers.'
'In a fallen world' interposed her mother.

'Yes, – because it is fallen,' answered the daughter. 'The wind has torn away these poor things from their fastenings, and they are growing wild whichever way they please; and I might perhaps once have argued, that if it were their *natural* way of growing it must therefore be the best. But I cannot say so, now I see the result. They are doing whatever they like, unrestrained; and the end is, – my beautiful GARDEN is turned into a WILDERNESS.'

Such sermonising created some extraordinary titles: *The Ministry of Flowers, being some thoughts respecting life, suggested by the book of Nature* to name one published in 1885, and 'Floral Decay: emblematical of man's mortal condition' in 1850. The latter appeared in a collection of *Poetical Trifles* by the Rev. R. Warner who aspired to a somewhat Byronesque pose in his frontispiece portrait, with quill and distant eyes. His trifles were no more trifling and lightweight than the gilded leather-bound album to which they had been entrusted. His interpretation of the summer jasmine could not have been more different from Rebecca Hey's (see page 57):

Ye *Jasmines* pure, of *modest white*!
　And *Odour*, passing *Araby*!
How soon ye'll vanish from my sight! –
　For, ye, alas! *must shortly die*!

nor his thoughts on the sunflower from those of Charlotte M. Yonge (a flower's moral was obviously very open to individual interpretation):

And, thou, *Bold plant*, that *lov'st* the sun!
　(*Emblem of human vanity*:)
Shalt, soon, thy *measured course* have run!
　For, *thou*, alas! *must shortly* die!

The last phrase was the joyless refrain for all seven verses.

The cycle of elements displayed in plant death, decay and reappearance in another guise (described by Shirley Hibberd on page 44), was a ready topic for J.S. Duncan in *Botano-theology*. Decay, like everything else, had a moral and a Design: 'Thus it has pleased Providence to display further diversity of power . . . that even in this world the general destroyer Death is controlled and bound by the will of the great Ordainer.'

The popular verse writer the Rev. F.H. Lyte was more gentle in his reminder of mortality:

Spare this flower, this gentle flower –
　The slender creature of a day;
Let it bloom out its little hour,
　And pass away:
Too soon its fleeting charms must lie
　Decay'd, unnoticed, overthrown,
Oh! hasten not its destiny,
　Too like thy own!

## In Judgement of Living Plants

In the belief that the tiniest natural details were part of a Design for 'good' or for moral instruction, the Victorians scrutinised the world about them for its accordance with their own rigorous code of conduct. Thus everyday natural events in field, hedge and forest were judged as sins and virtues and were turned into 'parables of plant life'. Writers like John Ellor Taylor wrote titles such as *The Sagacity and Morality of Plants. A sketch of life and conduct of the vegetable kingdom*. In this book he reflected on 'the works of the flesh' manifested in the battling vegetable world and the floral heroes who yet retained the standards of the day. Plants became almost transformed into bizarre caricatures in a morality play. Such well-meant efforts obviously made biological nonsense, with humanised interpretations of plant self-sacrifice, selfishness, ambition and craftiness.

In contrast to Rebecca Hey and Louisa Anne Twamley, Taylor designated the tulip a noble flower. Taylor agreed with earlier writers that it was the lily of the field mentioned in the Bible, except his conviction was based on what he saw as the commendable morals inherent in botanical aspects of the flower's structure. The calyx, usually green, unglamorous and leaf-like (as in the rose) was, in the tulip, as:

beautiful both in colour and streak as the petals of the flowers. Such plants have taken the calyx into partnership for floral attractive purposes; and hence we have the most beautiful flowers in the world developed by such co-operation. It is therefore not without reason the Great Teacher drew attention to the 'Lilies of the Field'.

Butcher's broom (*Ruscus aculeatus*) was another plant ennobled, but by suffering – in the traditional manner of the wronged Victorian heroine. This was on account of it being the only (and rather diminutive) English representative of the very ancient and stately group of plants which included the palms. Thus, it was 'submissively growing beneath the shade of trees which came into existence ages after its own family had occupied the proud position of aristocrats in the vegetable world. What a story of quiet suffering and struggling with these plutocratic newcomers . . .'. Taylor's image has more than a touch of the wronged aristocrat in reduced circumstances.

Another typical and likeable character was that ubiquitous hero of Victorian melodrama – altruism. The ideal in all its martyred glory was portrayed by the dark outer leaves of the sticky horsechestnut (*Aesculus hippocastanum*) buds of winter:

> They are leaves whose duty it has been to sacrifice for the benefit of those inner leaves they are thus protecting from the winter's cold. They will never see the 'promised land' of next summer – will never wave green in the gentle summer breezes, or be visited by the singing birds . . . The principle of *altruism* ('self-sacrifice' and 'heroism') is thus abundantly represented even in the vegetable kingdom.
>
> (John Ellor Taylor)

A plant's moral status was not always so clear, as in the case of cow parsley (*Anthriscus sylvestris*) and its kind. In this flower community the outer flowers of the head have larger petals than the rest and Taylor pondered over the motives of these privileged flowers. 'So far . . . it would appear as if their character were *egoistic* rather than *altruistic* – that they were aristocrats, or plutocrats, rather better off than their neighbours.'

Further down the moral scale were those blatantly displaying vanity and prodigality – the double flowers. These indulged in the frippery of extra petal 'robes' instead of getting on with the serious business of producing seed. (Their extra petals were formed at the expense of the reproductive parts of the flower which was rendered reprehensibly sterile.)

In *The Herb of the Field*, Charlotte M. Yonge did not mince her words on the double anemone:

> Mr Poppy anemone . . . has an endless variety of beautiful dresses . . . [and] is a great friend of the gardeners, who think they can get him to do anything to please them, and persuade him to alter his shape, wear all manner of flounces and furbelows, and disguise himself in such strange fashion that his best friends would hardly know him again. Sometimes, indeed, he wastes all his substance in thus doubling the folds of his robes.

A less frivolous Mr Poppy Anemone 'takes off all his beautiful red or purple garments, and rolls himself up in his plain working dress, very like a grey duffle cloak', later unravelling into a multitude of seeds. A similar indictment was given to the double snowdrop. In this flower the petals:

> have used up all the strength of the plant, and even consumed these really useful parts, so that, as every body knows, a double flower never produces good fruit, but only rejoices in its own finery for a time. Not unlike some people that I could tell you of.

By contrast there was the 'good, quiet, modest snowdrop, with its green and white robes in good order, and put to their proper use, of guarding and sheltering what is within them'. (See Figure 5.4.) For some moral naturalists there could be mitigating circumstances, as in the rose, which according to Charlotte M. Yonge: 'must be pardoned for being double, since their office is to be fragrant and beautiful . . . .'.

The plant world also had aggressive criminals who emerged tainted but victorious. Such characteristics were peculiarly appropriate to a time of economic progress and Empire-building. John Ellor Taylor avidly quoted Charles Kingsley:

> Through the great republic of the forest, the motto of the majority is – as it is, and always has been, with human beings – 'Every one for himself, and the devil take the hindmost!' Selfish competition, over-reaching tyranny, the temper which fawns and clings as long as it is down, and when it has risen, kicks over the stool by which it has climbed – these, and other 'works of the flesh', are the work of the average plant.

Taylor illustrated the point with the 'tyrranous, pines dominating ground flora by dropping on them a thick carpet of needles. In the same vein, he saw the shade of the tree canopy limiting the sunlight on the woodland floor (see Figure 4.6) in terms of rich trees and creeping beggarly plants:

> In the vegetable kingdom, therefore, Lazarus can only exist by the crumbs which fall from the rich man's table! The giants of the forest have won in the battle of life by sheer strength and bulk . . . Every Spring-tide there is taking place on the peaceful hedgebanks of our green lanes, and in the bosoms of our silent woods, a contest more actively fought out than ever was visible on a human battlefield!

He pictured the exotic far-flung forest habitats of the Empire as the worst offenders of all in terms of vegetable 'greediness' (see Figure 4.7). 'In equatorial forests, especially those of ancient standing, the bush-ropes strangle, the parasites bleed, and the epiphytes [mosses, orchids and ferns] hang on for a living . . . [a] selfish mass of vegetation'. Describing how the bush ropes had climbed and twined to gain height and light, he wrote of how they had 'cheated, and strangled, and done all kinds of vegetable crimes'.

Henry Walter Bates, who lived for eleven years in the jungle, was less emotional about the equatorial creepers using their neighbours:

> with reckless indifference as instruments for their own advancement. Live and let live is clearly not the maxim taught in these wildernesses . . . The competition exists also in temperate countries, but it is there concealed under the external appearance of repose which vegetation wears.

Bates referred to a German traveller who proffered a somewhat unorthodox reason (in modern eyes) for character differences between the South American and European peoples:

> the contemplation of a Brazilian forest produced on him a painful impression on account of the vegetation displaying a spirit of restless selfishness, eager emulation, and craftiness. He thought the softness, earnestness, and repose of European woodland scenery were far more pleasing, and that these formed one of the causes of the superior moral character of European nations.

**Figure 4.6** Gilbert White's 'Beech Hanger' at Selborne: 'Every Spring-tide there is taking place . . . in the bosoms of our silent woods, a contest more actively fought out than ever was visible on a human battlefield' – John Ellor Taylor's view of 'tyrranous' woodland trees taking the sun from the small plants beneath them.

The most effective climbers were seen to be the most reprehensible as their structure was often so flimsy they could not even support themselves – they lacked the support of physical fibre as well as the moral variety. 'The climbing habit', said Taylor was 'gradually developed by weak-stemmed, ambitious, and crafty plants.'

Parasitic plants such as the broomrape (*Orobanche* spp.), 'a vegetable blood-sucker', beautifully efficient and adapted to its life style in natural terms, came in for harsh criticism: 'What renders it more disgraceful . . . is the fact that the plants the Broom-rapes attack are naturally small and feeble, such as the Clover, etc.' The ivy retrieved its image, by at least being 'honest', and not penetrating the stem of its host with its clinging stem roots.

CLASPING ROOTS OF WIGHTIA.

**Figure 4.7** Vegetable greed. The 'most remarkable' Wightia with its grasping roots sketched by Sir Joseph Dalton Hooker at one of his encampments. (From *Himalayan Journals*, 1854 – by permission of Avon County Library (Bath Reference Library))

Worst of all vegetable offenders were the insect-catching plants, as they were 'instruments of destruction to the insect world'. They displayed varying degrees of spite to their victims: the catchflies (*Silene* spp.) with 'clammy joints and calyxes, entangle them to death' rather like fly papers, the sundews (*Drosera* spp.) killed 'without torture' (see Figure 8.17), but none were 'more cruelly destructive of animal life' than the North American perennial dogsbane (American Fly-trap, *Apocynum androsaemifolium*), grown in gardens since the eighteenth century. Inside the flower's innocuous-looking pink bell, 'cement' set on the mouthparts of an insect feeding on the nectar, detaining 'the poor prisoner writhing in protracted struggles till released by death'. Since the plant was frequently 'dusky from the numbers of imprisoned wretches' and its motivation was obscure, J.L. Knapp was convinced of 'a wanton cruelty in the herb'.

At least those which consumed their insect prey needed nutrition and their leaves were especially equipped for the purpose. The leaves of the pitcher plants (*Nepenthes* spp.) from India and the Far East (see Figure 9.1) were curled and folded to make lidded pots with sweet and slippery insides where captured insects accumulated and decayed. One naturalist actually proposed that their presence in the pitcher was due to the work of an apparently manic insect – an ichneumon fly, which 'would drag other flies, and hurl them over the edge of the pitcher to destruction, as a human murderer might throw a victim over a bridge'. Shirley Hibberd's explanation in *The Amateur's Greenhouse and Conservatory* was more realistic, but still a delightfully moral interpretation:

> Inside the pitcher are numerous hairs, which project downward; and it is found that when an insect enters, its downward course is easy, but escape is almost impossible . . . Ah! the way to ruin is smooth and sometimes pleasant, and to go down is easier than to go up: so perhaps the flies find it in the pitchers, as we do also in the conduct of life.

These vegetable criminals perplexed the natural theologians who sought to justify everything as 'good' or morally commendable. However, there was always one way out: the policy of pious ignorance, favoured by J.L. Knapp and Charlotte M. Yonge:

> how little of the causes and motives of action of created things do we know! and it must be unlimitable arrogance alone that could question the wisdom of the mechanism of him 'that judgeth rightly'; the operations of a simple

plant confound and humble us, and, like the handwriting on the wall, though seen by many, can be explained but by ONE. (Knapp)

And if we know nothing of what is so like and so near to ourselves, how should we know any thing of the hidden things of nature and of providence? They seem put there to show us how dim our eyes are, and remind us that a time may come when we shall see more clearly. (Yonge)

Insect-suffering and punishment at the hand of flowers could be interpreted as morally good if it was their just desserts for bad behaviour – curiosity, overestimating their own abilities, loitering or, worse still, supposedly stealing the flower's nectar. The priorities of the industrial age focused exaggerated attention on economy, function and machinery. Thus it was not surprising that scientific enquiry into flowers and their insect pollinators often became biased towards the industrial ideals of toil, profit, just reward and efficiency untainted by waste. As living exponents of this philosophy, it was the flower's task to 'prevent the insect from merely loitering about . . . in idle satisfaction' and put it to the main task of pollinating the flower in return for realistic payment rather than 'empty gratifications'. Efficient flowers welcomed insects advantageous to their own ends – those which shared efficiency by virtue of their speedy flight and large pollen-carrying potential. In contrast, less privileged insects which were likely to waste the flower's resources without offering an advantage were ruthlessly trapped, toppled or killed slowly. Ants and beetles were in the undesirable loitering category and the Victorians were fascinated by nectar-protecting devices (such as the barricading hairs visible in the sage, see Figure 9.10) and macabre traps developed by flowers against such insects.

Anton Kerner von Marilaun specialised in this aspect of flowers in *Flowers and their Unbidden Guests*. It was a standard work in the bookcase of the serious student of flowers and, although it was a factual and academic book, something of the seriousness and ethic of the industrial age shadows the plants. His ideal flower was an allegory of thrift, introduced in very Victorian style by his translator, W. Ogle:

Now Nature, who at first sight often appears a

**Figure 4.8** Industrial terminology extended even to flowers: a bee on a globe thistle 'toils' for its 'just reward'.

prodigal, is always found on closer examination to be the most rigid of economists . . . The brilliancy, the scent, and the nectar are only furnished when the flower is ready for its guests, and requires their presence; just as a thrifty housewife lights her candles when the first guest is at the door.

Kerner's targets were not the invited guests at this floral banquet but the uninvited ones: 'Guests might come who were not of sufficient importance, and the banquet be wasted on them . . . all insignificant and unremunerative visitors must be kept out.' These luckless insects, unable to pay for their feast 'creep in by the back entrance' or try to gatecrash at the 'main portal'. He recounted the athletic attempts of ants to climb to the catkins of a willow, *Salix daphnoïdes*, each sliding down 'as though in slippery ice, and often pays for its attempts to get at the enticing nectar by tumbling to the ground from heights of several metres'. The concept of a deserved judgement on insect marauders was widespread: Philip Henry Gosse's pitcher plant casualties 'paid the forfeit of their curiosity', while even Charles Darwin fleetingly succumbed to the idea. He was watching the common twayblade

orchid, *Listera ovata* (see Figure 4.9), which glues its pollen bags explosively on to its unsuspecting insect visitors. He found an extremely minute insect vainly struggling with its whole head buried in the hardened glue. 'The insect was not so large as one of the [pollen bags] . . . and after causing the explosion it had not force to remove them, and was thus punished for attempting a work beyond its strength, and perished miserably.'

## The Delicate Topic – Euphemisms and Evasions

There was one aspect of flowers which did not totally accord with the high moral tone of natural history: this was the unmentionable business of reproduction, which was unfortunately the *raison d'être* of the flower and thus difficult to ignore. Furthermore the vehicle bringing the study of flowers within the grasp of most Victorian amateurs – Linnaeus's classification – was actually based on the number and positions of the flower's sexual organs. In view of Linnaeus's explicit descriptions and definitions, the moral prospect seemed appalling. The fears of Henrietta Maria Moriarty in 1808 that 'those ingenious speculations and allusions, which, however suited to the physiologist, are dangerous to the young and ignorant' were echoed by John Ruskin. He advised 'the gentle and happy scholar of flowers' to have nothing to do with 'these obscene processes and prurient apparitions'. One of the heinous faults of many Latin and Greek plant names was, as he put it, a very serious one, being:

of the Devil's own contriving – (and remember I am always quite serious when I speak of the Devil), – namely, that the most current and authoritative names are apt to be founded on some unclean or debasing association, so that to interpret them is to defile the reader's mind. I will give no instance: too many will at once occur to any learned reader, and the unlearned I need not vex with so much as one . . . there is only one other course open to me, namely, to substitute boldly, to my own pupils, other generic names for the plants thus faultfully titled.

In practice, many books on Linnaean classifica-

tion surreptitiously lost the purpose of male stamens and female carpels and pistils in their enthusiams for counting them. Those dealing with the 'how' and 'why' of flowers were faced with a dilemma. Phoebe Lankester circumnavigated the issue with distant generalities. Her rendering of the bee's role in floral reproduction was demure and fleeting: 'we must not consider these little creatures as merely selfish seekers of their own gratification; they, in common with the whole of creation . . . carry out the designs of the Great Architect of all.' E. Bevan in *The Honey Bee* kept a safe and vague distance by quoting Sir James Edward Smith (tutor of Queen Charlotte) on the purpose of nectar: 'to allure these venial panders to the flowers'. A well-tried means of avoiding indelicacies particularly when instructing the young was to describe the mundanities of structure and sequence while studiously omitting any emotive key words. Thus one could understand the details of the meeting and fusion of the two partners without ever knowing that male and female were in any way involved. In *The Fairy-land of Science* Arabella Buckley prepared to remark on the reproduction of the primrose in this way:

> Now for the use of these yellow bags, which are called the *anthers* of the stamens . . . they have a yellow powder in them, called *pollen*, the same as the powder which sticks to your nose when you put it into a lily; and if you look with a magnifying glass at the little green knob in the centre of the flower you will probably see some of this yellow dust sticking on it.

She went on to the centre of the flower with its

> *ovules*, or little bodies which may become seeds. If they were left as they are they would all wither and die. But those little yellow grains of pollen, which we saw sticking to the knob at the top, are coming down to help them . . . they find a tiny hole and into this they creep . . . [and the ovule has] . . . all it wanted to grow into a perfect seed.

John Ellor Taylor alternately side-stepped and solemnised the issue: the appropriate chapter in his book on the moral behaviour of plants, coyly entitled 'Floral Diplomacy', commenced with the agreeably pure process of vegetative repro-

**Figure 4.9** The common twayblade orchid (*Listera ovata*) explodes its pollen on to unsuspecting insect visitors. Darwin noted it was 'so exquisitely sensitive . . . that a touch from the thinnest human hair suffices to cause the explosion'. (Photograph: Hampshire, June)

duction by cuttings and so on, with sex remaining discreetly at bay. His more irresistible approach was that of plant reproduction cloaked in something akin to marriage – which was not as unlikely as it would seem, given that Charlotte M. Yonge could transform the nest-building of birds into 'home-making' and their eggs into 'the dear fruits of happy love'. The act of pollination when it came was duly dignified into respectability:

> The Hops [*Humulus lupulus*] take their time [to flower] – leafing first, masking the hedgerows they have conquered by wood-craft with their beautiful leaves, then placing their flowers (always on separate plants) triumphantly in the best spots for the summer breezes to carry the pollen, and to act as their marriage priests.

And John Ellor Taylor's very proper flowers did not stop there in observing moral ethics: 'Nature has everywhere forbidden the banns of inter-marriage! Her decree is rigidly carried out whenever possible, from mosses up to men.' (Presumably he discounted the hybrids produced by plant breeders.)

Poetry provided an eminently respectable covering for the facts about reproduction. Phoebe Lankester contrived the pollination of the water-lily to emerge from under a modest classical veil, with all the images of purity appropriate to the subject:

> Like the sacred Lotus of the Nile, the flowers rise and expand as the sun gains strength, and close again in the evening; sleeping as it were through the hours of darkness until called into life again by the warm rays of light.
>
> Moore:  'Those virgin lilies all the night,
>       Bathing their beauties in the
>           lake,
>       That they may rise more fresh and
>           bright
>       When their beloved sun's
>           awake.'

The stimulus of the sun's rays seems to have relation to the fertilization of the plant. The pollen, if scattered beneath the water, would be washed away and decomposed, while on the expanded raised flower it is received without injury. This is truly the object for which –

> 'The water-lily to the light
>     Her chalice rears of silver white.'

And as it is with poets in sentiment, so it should be in our everyday life; each daily duty, if viewed aright, contains in it the elements of poetry, which may be made to surround the most prosaic acts of existence with beauty.

# Chapter 5

# BOTANICAL FASHION

## Floral Clocks

Several floral hobbies of the nineteenth century stemmed from the advances in plant identification made by the eighteenth-century naturalist, Carl Linnaeus. He had many less than down-to-earth speculations and enthusiasms, one of which was in evidence in the Victorian garden. He was obsessed with the idea of a botanical clock, an 'Horologe, or Watch of Flora' as he called it. The clock was made up of 46 flowers which opened and closed as the day progressed. In Uppsala, Linnaeus had kept records on the punctuality of wild and cultivated flowers, and his optimism of reading the time by them 'as accurately as by a watch' was such that a contemporary wrote to him: 'But pray consider what will become of the clock-makers, if you can find out vegetable dials.'

This 'pretty fancy of Linnaeus' lent itself to the Victorian passion for formal designs in bedding-plants for the floral timekeepers could be planted neatly in beds depicting a clock-face according to the hours they kept. John Claudius Loudon's 1822 *Encyclopaedia of Gardening*, required reading for new middle-class gardeners, shared Linnaeus's confidence in the punctuality of petal opening and closing for some of the 'Dial Plants' were allocated with times so accurate as to be only in the realms of fancy. One, the wild goat's-beard, *Tragopogon pratensis* (see Figure 5.2), a small pale dandelion-like flower, was listed as opening in the morning at '3 hours 5 mins'.

The clock flower-bed must have had little aesthetic appeal, as the mixture of flowers was incongruous and many of the wild plants used were similar to each other in form and colour – a consequence of many being closely related, reflected in their membership of the same modern botanical family, *Compositae*. The hallmark of the group is an appearance of a single flower-head which is actually a cluster of many tiny flowers, as in the dandelion which was one of the floral 'timekeepers'. Most of the other composite flowers were yellow and to the uninitiated many are as alike as their names: hawkbits (*Leontodon* spp.), hawkweed ox-tongue (*Picris hieracioides*, see Figure 5.1) and hawk's-beards (*Crepis* spp.), all subtle variations on the dandelion theme, some with tall branched stems, and mostly growing wild in dry grassy places. From the same wild habitat came paler yellow flowers to fill the clock-face: mouse-ear hawkweed (*Pilosella officinarum*, also called *Hieracium pilosella*), with white-backed hairy leaves creeping along the ground, and nipplewort (*Lapsana communis*), with diminutive flowers on many wiry branches. Some of the more pernicious weeds of cultivation were introduced into the flower-bed, such as the yellow tufts of common sowthistle (*Sonchus oleraceus*) alongside the now rare spotted cat's-ear (*Hypochoeris maculata*), with its dandelion-type head and purple-spotted leaves. Two wild composites of today's grassy roadsides would have contributed a contrast of colour and form to the floral clock: blue chicory (*Cichorium intybus*), and goat's-beard, with its distinctive stiff pointed leaves sheathing a straight stem all the way up to a diminutive yellow flower sinking within its green pointed crown.

Goat's-beard (and its cultivated relative salsify) was said to close so regularly at noon that it was

**Figure 5.1** Hawkweed ox-tongue (*Picris hieracioides*), a plant of Linnaeus's 'Horologe or Watch of Flora'. According to Linnaeus in Uppsala, it opened its petals at 4–5 a.m. and shut them punctually at 12 noon. (From *English Botany* by James Edward Smith and J. Sowerby, 1790–1814 – by permission of Avon County Library (Bath Reference Library))

*190*

small flowers of scarlet pimpernel and bell-vine (bindweed – *Calystegia* spp.), and the mauve hollyhock-shaped flowers of mallow, *Malva sylvestris* (see Figure 8.5).

Old and new cultivated flowers gave the floral clock a touch of the dazzling colour that Victorians demanded in their other flower-beds. There were several species of mesembryanthemum, there was the old-fashioned marigold (*Calendula officinalis*), and the day lily (*Hemerocallis* spp.) which still had some novelty value as a newcomer to Britain, having been introduced at the end of the eighteenth century. Some of Linnaeus's clock-flowers presented the pedantic Victorian gardener with a certain amount of inconvenience and difficulty: some catchflies could contribute to timekeeping only by night, when the shrivelled, dead-looking flower of the day opened out into a white star-shaped flower resembling a campion. The white water-lily (*Nymphaea alba*) presented particular problems. Reading the garden clock would have been fairly complicated as the times the particular flowers stayed open varied from five hours in the chicory to ten or eleven hours in the spotted cat's-ear, so the sequence of opening times was completely different from that of closing: cross-reference between flowers was thus essential. The more romantic Victorians believed implicitly in the punctuality of the garden clock, as was portrayed in the often quoted verses by Charlotte Smith:

In every copse and shelter'd dell,
Unveil'd to the observant eye,
Are faithful monitors which tell
How pass the hours and seasons by.

See Hieracium's various tribe     [hawkweeds]
Of plumy seed and radiate flowers;
The course of time their blooms describe,
And wake or sleep appointed hours.

Broad o'er its imbricated cup
The Goatsbeard spreads its golden rays,
But shuts its cautious petals up,
Retreating from the noontide blaze.

Although John Claudius Loudon gave goat's-beard's opening time (in Uppsala) as '3 hours 5 mins', other sources of information varied by as much as two hours, which allowed the less romantic some doubt on the existence of mass floral synchrony. Some complained the time

an accepted fact of country routine that 'the ploughboy regulates his mid-day meal by it'. There was a long tradition of this particular flower's punctuality in its alternative names, 'Jack-go-to-bed-at-noon' and 'Go to bed at noon'. Wild flowers from different flower families provided some relief from the yellow *Compositae* in the floral clock: these were the

'monitors' were far from faithful, as, for instance, dandelions did not open at all in the rain. Lack of 'appointed hours' was an inevitable aspect of the botanical clock because of the different mechanisms opening and shutting the flowers. In the first half of the nineteenth century the factors affecting plant movements were unknown. Ideas circulating at the time included those of an eighteenth-century writer who directly equated the closed flower with sleep and believed flowers therefore to have a 'voluntary power: for without the faculty of volition, sleep would not have been necessary to them'. The ancient Greek, Theophrastus, had been closer to the truth when he tried to explain flower movements in terms of temperature change. Long after the fashion for planting botanical clocks, floral timekeeping became better understood.

Temperature is the regulating factor in the case of the white water-lily. Dandelions need a minimum temperature of 10 to 12 °C to open at all and only open fully at 18 °C. The daisy requires a higher temperature and, as one would therefore expect, opens later and closes earlier in the day than the dandelion. Temperature and moisture govern the chicory's opening and closing, as well as the scarlet pimpernel (or Poorman's-weather-glass). The evening-opening catchflies depend on dampness alone, only remaining open during the day if it is raining or there is a very wet atmosphere. Light intensity alone controls many of the clock-flowers, such as the mouse-ear hawkweed and its kin, and the marigold. Light, warmth and the rain clouds in the distance present the least ambiguous conditions for telling the time by flowers – just the sort of day that Victorian ladies would have been tempted to muse on such possibilities. Linnaeus's idea was indeed just a 'pretty fancy', but it somehow captured the mood of Maurice Maeterlinck's, writing of the 'fair hours of the year' in *Life and Flowers*. He wrote:

> Let us have for these privileged hours a nobler measure than that into which we pour the ordinary hours . . . [Time] takes shape, acquires its substance and its value only in complicated forms of apparatus which we have contrived in order to render it apparent; and, having no existence in itself, it borrows the taste, the perfume and the shape of the instrument that rules it.

**Figure 5.2** Considered to be one of the more reliable plants of the floral clock: goat's-beard (*Tragopogon pratensis*) or Jack-go-to-bed-at-noon. Its closing was the signal for the ploughboy's lunch. (This particular flower remained open, however, until 1.30 p.m.; photograph taken in Wiltshire, June)

A dial of flowers was 'worthy to measure the splendour of the months of green and gold . . . all the blissful intensity of the cornfields, . . . the scent of the flowers hastening to finish a day of scorching beauty . . .'.

## Linnaeus: Identifying Plants as Entertainment

In drawing rooms and front parlours the simple plant-classification system of Linnaeus played a part in botanical fashion. It had been the important factor in the transformation of botany from 'an abstruse science' in the mid-eighteenth century to a fashionable hobby of Queen Charlotte and many aristocrats by its close. Botanical books for ladies became more popular. They were of varying degrees of merit and patronage: the remotest improprieties were scrupulously avoided, heavy facts were diluted such that it was dubious that gentlemen could actually gain from their pages, while dedications flattered the botanical expertise and physical beauty of the readers. The 1843 dedication of *The Little English Flora* by G.W. Francis was typical of these books:

> To the young ladies of England, whose occupations, tastes, and sensibilities, render The Science of Botany so peculiarly a proper object for their study, this work is respectfully dedicated, as an entertaining and scientific introduction to the simple, the elegant, and the sweet little flowers of our native land.

With such a pedigree, plant identification further progressed from 'an agreeable amusement to persons of leisure' to a social necessity for Victorian middle-class families eager for genteel attainments and respectability. For even an amateur of little intelligence could indulge in the time-consuming entertainment of Linnaean botany in the name of learning. (Acquisition of some knowledge was essential for amusement for its own sake smacked of vulgarity.)

Linnaeus's system simply involved counting first the male parts of the flower, the stamens, then the female parts, the carpels or stigmas, and in a few cases noting particular placings of both within the flower. These numbers fitted the plant into a vegetable filing system (see Figure 5.3); for example, the Victorian bedding-plant, canna, had one stamen and was thus allocated to Class *Monandria*; another favourite, the salvia, had two stamens which put it in Class *Diandria*. Linnaeus's system provided a striking contrast to the vagueness of the several independent systems of sorting and naming used previously; according to the *English Cyclopaedia* (1856-72), he had 'purified botany of the endless varieties of the gardeners and herbalists'. Victorian amateurs and ladies continued to use Linnaeus's simple classification long after it was discarded by serious botanists. It contributed to the modern method and his binomial system of naming remained and is still in use. (He gave every living thing two Latin names, one a general group name and the other a specific name.) His industry had been immense; he named, catalogued and described over 12,000 species of plants and animals and he was little less than eulogised by flower-spotting ladies as late as 1887.

Instruction in plant classification closely followed the example of the Age of Elegance where it had begun. The conversations of 'a Lady' of 1797 set an awe-inspiring example for the middle-class writers who followed her and their nineteenth-century readers. The Lady's daughter, Harriet, enquired if it was necessary for her to learn Linnaeus's difficult class names:

> *Hortensia [mother]*: if you will take the trouble to familiarize yourself with them at first, you will soon find they appear not very uncouth to you.

> *Harriet*: I shall not think any thing too much trouble, that you recommend to me, Ma'am, but sometimes I feel a little afraid of being found dull; and I think I have heard of botanical books written for ladies, which make all the hard words easy. (Jackson, *Botanical Dialogues. . .*)

Hortensia and many Victorian botanist-mothers tended to spurn these 'pretty round-about ways' which had been concocted 'to level the science to the capacity of ladies', and in an increasing quest for thoroughness later *Conversations* were crowded with disjointed tit-bits of information amongst the Linnaean class names. Traditional and contemporary uses of the plants featured alongside idiosyncrasies of vegetation and the diets of 'savages' in remote Van Dieman's Land (Tasmania). The miscellany of irrelevancies in botanical works was the object of John Ruskin's magnificent satire, in *Proserpina*. Wishing to clarify whether his poppy specimen with two smaller and two larger petals was typical, he consulted:

> an excellent little school-book on botany – the best I've yet found, thinking to be told quickly; and I find a great deal about opium; and, apropros of opium, that the juice of common celandine is of a bright orange colour; and I pause for a bewildered five minutes, wondering if a celandine is a poppy . . . going on again . . . I am told to 'observe the floral receptacle of the Californian genus Eschscholtzia'. Now I can't observe anything of the sort, and I don't want to; and I wish California and all that's in it were at the deepest bottom of the Pacific. Next I am told to compare the poppy and water-lily; and I can't do that, neither – though I should like to; and there's the end of the article; and it never

**Figure 5.3** Linnaeus's Table of Plant Classes. Flowers with one stamen were in Class 1, *Monandria*, flowers with two stamens in Class 2, *Diandria* and so on. Class 14 had two long stamens and two short, Class 15 four long and two short, after which the diagnostic feature was the fusion of stamens into 'bundles', as in the sweet pea in Class 17. The catkins and plants with unisexual flowers on the same or separate plants were in separate classes, and last of all came Class 24 – Linnaeus's secret marriages of plants without flowers such as mosses, ferns and toadstools. (From *The Little English Flora* by G.W. Francis, 3rd edition, 1849 – by permission of Avon County Library (Bath Reference Library))

tells me whether one pair of petals is always smaller than the other, or not.

Delight in flowers seemed to be lost in disciplined drudgery and for half a century the child prodigies of the instruction books continued to be pretentiously well mannered and thirsting for knowledge, as in the *Conversations on Botany* of 1820:

> *Edward.* What a thick calyx this flower has, with such delicate petals?
> *Mother.* The design of the calyx is to give security to the other parts of the flower before it opens, and afterwards to support them in their proper places.

Father could mete out similar floral information from a similar male volume written by Robert John Thornton, creator of the famous book, *The Temple of Flora*.

As well as talk of Linnaean classification, conversations included discussions on the workings of the plant, practical advice on how to water them and why one should not eat unripe apples, and somewhat bizarre exchanges such as:

> *Teacher.* To us the flowers are more beautiful than useful; but many of them are employed as a medicine, such as cammomile flowers. Can you tell me by which of our senses we enjoy flowers?
> *1st Child.* By our sight and by our smell; for they are very pretty to look at, and very nice to smell.

(Jane Marcet, *Lessons on Animals, Vegetables and Minerals*)

Books for adult instruction were similarly banal and were diluted with sentimental poems that completely overshadowed the botany.

From the first introduction of books popularising Linnaeus's plant classification in the eighteenth century, the moral respectability of the subject had been emphasised. This high moral tone and the Victorian avoidance of the reproductive function of the flower was, in fact, quite out of keeping with Linnaeus's own descriptions of his various classes of plants. The calyx introduced so demurely to Victorian readers by Edward and his mother was a far cry from Linnaeus's own introduction to the flower structure:

We see then how the great Creator has enriched the most innocent nuptials of plants with the most singular superb ornaments. Let us behold the marriage bed, or *calyx*, with what art it is constructed . . . (*The Elements of Botany*)

The petals within he saw as:

> precious bed-curtains, and perfumed with so many sweet scents in order that the bridegroom and bride may therein celebrate their nuptials with the greater solemnity. When the bed has thus been made ready, then is the time for the bridegroom to embrace his beloved bride and surrender himself to her . . . (*Praeludia Sponsaliarum Plantarum*)

The already *risqué* exposure of floral romance became even less solemn when Linnaeus further brought to life – and scandal – his interpretation of stamens and pistils as husbands and wives with permissive ideas ahead of their time; in gay abandon the salvias of the parterre each had two husbands in bed with the same female. In Victorian botany books all the mid-eighteenth-century scandal of floral polygamy, concubines, harlotry and eunuchs was somehow expurgated, together with the attacks on Linnaeus by 'numerous and rancorous adversaries, who cowardly and morosely [had] addressed the prejudices of the vulgar against him'. Some of Linnaeus's lewder naming of flowers from their superficial resemblances were forgotten and most nineteenth-century botanisers concentrated on the dry business of counting stamens rather than thinking of their purpose. Few thought that their botanical pursuits were once seen as a 'licentious method' of classifying flowers.

Even without this past scandal, Linnaeus's life and controversial personality afforded an abundance of entertainment to keep the attention of those bored by the facts of his 24 classes. Eulogies in the first decades of the century spoke of 'this indefatigable man, born to be nature's historian', and 'a meteor' of the North, the 'brightest ornament' of Botany. Seventy years later, admirers could relive a lady's pilgrimage to the Swedish countryside of Linnaeus's childhood and imagine how it must have all begun:

> his classifying infant eyes can spy the minute green butterfly, invisible to anyone else, upon

**Figure 5.4** The structure of the snowdrop. 'Mother's' prim flower with its parts supported 'in their proper places' or Linnaeus's 'marriage bed' with its 'precious bed-curtains'.

the whortleberries . . . beneath the trees, sheltering the cooing doves, and the dryad's hair of the silver birch, his feet lapped in leaves of the wild lily of the valley with miniature racemes.

(The lapse from sentiment to botanical jargon depicts a main axis stem bearing stalked flowers.) Even the boulders were described 'which served little Carl for seats and tables!'

On his visit to England, Linnaeus had been immensely moved by humble gorse flowers and the image of this event in 1736 appealed greatly to Victorian ladies – publications such as *Aunt Judy's Magazine* featured poems on the incident. The eminent man had fallen down and wept, praying at his first sight of a gorse-covered hillside. 'The rapture of Linnaeus when he knelt on the sod thanking God for its loveliness, can be well understood by the lover of flowers', wrote another admirer, Anne Pratt, who had this poem written by Mary Isabella Tomkins for her large work on wild flowers, *The Flowering Plants of Great Britain*, published in 1855:

A strong man kneeling, and in tears,
Beneath June's azure sky,

.     .     .     .     .

Is it a pilgrim who hath sought
Some deeply hallow'd spot,

.     .     .     .     .

Is it a warrior on the plain
Where meeting myriads fell?

.     .     .     .     .

No; none of these – the naturalist
By his true heart impell'd,
Could not this meed of praise resist
For what he then beheld;
An open heath, where thick was spread
The Gorse of golden hue,
With heavy perfume round it shed,
That well the wild-bee knew.

Those with more inclination to gossip could ease the burden of botanical learning with Linnaean anecdotes of plant-naming. He had a tendency to pass adverse comments on colleagues and adversaries via the immortal snub of a flower name. For instance, he repaid a famous critic of

**Figure 5.5** *Bufonia tenuifolia* (Slender *Bufonia* or Toadgrass), maliciously named by Carl Linnaeus after his opponent, Count Buffon. (From *English Botany* by James Edward Smith and J. Sowerby, by permission of Avon County Library (Bath Reference Library))

the time, Johann Siegesbeck, by giving his name to an unpleasant weed with a small flower. He deliberately altered the spelling of an old generic name, *Buffonia*, and named a plant *Bufonia tenuifolia* (see Figure 5.5) after his ardent opponent, Count Buffon, 'because its slender leaves were typical of the slender attainments made by the naturalist in botanical science'. He contrived a worse insult yet from the name *Bufonia tenuifolia*, for as well as the image of 'slenderness' being immutable in its specific name, 'tenuifolia', Linnaeus also 'rather maliciously' according to the classic, *English Botany*, dropped one 'f' in the generic name making it a pun upon *bufo* a toad. 'The latter idea' it was noted in *English Botany*, 'has been confirmed by the authors of the Botanical Arrangement, who call it *Toad-grass*.' (*English Botany* politely retained the old spelling, but today it is spelt Linnaeus's way.) It made a bizarre memorial for the courtier naturalist dressed decorously to write his magnum opus (see page 4).

These 'studies' of the Linnaean classification also rendered the essential health-giving walk more bearable, for 'a walk without an object' was, and appeared to be, idling time away and 'a poor exercise'. Better still, there was something to show for one's efforts and the making of a pressed-flower collection was ideally suited to supposed female abilities. The stonemason–geologist, Hugh Miller, giving advice to his fiancée in a letter, sums up the motivation of the majority:

> Take little thought and much exercise. Read for amusement only. Set yourself to make a collection of shells, or butterflies, or plants. Do anything that will have interest enough to amuse you without requiring so much attention as to fatigue.

Fortunately for the future of botany, there were those who took their collections far more seriously.

## Collections in the Making

### Botanical Families

Serious collecting and botanising remained a favourite occupation of many upper-class families through into the nineteenth century. A typical (and eminent) example was the Talbot

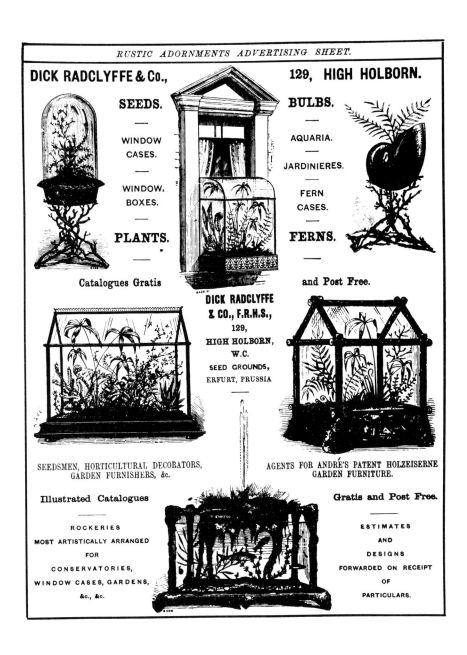

**Figure 5.6** A page from William Henry Fox Talbot's notebook. (From the Lacock Abbey Collection, the Fox Talbot Museum, The National Trust)

family (the most famous member of which was William Henry Fox Talbot FRS, MP, inventor of the negative-positive system of photography, mathematician, etymologist and researcher in optics), and the related family, the Fox-Strangways. Most of them (see Table 5.1) botanised and corresponded on the subject. In common with like-minded enthusiasts all over

**Table 5.1**  Botanical interests across families

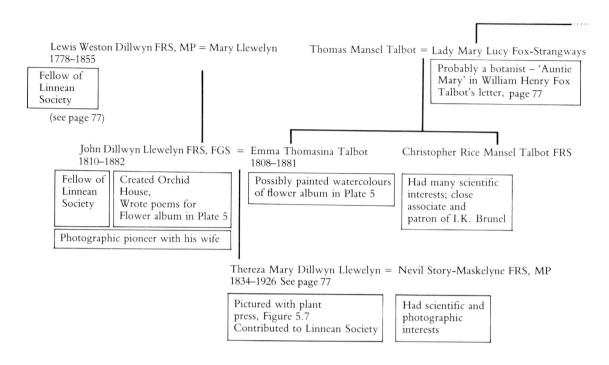

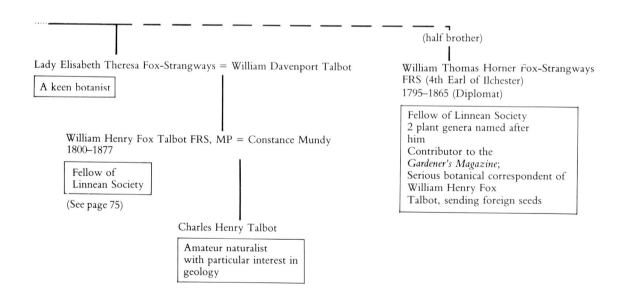

the country, William Henry Fox Talbot kept meticulous day-by-day accounts of the progress and flowering of wild (see Figure 5.6) and cultivated species. He had a botanic garden at his home, Lacock Abbey, and was a member of the Royal Horticultural Society.

Fox Talbot had a large herbarium partly compiled by his mother as well as some pages from a purchased collection. However, his talent and perfectionist attention to detail took him far beyond the routine activities of the serious collector. His first 'contact photographs', which he termed 'photogenic drawings', of 1835 included many plant subjects (see Figure 8.1), and he recognised the potential of photographic techniques in botany. His botanical distinction was acknowledged in his election as a Fellow of the Linnean Society. His comments on botany as a science are especially interesting for their revelations of popular misconceptions of the subject in 1814:

[botany] is a science which extends pretty far & which by no means consists entirely of nomenclature. It affords excellent exercise to the powers of discrimination, & practices [sic] the memory very much. I am sure that I shall find Euclid much easier, after having accustomed myself as I do here, to the attentive examination of plants, in the descriptions of which, every term & expression must be well weighed in the mind, & thoroughly understood. . . . Aunt Mary says there is a difference between a philosophical & a *stupid* botanist. The variety of wonderful contrivances which Nature employs for the protection of the flower, & due ripening of the seeds &c. excite one's admiration at every step, & though not so useful, Botany is as engaging as any science I have yet read about.

These were the thoughts of a 14-year-old schoolboy in his letter home. At the time he was jointly writing a Flora of Harrow with a contemporary. His detailed knowledge of plants later reached the expertise of recording new species, one of which he grew at Lacock from seed collected by a traveller in South Africa – it was subsequently named *Talbotia elegans* after Talbot. Throughout his life he felt joy and excitement over flowers and his sensitive aesthetic descriptions matched his botanical accuracy.

One of Talbot's distant relatives was Lewis Weston Dillwyn, a botanist of distinction whose son John, and grand-daughter, Thereza Mary inherited his talent and interest in botany. Thereza Mary Dillwyn Llewelyn was photographed holding her botanical press by her father; an eminent photographic pioneer (see Figure 5.7). She did more than just compile a herbarium of pressed flowers: she noted their minutest details. She had a paper read at the Linnean Society in March 1857 on 'curious leaf-plants' of *Cardamine hirsuta*, with encouragement from George Bentham of Kew and Flora fame (whose friendship with the family had begun with swapping plants and Welsh tweeds at the 1848 meeting of the British Association for the Advancement of Science at Swansea).

Talbot's schoolboy botanical correspondence with Lewis Weston Dillwyn and its developments illustrates the network of botanical friendships and patronage which existed at the time. A questionnaire had been circulated round the network to gather botanical records which Dillwyn had published in *Botanist's Guide through England and Wales* in 1805 with Dawson Turner, a banker and an expert on mosses and lower plants. Turner was the father-in-law and patron of William Jackson Hooker who in turn introduced Talbot to the Rev. James Dalton, an authority on sedges and mosses. Through the botanical brotherhood and because of his habit even as a youth of consulting only experts on serious matters, Talbot became friends with Sir James Edward Smith and corresponded with Charles Darwin's friend and fellow enthusiast, John Stevens Henslow, Professor of Botany at Cambridge and father-in-law to Joseph Dalton Hooker; also George Bentham and many others, including John Lindley (who contested the Directorship of Kew against Hooker when it passed to the nation). Talbot was instrumental in saving Kew and much of its exotic collections from destruction at the beginning of Victoria's reign by marshalling a petition to the House of Commons from the Council of the Linnean Society.

At this time Kew had its own family network of botanists. William Jackson Hooker with the help of his son (from the age of twelve) had compiled the largest single collection of herbarium specimens, which in 1849 occupied thirteen rooms of his private house. (He founded three journals, *Botanical Miscellany*, *The Journal of*

*Botany* and *Companion to the Botanical Magazine*, in order to share the knowledge of his plants.) Hooker's herbarium was moved to Kew and formed the basis of the Royal Botanic Garden's immense and definitive collection. Its arrival in fact marked Kew's beginnings as the permanent reference point for plant knowledge. When William Jackson Hooker died, his son, Joseph Dalton Hooker, took over and further extended Kew's role in keeping identification records. He was followed by his son-in-law, Sir William Thiselton-Dyer. All three men were knighted.

Lady Thiselton-Dyer (née Harriet Ann Hooker) entered the botanical enclave when she stood in for a time as illustrator of the famous *Curtis's Botanical Magazine*. This periodical, like Kew whose plants it largely featured, had become another Hooker family effort, with William Jackson Hooker taking over its direction and illustration in 1826, being succeeded by Joseph. William Jackson Hooker's protégé and Kew's draughtsman, Walter Hood Fitch, was responsible for the fine illustrations between 1834 and 1877 (see Plates 11 and 13). The descriptive and scientific text included details of a flower's origin and culture with the occasional homely comment such as: 'I received flowering specimens of this plant from my friend Mr Darwin, in April last', as befitted a regular communication between the friendly network of the widening circle of the nineteenth-century 'botanical family'.

*Collecting and Clubs*

Two books spurred Victorian collecting and were the models for many aspiring authors. One was Gilbert White's *The Natural History and Antiquities of Selborne*. Although published in 1788 the book remained more or less unknown outside the *cognoscenti* until its 1827 edition when it became the vogue for the middle classes. To everyone's surprise the day-to-day events among the weeds and common animals 'read like any novel'. For those with the sensitivity there was also understanding and respect for plants and animals. The second book, J.L. Knapp's *The*

*Journal of a Naturalist*, had similar characteristics and was another masterpiece. By 1831 both books were selling in their thousands and their authors made glittering examples for amateur botanists all over the country. They set out armed with a *Flora*, drying papers and vasculum, or at least instructions on alternatives: 'be careful to gather the specimens in fine weather; they may be brought home in the hand as a nosegay, or, what is much better, put into the crown of the hat, or in a tin sandwich box'.

Enthusiastic collectors noted the details and whereabouts of their local plants, with varying degrees of accuracy and usefulness. For instance, in some of its plant sites, Charles Cardale Babington's *Flora Bathoniensis* of 1834 conveyed an air of delightful rustic vagueness: 'Brittle Bladder Fern . . . On an old wall near the top of Widcombe Hill, – Dr. H. Gibbes. Walls near the Horse and Jockey – Dr. R.C. Alexander.' Compared to the modern grid system such directions after the manner of Gerard's Herball seem quaint, but with the bringing together of information of many peoples' finds, here were some beginnings of detailed records of wild flower distribution.

Others went in search of the few: rarities and ancestral flowers. One of these was Canon Ellacombe. The ancestral carnation, originally a wild plant of south Europe, was introduced to England by the Normans and the Canon, 800 years later, went in search of the relics of the plant's journey. A Victorian flower spotter *par excellence*, he found the carnation still growing in a wild state on the castle walls of Falaise, the birthplace of William the Conqueror. Leaving no stone unturned, the intrepid gentleman went on to inspect the castles of England and Wales and noted the same species growing on the ruins of Rochester, Dover, Deal and Cardiff, all of which are Norman. (The specimen illustrated by Sowerby in *English Botany* in 1794 had been 'gathered on the walls of Rochester Castle', and a century after Ellacombe the plant apparently still retains its hold there and at Dover.) Whether the flower was deliberately planted by the newcomers or whether it was incidentally introduced with the Normandy stone used to construct parts of these castles does not detract from the interest of the Canon's discovery of a real living link with the past.

Shared enthusiasm in finding plants and learning about them lay at the heart of the nineteenth-

**Figure 5.7** Lewis Weston Dillwyn's grand-daughter Thereza Mary Dillwyn Llewelyn holding a botanical press. She had a paper read on *Cardamine hirsuta* at the Linnean Society. (Photograph by John Dillwyn Llewelyn, c. 1854)

century Field Club. On the one hand there were the gentlemanly natural history societies with aspirations of premises, published Transactions of their discussions, a museum and a library of rare books and thus an inevitably high subscription. The first of these was formed in the 1820s. On the other hand there were clubs, often not even formally acknowledged as such, which habitually met on a Sunday at a particular public house, exchanged plant specimens and jointly bought botany books. The joint purchase of books was an essential rather than a pretentious trimming as the members of these clubs were poorly paid manual workers such as jobbing gardeners and factory operatives. As in the Florists' Clubs and Floricultural Societies, hand loom weavers and other textile workers formed a large proportion of the members. The clubs were prevalent in the Manchester area and some had been thriving since the 1770s, while Sir James Edward Smith described a botanising group among Norwich tailors and weavers which had had a long tradition before 1760.

Happily the natural history societies and the clubs combined to their mutual advantage in the Field Clubs, the forerunners of today's Naturalist Clubs. These clubs were based on the botanical excursion which involved meeting in the field in the morning and going for a day-long expedition. A mere few shillings a year subscription opened the door to all enthusiasts. The first Field Club, formed in 1831, was the Berwickshire Naturalists's Club: the Scots did not feel the same embarrassment over class divisions as the English. From this beginning, local clubs of botanists blossomed even to the extent of hiring trains for distant explorations. Here are some of the excursions made by the Bath Natural History and Antiquarian Field Club (see Figure 5.8):

24th April 1856. Train to Bristol, botanising walk to Westbury and Henbury, in search of *Draba muralis* [wall whitlow grass], in Musgrove Paddock.
5th March 1857. Bury Wood Camp; *Daphnae*

**Figure 5.8** Field Club outing, 1890. Bath Natural History and Antiquarian Field Club excursion to see Burrington Combe in the Mendip Hills, Somerset (By permission of Avon County Library (Bath Reference Library))

Burrington Combe

G.J.P
/1890

*Mezereon* [Mezeron] found in flower in South Ditch.

28th May. Spy Park for *viola palustris* [sic] [bog violet] (found).

It could be the programme of any of today's County Naturalist Trusts.

The membership of this club, like many others, was all men and in the 1870s consisted almost exclusively of senior military officers, clergymen and gentlemen (one of whom was Fox Talbot's son, Charles, an amateur geologist). The club's early membership was the subject of later reminiscences:

Many of the first members, as is well-known, were gentlemen in the military and civil services, returned from India, who, although advanced in years, possessed wonderful physique and mental activity, and having toiled in foreign service thoroughly enjoyed . . . active outdoor researches . . . Then fortnightly walks were undertaken . . . they visited the various villages in the surrounding district in search of objects of natural history, archaeology, and geology.

In the 1870s there were over a hundred Field Clubs based, at least theoretically, on field excursions. Field botanising had in some cases deteriorated as in the 1860s more lavish societies emerged which must have attracted the middle classes with a greater sense of frivolity than botanical ardour. Picnics, dancing, bands and beverages featured prominently in between viewing the appointed sights, all in the decorative presence of the ladies. It was just such an affair – organised by the Thurso Society for the Study of Natural History – which prompted Robert Dick to comment:

I am very glad that I did not consent to go a-gowking to Dunnet Hills. The party went off in gigs, single and double; and what they saw, in crossing the sands, I know not. Certes, no one ever heard of objects in natural history being collected *in gigs*! The Society went to the inn and had dinner, and they did not rise until it was late. In coming back across the sands, they drove their gigs into the sea!

In the face of such middle-class social outings the separate social strata were forcibly brought together for serious natural history study by a pioneering few, one of whom was Charles Kingsley, Canon of Chester (who nevertheless did not extend his call to ladies). Grocers, clerks, clergymen, doctors, blacksmiths and shop assistants could sink their differences in the joy of finding and identifying plants and animals. Natural history magazines carried lists of enthusiasts, enabling collectors from all over the country to correspond and exchange specimens.

*Humble Collectors*

More than 100 years later little survives of these ordinary peoples' feelings, written to communicate rather than to publish, or their enthusiasms for plant-seeking. However, the modern reader can catch a glimmer of unselfconscious plant-collecting from the published diary and private letters of two working men, Joseph Gutteridge, a ribbon weaver, and Robert Dick, a baker. Both radiate sheer joy at first finding a flower: nature was a sacrifice but also a solace from dreadful realities for both of them – as it must have been to many of what Gutteridge called the 'poor working bees of the human hive'.

Idling away the hours was a rich man's problem which many working men were forced to share when work was scarce. Several times Joseph Gutteridge experienced the rigours of near-starvation and of winter nights spent huddled on bare boards, yet throughout a life of dreadful hardship and mishap he was sustained by his love of nature and his collections of plants, fossils and shells. Since boyhood he had hunted the lanes and hedgerows 'in quest of natural productions. The finding of a choice or rare specimen . . . would enhance the pleasure a hundredfold'. At school he painted in watercolour and 'experienced great delight in delineating the forms and colours of plants and flowers' – which he later found a useful aid in memorising a plant's characteristics. He also collected leaf impressions on paper, each marked with habitat and name which he gleaned from an old edition of Culpeper. As a young man in 1835:

scarcity of work afforded opportunities for pursuing studies . . . By this time I had got a smattering of botany, and began after a fashion, as best I could without a tutor to arrange specimens of flowers by the aid of

**Figure 5.9** Herbarium page of bear berry (*Arctostaphylos uva-ursi*), meticulously arranged with an eye for beauty as well as botanical identification by Robert Dick. (By permission of Thurso Museum)

an . . . [old book with obsolete terms] published in 1776, obtained from an old book stall . . . Had means allowed, I should have studied the science more closely and systematically, if only for the love of flowers.

Walking in the Scottish countryside was a part of work for the apprentice-baker, Robert Dick, another self-taught botanist, who had to travel to deliver bread. He later compiled a beautiful and extensive herbarium of over 3,000 specimens. His herbarium was his delight and he captured the essence of serious Victorian plant-collecting when he wrote to a fellow collector:

Your first favour of a mistletoe is in its appointed place . . . You may rely upon it, you bestow the specimen on one whose very life is bound up with those things; and I can in all sincerity say:
For them I panted, them I priz'd
For them I've gladly sacrificed
    Whate'er I lov'd before;
And shall I see them sacrificed?

Dick often expressed himself in verse, quoted or original.

The way in which Dick presented his herbarium pages was typical of the ornate manner of the time. To obtain the neatest lettering for the collection site, he often cut letters and words of newsprint from the Thurso newspaper. Sometimes a leaf was carefully draped round a label and he exercised the utmost artistry in arranging his material. The display might be strictly symmetrical or fancifully composed, such as his red bear berry (*Arctostaphylos uva-ursi*) which he draped in pretty flowing arches, framing small bunches (see Figure 5.9). He showed an unusual sense of artistic composition and sensitivity to the natural flow of his materials; his page of a sweet-briar rose (see Figure 5.10) would not have disgraced any of the artistically inclined albums of the ladies. Three-dimensional flowers which have a flat mushroom-like top, like cow parsley and angelica (*Angelica sylvestris* see Figure 5.11), present great difficulties in pressing – every small flower-stem and petal seems to need individual attention simultaneously as one applies the weight. Robert Dick's specimens are perfect, with stems tilted and each petal beautifully placed. Like many of the gentlemen writing county Floras, he was not merely a collector or

**Figure 5.10** Robert Dick's specimens of the small-flowered sweet-briar rose, collected about 1848. (By permission of Thurso Museum)

plant spotter; he visited the same plants frequently, noting their growth and development and small variations under extreme conditions from one season to the next.

Dick was one of those privileged to find a new plant for the British Flora, though as he was only a working baker his discovery was initially received with scorn. In 1834 he recognised holy grass (*Hierochloe odorata*) on the bank of the River Thurso, only to discover that it was theoretically absent from Britain, having been deleted from the British Flora as unsubstantiated. Little was known of the area and books perpetuated old errors. Robert Dick always started with the living evidence and had the unusual courage to

**Figure 5.11** Robert Dick's carefully splayed head of wild angelica (*Angelica sylvestris*). (By permission of Thurso Museum)

less dedicated amateurs carrying out nature study on a Grand Tour of the country. Their attentions and correspondence were unwelcome for time was short and Dick had such long distances to cover in between baking.

To a collector, the treasures he has collected are a part of himself. Besides its own appeal each specimen brings its special memory of acquisition and 'cost a good deal of search and labour'. For poor collectors, when life dropped to the level of survival, the toil, patience and love manifested in their collections was always the last asset left to sell. For example, having first lost his boyhood treasures at the hand of an unsympathetic stepmother, Joseph Gutteridge was later compelled by adverse circumstances to part with plants and coal fossils spanning some 20 years. Much later at the age of 77 he still regretted their loss. Robert Dick was also forced to sell his fossil collection, gathered over 30 years, in order to sustain the loss of his flour in a coaster which broke in two while entering harbour under a drunken helmsman. Ironically, after his death in 1866, his other collections, donated to the town, were little valued. His treasured herbarium was carelessly left in a corner and the grasses, his pride and joy, were largely ruined by moths and grubs. Fortunately, much of the rest was eventually salvaged from neglect and treated more appropriately so that today it is treasured once more and one can still browse among his gentians and foxgloves (still retaining their beautiful blue and purples), and marvel at the variety of British plants and the immense achievement under hardship of their humble collector.

Ferns were one of Robert Dick's great passions. They were a firm favourite for Victorian interiors, ferneries and garden grottoes, too, but fashion was the least consideration of this down-to-earth man.

### The Fascination of Ferns

The nineteenth-century love of ferns is an enigma to many twentieth-century writers who invoke causal factors from many sources, but much of the cause of their popularity must lie in the nature of the plants themselves. Sir William Jackson Hooker's enthusiasm for ferns was obvious from the adjectives he used to describe them: 'pretty', 'delicate', 'most beautiful' and

discount the textbooks when the two failed to coincide. An Edinburgh Professor of Botany jeered at a Caithness plant list presented by a Thurso student based on Dick's findings, but Dick was always amused by such 'fireside botanists'. It was not until 1854 when a visiting botanist saw the holy grass specimen in Dick's herbarium that Dick was persuaded to publicise his historic find. After the publication of his paper, collectors from all over the country were clamouring for specimens for their herbaria and Dick's humble bakehouse with its charcoal sketches of Greek sculpture and religious subjects on the walls became a fashionable curiosity for

**Plate 1** 'Convent Thoughts' by Charles Collins
By permission of the Ashmolean Museum, Oxford

Plate 2 Frontispiece of *Flora's Gems; or the treasure of the parterre* 'drawn and coloured from Nature' by James Andrews, *c.* 1837
By permission of Cambridge University Library

| Ragged Robin | . | . | . | *Wit.* |
| Ranunculus | . | . | . | *You are radiant with charms.* |
| Ranunculus, Garden | . | . | *You are rich in attractions.* |
| Ranunculus, Wild | . | . | *Ingratitude.* |
| Raspberry | . | . | . | *Remorse.* |
| Ray Grass | . | . | . | *Vice.* |
| Red Catchfly | . | . | . | *Youthful love.* |
| Reed | . | . | . | *Complaisance. Music.* |
| Reed, Split | . | . | . | *Indiscretion.* |
| Rhododendron (Rosebay) | . | *Danger. Beware.* |
| Rhubarb | . | . | . | *Advice.* |
| Rocket | . | . | . | *Rivalry.* |
| Rose | . | . | . | *Love.* |
| Rose, Austrian | . | . | *Thou art all that is lovely* |
| Rose, Bridal | . | . | . | *Happy love.* |
| Rose, Burgundy | . | . | *Unconscious beauty.* |
| Rose, Cabbage | . | . | *Ambassador of love.* |
| Rose, Campion | . | . | *Only deserve my love.* |
| Rose, Carolina | . | . | *Love is dangerous.* |
| Rose, China | . | . | *Beauty always new.* |
| Rose, Christmas | . | . | *Tranquillize my anxiety.* |

36

Plate 3 A page from Kate Greenaway's *The Language of Flowers*

**Plate 4** A Christmas card, with Valentine message
By permission of Bath Reference Library

**Plate 5** Burnet rose — a page from a Flower Album. Poem by John Dillwyn Llewelyn, watercolour by his wife, Emma Thomasina, or his sister, Fanny

**Plate 6** 'Dwarf Cavendish' banana (Paxton's *Musa Cavendishii*, now known as a cultivar of *M. acuminata)*: detail of hand-painted Chinese wallpaper
By permission of the Trustees of the Chatsworth Settlement

**Plate 7** *Rhododendron dalhousiae*, frontispiece of the *Rhododendrons of Sikkim-Himalaya, 1849-51*, illustrated by Walter Hood Fitch after field sketches by Sir Joseph Dalton Hooker
By permission of Cambridge University Library

'very remarkable'. More sentimental writers ventured into the realms of 'Worthy to be handmaids to this dainty lady. . .' in describing a fern, in this case sea spleenwort (*Asplenium marinum*) (see Figure 5.12). For the herbarium collector ferns have an especial appeal as they press with ease and perfection, so that when uncovered from the press, dried and crisp, their intricate pattern and symmetry is the more striking for the loss of fresh green. They have the mathematical fascination of a near artificial shape of straight lines, softened by the most subtle of curves. Theirs is an essential beauty of outline, enabling the most unartistic to recreate their graceful growth on the page.

The patterning of ferns dominated Thomas Hardy's image of them in *The Return of the Native*: 'The ferny vegetation around . . . though so abundant, was quite uniform: it was a grove of machine-made foliage, a world of green triangles with saw edges, and not a single flower.' A less objective view was of ferns drawing the naturalist to ruins and romantic places, in the footsteps of William and Dorothy Wordsworth. Ferns lured the botanist and collector 'from the parterre and the field, to converse with nature in her native garb, on heath and mountain' (the words of Rebecca Hey). These echoes of the Romantic era were more at one with those of a nature lover forced to live without a garden or far from the sight of wild places. For reluctant town-dwellers, whether of this century or the last, the green luxuriance of ferns can evoke a whole landscape. It was Shirley Hibberd's regret that 'we cannot grow the scene as well as the Fern'. Anyone who has walked over apparently unending moorland and then stumbled upon a cleft hiding a natural fernery can understand Hibberd's sentiment and the appeal of ferns in a natural setting: 'the lovely secluded spots which they seek out – shy wood-sprites that they are'. Only Hibberd's very nineteenth-century superlatives were suited to describe their habitats: 'they do haunt the greenest and coolest nooks, the most mossy and ancient banks'. Ferns suggested such scenes, whether witnessed or dreamed of, and kept 'a coolness in the brain and a freshness in the heart – breathings of a fragrance from the green world that sweeten the resting-places in the march of life'. Ferns, decided Hibberd, were appropriate candidates for cultivation by 'our first parents' in 'their happy garden'. He was in no doubt at all that a Victorian-style fernery was

**Figure 5.12** On a rainy day in April, Robert Dick clambered over 'the edge of the precipitous cliffs of Dunnet Head . . . I gazed upward in wonder and admiration . . . It is not every day that one stands at the foot of such a cliff. I moved westwards. I passed along delighted. The scene was grand and unusually striking. I came at length to a narrow fissure, up which I forced my way in quest of Ferns. Yes, Ferns! Ferns grow green on Dunnet Cliffs all the year round . . . It was the Sea Spleenwort that I wanted, and sure enough I found it growing green in all its glory. I gathered a few, and left the rest.' (By permission of Thurso Museum)

'one of their choice delights' as 'few rustic adornments would better have become their sylvan home, where shade and coolness, fragrance and verdure softened the song of love and the hymn of praise'. (*Rustic Adornments . . .*)

The natural rocky fissure encrusted with a mosaic of mosses and ferns, natural waterfalls, pools and precariously overhanging trees defy gardening mimicry, although many Victorians tried. For them, ferns – whether in an aquarium, a fernery or growing wild – carried the imagery of fresh green grottoes, cool shadows and glistening silver cascades: places for classical nymphs, nostalgia and solitude. Quietness amidst nature's beauty was at the very heart of Robert Dick's character and his ferneries were particularly special for that age of collecting mania, for rather than taking from nature, he was one of the few who gave.

In the bleak landscape of Caithness Dick had found natural ferneries in miniature and he nurtured and expanded his favourites; he transplanted ferns and brought spores from all over the county to these few sheltered places in order that they might spread. One such site he especially treasured and kept secret but his joy ended in disappointment when someone discovered it and cleared it of the 'weeds'. He revealed the motivation of his 'wild gardening' in a letter to a friend:

I felt considerable chagrin when you returned from the West, and brought no root of *Phyllitis scolopendrium* [Hart's-tongue Fern] with you. I did not want it for myself, but for science and Nature . . . I know favourable spots where I think it would live, and gratify the weary souls of lonely pilgrims, long after you and I are singing hallelujah with the angels.

At last the fern (see Figure 5.13) arrived and was planted: 'What beautiful green fronds! How handsome and picturesque! My only regret is that I cannot sow it broadcast over the whole land.' When more of the ferns were available Dick planted them far and wide across the county:

I prefer the fatigue of planting them as widely apart from each other as possible, so that they may scatter their colonies. . . . It was not for vanity that I begged them from you. No. It was the certainty that in generations yet unborn the feeling that 'vanity of vanities, all is vanity', would weigh down and oppress, and that some wanderer sad might be made

**Figure 5.13** Hart's-tongue fern (*Phyllitis scolopendrium*). 'I have planted it among the magnificent crags of Dunnet Head. A bronze pillar should reward the person who introduces into a county such a lovely plant as the Hart's-tongue fern, ever verdant, ever gay.' (Robert Dick) (By permission of Thurso Museum)

happier by seeing them. For is not a 'thing of beauty a joy for ever'?

He planted the royal fern (*Osmunda regalis*, see Figure 5.14) and maidenhair (*Adiantum capillus-veneris*) in his secret fernery ten miles west of Thurso, in the Dorery hills and on Morven mountain (2,313 feet), the other side of the county. The 60-mile walk to Morven and back across rough moorland, dykes and stone walls was a time-consuming journey for a baker working in Thurso: on one occasion he records setting out at 2 o'clock in the morning, reaching the summit at 11 a.m. and leaving at 2 p.m.

And yet the light of day was gone and the moon was up long, long before I gained a civilised road. The night became windy and stormy. Tremendous sheets of hailstones and rain impeded my progress so much so that I thought, as Burns says, that 'the De'il has business on his hand', and that he was determined to finish my course with Morven. But no! In spite of hail, rain, wind and fire (in fact I had them all), I got home at three o'clock on Wednesday morning, having walked with little halt for about twenty-four hours. I went to bed, slept till seven o'clock, then rose, and went about my work as usual. Sixty miles is a good walk to look at a hill. Oh, those plants, those weary plants!

In contrast to Robert Dick spreading wild ferns for future generations, most Victorian fern lovers were in the process of destroying many of them: dealers spoke in terms of tons of ferns from a single foray. Suggested lists of wild ferns suited to growing in pots for the garden, house and conservatory read like an inventory of today's rarer and local species. Creators of garden aquaria, indoor freshwater tanks and fountains were advised that the beech fern, oak fern, lady fern, maidenhair, hard fern, spleenworts, rusty-backs and many more 'must be sought in the native marshes, or by the sides of the clear streams that "Go singing in fine lines" '. 'My Lady Fern', wrote Charlotte M. Yonge, 'is too choice and elegant to be very common'.

Also to be taken from the wild for indoor enjoyment were 'the mosses of our own moors', while readers were advised by Shirley Hibberd that most bog-plants such as the several species of insect-eating sundews bloomed well in Wardian cases. There were also for the taking 'the traditional glories of our own old English water scenes . . . and if you will, the bonny flowering rushes [see Figure 2.6], over which, in the green old time, the bride walked in fragrance to the altar.' Victorian acquisitiveness and adoration of God's nature allowed no place for conserving it for future generations. However, in partial mitigation of the horticultural writers and their followers, it should be said they believed that every detail of nature was being carefully steered from above: thus extinction of a species was

**Figure 5.14** 'I can yet recollect how happy I was when I found the first *Osmunda*. I was wearied, and sore, and sick, and nearly tired of this world, and all that's in it, when I caught sight of that glorious Fern, large, radiant, and Flourishing, among the red sandstone cliffs of Dunnet. What a beauty!' Robert Dick's specimen of the royal fern (*Osmunda regalis*), collected by clambering 200 feet down the sheer cliffs of Dunnet Head, Caithness, Scotland. In the 1840s this fern was common. (By permission of Thurso Museum)

presumably either impossible or an inevitable part of an overall heavenly plan. Ferns, after all, had been created for the enjoyment of man – and, more importantly, made an interest for his womenfolk.

87

**Figure 5.15** Some wild plants such as the wood anemone (*Anemone nemorosa*) were transplanted successfully into nineteenth-century gardens and conservatories. Many soon died but were still regularly 'snatched from the wild and cherished . . . albeit for a limited time'. Under this pressure the royal fern (Figure 5.14) which was a middle-class status symbol became extremely rare or extinct (in England) and remains so today. This is an illustration for 'Gefunden' [Found] by Goethe in *The Baby's Bouquet. A Companion to the Baby's Opera*, decorated by Walter Crane.

## Ferneries and Aquaria

Charles Kingsley, obviously writing for a male readership in 1855, explains the ladies' penchant for ferns:

> Your daughters, perhaps, have been seized with the prevailing 'Pteridomania', and are collecting and buying ferns, with Ward's cases wherein to keep them (for which you have to pay). . . 'Fancy-work' has all but vanished from your drawing-room since the 'Lady-ferns' and 'Venus's hair' appeared; and . . . you could not help yourself looking now and then at the said 'Venus's hair', and agreeing that Nature's real beauties were somewhat superior to the ghastly woollen caricatures which they had superseded.

The expense of the Wardian cases was not an idle luxury in the age of gaslight and coal fires for the polluted atmosphere soon killed subjects as delicate as the lady fern: 'so tender is she, that it is nearly impossible to gather and carry her home without her withering'. Charlotte M. Yonge described 'her bower' as:

> Where the copsewood is the greenest,
> Where the fountains glisten sheenest,
> Where the morning dew lies longest.

To keep such an elusive plant as the lady fern bright and fresh, day after day, in a city house seemed an impossible dream for the inventor of the Wardian case, Nathaniel Bagshaw Ward:

> Impelled by such instinctive love, and still further actuated by an ardent zeal for the science of botany, Mr. Ward had for years striven to realise the '*rus in urbe*'. . . The only resource left him was, on each occasion of a visit to the country, to bring back a fresh relay of plants, and thus maintain a fluctuating appearance of freshness and verdure. (Shirley Hibberd, *Rustic Adornments*)

In 1830 Ward accidentally invented a closed microcosm of clean air in which ferns could live for years. He had put a chrysalis in a jar with some earth and replaced the stopper. After some time a fern and a grass appeared, both of which lived for four years. (They finally died not because of mould or stagnation but as a result of an unfortunate mishap while Ward was away on holiday.) Light, consistent moisture and still air without dust and with an occasional change of air were the essentials. It was important that the plant container was closely but not hermetically sealed. In 1833 Ward made some dramatic preparations: he planted ferns and grasses in two plant cases and watered in some ferns and mosses in a stoppered jar. The jar had no more water added and went on show eighteen years later at the Great Exhibition and the two plant cases were put on a ship sailing for Sydney. The plants were still alive on arrival in Sydney and this was to be one of the most significant horticultural events of the century. The safe transit of the plants opened up the way for the importation of floral wealth for gardeners and for the introduction of economic plants to new growing areas, providing actual wealth for entire countries.

Of more immediate importance in the eyes of most Victorians was the delight and status of plants thriving indoors in an extravagant and new container. By the 1840s the fashionable wealthy were growing exotic plants and ferns in Wardian cases which allowed the plants to flourish for the first time and in profusion. In the 1850s fern cultivation caught the imagination of the newly affluent middle classes and ferns and Wardian-type cases became inseparable essentials in the respectable household. Some cases had a lower compartment which could provide heat

via a gas jet and others had gadgets for concentrating the sunlight. Equally extravagant were designs finished in gilding and enamel, and those mimicking Gothic cathedrals or even the Crystal Palace. Others were fashionably rustic, apparently constructed of slender branches and twigs, like miniature bandstands topped with acorns. There were stands with grotesque cabriole legs carved with deep scrolls and roses, plinths with cherubs, maidens or shells, and bases contrived of fishes, twiggery and all manner of Victorian excess. Alternatively the case stood on a stately turntable of red plush. Like flowers, plant cases were allocated strict social strata. The more common rustic designs of plain slatted wood and twigs were considered adequate to serve the 'modest sitting-room of the City clerk or artisan'.

Inside them all was a living world in miniature, with water cycling naturally through root, leaf, air and soil. Pride of place went to the insectivorous plants which had dramatically wierd shapes, particularly the North American sarracenias which seemed to rear up like glossy green and red cobras. Species from British moorland and bogs had a quite different attraction: tiny, red, spoon-like leaves covered in droplets like a permanent dew which Charles Darwin described as 'Glittering in the sun', hence the plant's 'poetical name of the sun-dew'. Another was the romantically named grass-of-Parnassus, where the greenish centre of the pretty white flowers was ringed by a crown of glistening knobs (at that time erroneously thought to consume insects, but actually attracting them). The fascination of these plants was not so much their extraordinary shapes and lustrous shine but their habit (supposed, in the case of the grass-of-Parnassus) of trapping insects – down slippery sided pitchers or entangled in the viscous dewdrops. The genteel onlookers could cringe in horror at the spectacle of the hideous spiked maw of the Venus' fly-trap (see Figure 8.16) irreparably snapping shut on an insect and watch it fluttering and floundering behind a portcullis of vegetable teeth.

Watching the slow demise of helpless insects must have been a singularly depressing sight for the one section of Victorian society which was supposed to derive the most benefit from Wardian cases. For at the time, in Shirley Hibberd's words:

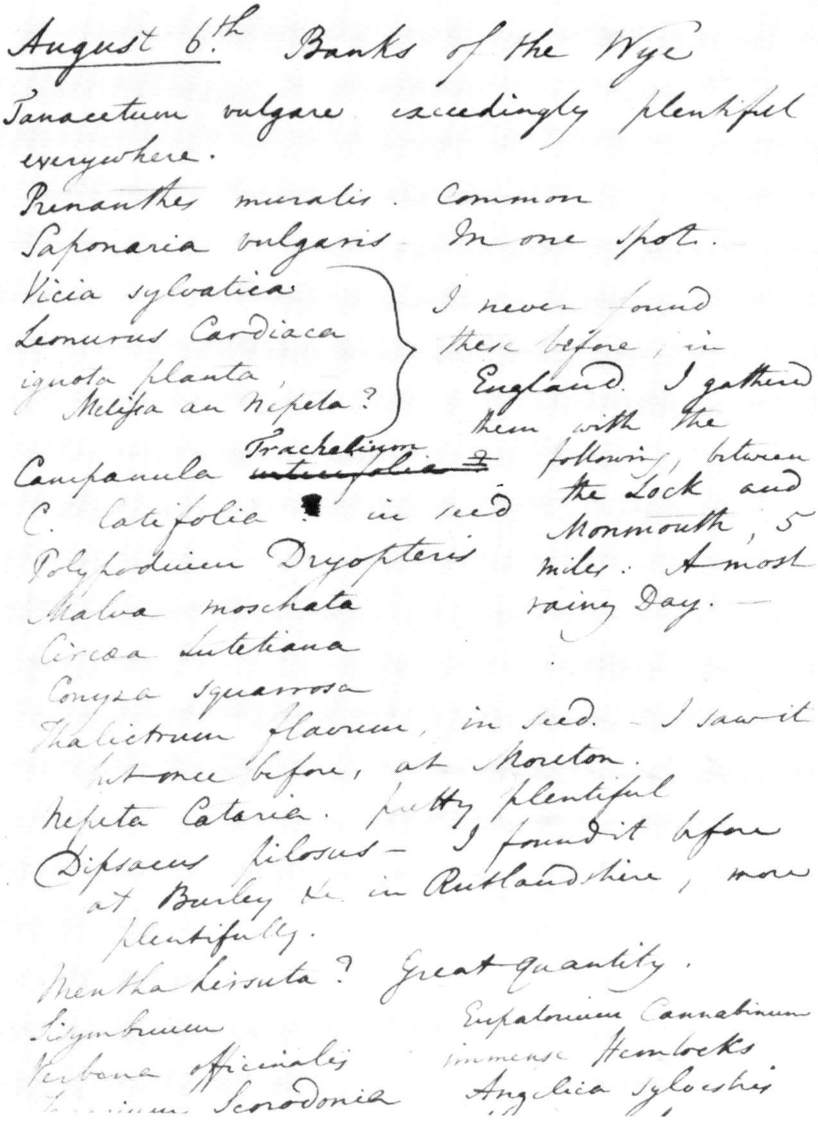

August 6.th Banks of the Wye
Tanacetum vulgare exceedingly plentiful
everywhere.
Prenanthes muralis. Common
Saponaria vulgaris. In one spot.
Vicia sylvatica
Leonurus Cardiaca
ignota planta,
    Melissa an Nepeta?
Campanula Trachelium
C. latifolia    in seed
Polypodium Dryopteris
Malva moschata
Circea Lutetiana
Conyza squarrosa
Thalictrum flavum, in seed. — I saw it
    at once before, at Moreton.
Nepeta Cataria. pretty plentiful
Dipsacus pilosus — I found it before
    at Burley &c in Rutlandshire, more
    plentifully.
Mentha hirsuta? Great quantity.
Sisymbrium
Verbena officinalis
    ... Scorodonia

I never found
these before, in
England. I gathered
them with the
following, between
the Lock and
Monmouth, 5
miles. A most
rainy Day. —

Eupatorium Cannabinum
immense Hemlocks
Angelica sylvestris

**Figure 5.16** An advertisement for Wardian cases, 1870.

Who is there that has not some friend . . . confined by chronic disease or lingering decline to a single chamber? . . . now through sickness dependent . . . for her minor comforts and amusements on the angel visits of a few kind friends, a little worsted work, or a new Quarterly.

He conveys a vividly dated picture of the consumptive maiden tending her plants:

happy in the possession of some fresh gathered flower, and in watering and tending a few pots of favourite plants, which are to her as friends, and whose flourishing progress under her tender care offers a melancholy but instructive contrast to her own decaying strength. (*Rustic Adornments*)

The physician enters the melodrama and orders the removal of the supposedly deleterious plants from the sick room but smiles on the ferns growing in the safe isolation of a Wardian case. '. . . Will our lady readers take the hint here kindly offered?' Tales like Hibberd's abounded in books on natural history as well as indoor gardens and, true to the sentimental mode, the sick were always beautiful young maidens, little children and dear old mothers.

In addition to ferns, water plants and animals were taken from the wild to recreate the excitement of natural habitats in the drawing room. In 1841 Ward had shown that animals could also thrive in closed glass tanks, their survival being dependent on the plants. A robin (initially trapped in there by accident), a toad and a chameleon thrived in his large fern 'house'. Of particular significance, he had a tank containing fish, pond snails and aquatic plants. The fish lived in the same water for almost a year and the aquarium was born. (Philip Henry Gosse made the same discovery independently and under his guidance front parlours of the 1850s added sea anemones and seaweeds to their collections.) The flowers sought for freshwater aquaria were water ranunculus (crowfoots, *Ranunculus* spp.), 'a most elegant creature of the water', *Vallisneria spiralis* (used by Ward in his experiment), and duckweed (*Lemna* spp), 'a graceful and cheerful ornament, and though very common, both beautiful and useful in an in-door lake'.

The number of plants was not purely for embellishment, but to create a microcosm: a self-sustaining community in the indoor aquarium. This balance of producers and consumers provided Shirley Hibberd with the vague mystery that was an essential and alluring part of his science. His writings reached the heights of pomposity and Victorian complacency but, in spite of this, his ludicrously verbose manner and loving passion for all aspects of plants and their associated creatures make him an irresistible soulmate. He explains the water community as 'a fair balance between the animal, vegetable, and aqueous contents . . . the one purifying and refreshing the other in a charming circle of mysterious operations'. The suggested animal contributors to this magic circle included six goldfish, two British carp, four small tench, some small perch and bleak, three dace, four small eels, two chub, four roach, twelve minnows, twelve gudgeon, two dozen stickle-backs, six newts and quantities of water beetles and pond snails. Victorians were always thorough,

even in their recreations. Hibberd wrote:

During summer the play of the sunlight on the green-tinted water, the sparkling iridescence of the finny creatures, sporting and gambolling among the thread-like roots . . . now darting at each other in play, or assembling in shoals at the surface, like mimic fleets drawn up for battle, form an assemblage of living objects unsurpassed in beauty, and of inexhaustible interest.

His message was essentially the same as that of Keats:

. . . watch intently Nature's gentle doings:
They will be found softer than ringdove's
   cooeings.

Their world of nature, with its poetic 'natural sermon', was truly a picture of when the world was young; creatures sported, frolicked and sang for joy:

The ripples seem right glad to reach those
   cresses,
And cool themselves among the emerald
   tresses;
The while they cool themselves, they freshness
   give,
And moisture, that the bowering green may
   live:
Thus keeping up an interchange of favours,
Like good men in the truth of their
   behaviours.

(Keats)

Territorial statements and threats belonged only to the world of men: coexistence and survival through 'Nature red in tooth and claw' seemed a long way off.

Hibberd wrought entertaining instruction out of every detail of this delightful segment of nature in the front parlour: 'the water is clear and sparkling, and the fountain falls over the tender fronds of the ferns in gentle trickling drops, each drop a prism, illustrative of Newton's triumph in analysing the laws of light.' The clarity of the water which allowed the light to be split into its rainbow components, was, Hibberd explained, due to the inclusion of the water snails. These were a vital link in the cycle of growth and decay, consuming slime and decaying matter.

**Figure 5.17** 'The grandest consummation of all' in a fresh water tank was a variety of 'the most delicate ferns'. An indoor aquarium and fernery combined. (From *Rustic Adornments for Homes of Taste* by Shirley Hibberd)

**Figure 5.18** Mrs Hibberd's fernery with the essential accessories of rockwork and hanging baskets. (From *Rustic Adornments for Homes of Taste* by Shirley Hibberd)

Having mentioned unmentionables, ruffled Victorian sensibilities were quickly smoothed:

> As there can be no success without these 'nasty things', we must beg our fair readers to endeavour to reconcile themselves to the idea of snails in-doors, and perhaps a little attention paid to their habits, may endear at last that which was at first repugnant.

For those who could view water snails without repugnance some had fascinating details such as a hard lid for shutting the shell, incomparably described by John Clare in *Natural History Letters* in 1825 as fitting 'as close as the lid of a snuff box and [it] keeps out the water when ever it chuses . . . or wants to be dry in its boat'. Attached 'under the chin' this manoeuvrable door brought 'no more inconvenience than a mans [sic] beard when it is open . . . [and served] the double purpose of clogs or shoes to keep the sharp gravelly bottom of the brooks from hurting its tender flesh'. The lowly status of the cleansing water snails of the drawing-room aquarium-fernery was no doubt raised by their accommodation comprising some fashionable 'raised rock-work, or the model of some old ruin', and their carved likenesses adorning the wooden case (see Figure 5.17).

Outside in the garden, ferns mimicked their wild origins, adorning 'water-scenery', in keeping with 'their proper character of wildness and simplicity', or growing from tree stumps or 'boldly designed rock-work'. In the last decades of the century, woodland gardens with naturalised bulbs and wild flowers made a less contrived setting. Under glass, there were complete fern gardens (see Figure 5.18), featuring exotics – tree ferns towering over a humid jungle of symmetry and pattern, from shrub size to fronds barely the size of toadstools. There were fern baskets hanging on chains of acorns or horse chestnuts and especial fern bricks for building into conservatory walls with planters shaped like shells.

The fernery, like the conservatory, was almost a happy coincidence of historical timing. Wardian cases had proved their worth for transporting exotic plants in 1833, which was also the year that new methods of glass manufacture became known. Twelve years later an old and prohibitive glass tax was removed and later novel construction methods were introduced, so the way was opened for cheap glass and better glass-houses just as exotic ferns and flowers were becoming more available. The combination of events and opportunity happily manifested itself in the fern craze and the passion for foreign exotics.

# Chapter 6

# FOREIGN EXOTICS

## The Essential Greenhouse

Alongside the naturalistic habitats and rustic appeal of ferns the Victorians loved plants and garden embellishments that epitomised formality and the artificial conditions of horticultural expertise. No Victorian gentleman worthy of the name kept a garden without a range of glass-houses to suit the special needs of each of the fashionable plants. There were the functional greenhouses for raising tender bedding-plants for the mid-Victorian fashion of formal carpet bedding (see Figure 6.1) in parterres as well as individual houses for carnations, petunias and geraniums, a cactus house, at least one fruit-forcing house of peaches, pineapples, bananas and nectarines, a fernery, a camellia house, an orchid house, and an orangery. This and the essential vinery lent themselves to architectural interpretations appropriate to the warmer climes they mimicked (see Figure 6.2), as well as demonstrating the wealth and thus good taste of their owner. On a large estate there might also be a pine stove, a bulb house or a heathery full of Cape heaths introduced by Francis Masson, but always in gardens great and small there was the *pièce de résistance* – the conservatory, attached to or very close to the house. Some, with their ornate pillars and supports, more closely resembled a ballroom than a greenhouse (see Figures 2.2 and 2.3).

By the 1850s the social desirability of a conservatory extended down the social scale well below the status of a gentleman with wealth; by this time, orchids were readily available in nurseries, there was a gathering momentum of

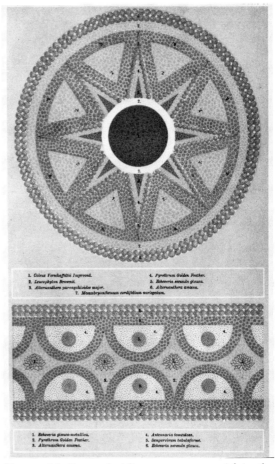

**Figure 6.1** Carpet bedding was an essential in the mid-Victorian garden and the tender exotics to keep it filled through the year demanded extensive green-houses. (From *The Gardener's Assistant: Practical and Scientific* by Robert Thompson, c. 1880)

**Figure 6.2** A parrot-house and vinery for the fashionable garden, 'where under the shadow of purple grapes a large number of choice birds will find sufficient room to be happy. . . A collection of parrots and paroquets would have a splendid effect in such a building and give it a truly oriental appearance.' (1856) Shirley Hibberd, *Rustic Adornments for Homes of Taste*

exotic plant imports, and cheap, efficient glass enabled heated greenhouses and conservatories to become an integral part of middle-class gardening. For the suburban majority one greenhouse or a conservatory was sufficient. It was here, particularly in the winter months, that the ladies of the house could dabble at gardening without sullying their decorum or their fashionable and voluminous attire. The compulsory sollyas, aspidistras, cinerarias, pelargoniums and fuchsias did not demand that one was either a passionate plant collector or an expert horticulturalist. The conservatory gave enjoyment, and above all, it bestowed 'a certain claim to distinction on its possessor'. To qualify for the distinctive title of conservatory rather than greenhouse, this glass extension to the house had to be able to accommodate trees. At the height of the social scale it was linked to a mansion by spacious glass doors. At Broughton Hall (see Plate 8) the conservatory is visible even from the main entrance, presenting an oasis of light and green through large curving windows as one enters. (Its small trees are eucalypts and the wild

African amaryllis growing below them are an interesting link with Victorian history: they were brought home from the Boer War by a young member of the family in his subaltern's knapsack.) On a much smaller scale, a small extension on a suburban drawing-room aspired to be a conservatory by judicious furnishing of the room with 'mirrors and bulbous flowers in water glasses', heightening the effect of 'growth, verdure, gay colours and fragrance'. It all blended delightfully with books, sofas and other 'accompaniments of social and polished life' (see Figure 6.3).

The conservatory had another very Victorian attribute – namely 'the moral effects naturally attending a greenhouse'. William Cobbett (who had been a gardener at Kew under William Aiton) explained this aspect in *The English Gardener*:

How much better during the long and dreary winter for daughters and even sons, to assist or attend their mother in a greenhouse than to be seated with her at cards or in the blubberings

**Figure 6.3** A small conservatory adjoining the drawing room.

**Figure 6.4** Plants succumb to architectural embellishment.

over a stupid novel or any other amusement that can possibly be conceived! How much more innocent, more pleasant, more free from temptation to evil this amusement than any other? . . . the taste is fixed at once and it remains to the exclusion of cards and dice to the end of life.

At the time Cobbett was expounding these views, the revolution in greenhouses was beginning. In 1833 new methods of glass manufacture completely changed greenhouse design and efficiency. Previous to that date the small glass sheets available were never perfectly flat, were of varying shades and contained air bubbles and streaks. Light intensity was further reduced by the large number of overlaps and supporting bars that were necessary in construction (dirt also accumulated in between them). There was also a glass tax so that there was little incentive as well as little possiblity of making a glass-house as full of light as the garden outside. Eighteenth-century and early nineteenth-century greenhouses had thus emphasised masonry and style rather than light: many such edifices aspired to the architecture of cathedrals or ancient tombs (see Figure 6.4), with only a flat opaque roof as a concession to the plants within.

After 1833, thin, flat, uniform sheets of good quality glass were combined with new methods of iron construction and 'ridge and furrow' roofing to create the Victorian iron and glass conservatory, and many other buildings besides. The new system of 'ridge and furrow' dispensed with the raftered supporting roof. This and the improved glass increased the light inside. Sir Joseph Paxton developed the new design, transforming greenhouses into sophisticated microcosms for tropical plants and opening the way to eccentric fantasy worlds full of luxuriant plant splendour, such as his Great Conservatory, built at Chatsworth between 1836 and 1839. It housed a complete grand tropical landscape in an area of 277 feet (85 m) by 123 feet (38 m), and 67 feet (21 m) high.

## The Romance of Foreign Climes

### The Orient

The flower world under glass encompassed the romance and danger of distant places, the excitement of new flower discoveries and the fancies of fashion and competitive gardening. It also satisfied the Victorian preoccupations with novelty, the exotic and forming collections. The charisma of new flowers such as orchids, the royal water-lily, acacias and wax begonias was illustrated by the melodramatic début of the golden-rayed lily of Japan (*Lilium auratum*, see Figure 7.2) in 1862. Japan, closed to Europe since 1639, had only just been opened to collectors. With the sudden opening up of a country with such plant potential, there was a rush of collectors in 1860 and 1861 which inevitably brought overlaps and four collectors independently sent home the flower. The British collectors were the nurseryman, John Gould Veitch, and Robert Fortune, both of whose activities were subject to the political limitations of nursery and garden visits within a small prescribed area, although *Lilium auratum* was one of Fortune's exceptional plants, collected from the wild. The difficulties of collecting in Japan lent the flower an aura of inaccessibility in addition to the beauty of waxy white petals spotted reddish-purple and striped with gold, and green stamens bursting with red pollen. John Lindley's contemporary description touched with the Australian goldrush gives a far more vivid picture:

If ever a flower merited the name of glorious, it is this, which stands far above all other Lilies, whether we regard its size, its sweetness, or its exquisite arrangement of colour. Imagine, upon the end of a purple stem no thicker than a ramrod, and not above two feet high, a saucer-shaped flower at least ten inches in diameter . . . [Each petal bears] a broad stripe of light satiny yellow, losing itself gradually in the ivory skin. Place the flower in a situation where side-light is cut off, and no direct light can reach it except from above, when the stripes acquire the appearance of gentle streamlets of Australian gold, and the reader who has not seen it may form some feeble notion of what it is. Fortunately ten thousand eyes beheld it at South Kensington. . . From this delicious flower there arises the perfume of orange blossoms sufficient to fill a large room, but so delicate as to respect the weakest nerves.

(quoted in *Curtis's Botanical Magazine*)

At this first London appearance of 'the most attractive object of the present floral season',

gentlemen removed their hats in deference to its exquisite beauty.

Simultaneous events were paradoxical and epitomised the dangers surrounding the introduction of such flowers into Victorian conservatories and gardens for back in the lily's homeland there was butchering of foreigners by Japanese Samurai, followed by British revenge. In the vein of a popular novel, Fortune did not stop at guile, bribery, or Hornblower-style heroics in order to collect what he wanted. He was an old hand at overcoming petty restrictions, having several times penetrated deep into the forbidden countryside of China some years before, totally disguised with shaved head and pigtail, on occasion unable to eat for fear of giving himself away by his chopstick technique. Such tales further increased the acquisitive cravings of plant fanciers for the hard-won plants of the Orient. Transporting the plants across the globe had presented other problems (90 per cent of plants had died in transit in Sir Joseph Banks's time), but the invention of the Wardian case (see Figures 2.7 and 5.16), in which plants were cocooned in their own microclimate was now proving its real worth in long-distance plant travel.

### The Himalayas

In addition to Japan, the central mass of Asia remained one of the great unknown areas of the world, with an inevitable magnetism. The strange emotion of the sublime brought romance to species of remote mountain wildernesses, such as the giant lily, *Lilium (cardiocrinum) giganteum*, from the Himalayas, with its glittering wet-looking rosette of leaves and flowers nine inches long. It became known in Europe in 1820 and was introduced by Nathaniel Wallich, a supplier of plants and botanical information to Sir Joseph Banks, and director of the Calcutta Botanic Gardens. Like the plant collectors in Japan he obtained plants in the face of politics and limited access. He was the first to obtain a glimpse of the Himalayan plant potential and saw the giant lily first in Nepal, abundant in 'thick deep forests' at 7,500 to 9,000 feet, growing 'sometimes to a size quite astonishing' – around ten feet. The flower itself, praised as 'the Prince of Lilies' by Sir William Jackson Hooker, was astounding enough without its magnificent mountain setting, as described by Sir William's son, Sir Joseph Dalton

Hooker, during his historic plant-collecting expedition in 1848:

> The most eloquent descriptions I have read fail to convey to my mind's eye the forms and colours of snowy mountains, or to my imagination the sensations and impressions that rivet my attention to these sublime phenomena when they are present in reality . . . the precision and sharpness of their outlines . . . the wonderful play of colours on their snowy flanks . . . the glowing hues reflected in orange, gold and ruby, from clouds illumined by the sinking or rising sun . . . the ghastly pallor that succeeds with twilight, when the red seems to give place to its complementary colour green. Such dissolving-views elude all attempts at description, they are far too aërial to be chained to the memory, and fade from it so fast as to be gazed upon day after day, with undiminished admiration and pleasure. . . . In the early morning the transparency of the atmosphere renders [the] . . . view one of astonishing grandeur . . . a dazzling mass of snowy peaks, intersected by blue glaciers, which gleamed in the slanting rays of the rising sun, like aquamarines set in frosted silver.

The idea of such vast and dangerous peaks guarding rare and exquisite flowers fulfilled every requirement of the lofty emotion of the sublime: a sense of awe and a thrilling shiver down the spine (see Plate 7). Sir Joseph Dalton Hooker sensed this when he wrote: 'The scenery is as grand as any pictured by Salvator Rosa; a river roaring in sheets of foam, sombre woods . . . flanked and crested with groves of black firs, terminating in snow-sprinkled rocky peaks.' The cult of nature worship had always been associated with mountains and in the picturesque gardens of the late eighteenth century the sort of features Hooker described had been used in an attempt to create this atmosphere of awe and gloomy foreboding; middle-aged Victorians and those of Romantic inclination must have revelled in reminiscences of sublime escapism. Jane Loudon heightened the melodramatic picture in *Facts from the World of Nature*:

> Here is concentrated all that is sublime in the scenery of nature. On every side rise snowy summits of stupendous height . . . and rugged and frightful precipices. . . . In some places these paths would be quite inaccessible, if it were not for the help of the natives, who carry travellers in wooden chairs upon their backs. Even with this assistance we may easily imagine the terror and inconvenience to which travellers are exposed in traversing those fearful regions . . . we may almost wonder how human beings can ever live through the perils of such a journey, particularly Europeans.

Then followed a delightful picture of the armchair rides of the stiff-upper-lipped Europeans, with a touch of 'sublime' drama in the left-hand bottom corner! (See Figure 6.5.) Such speculations were a comfortable contrast to the realities of plant-collecting and exploring in unknown terrain.

The ethereal magnificence of the Himalayas was imprinted on rhododendrons as well as lilies. After Sir Joseph Dalton Hooker's historic expedition to Sikkim Himalaya in 1848, the rhododendrons he discovered became an integral part of the British garden and the romantic Victorian dream of exotic beauty. Kew's rhododendron dell was started, and even before Hooker returned home, his seeds had produced young plants, some of which the Queen had growing at Osborne. Some rhododendrons were only suited to greenhouse cultivation such as the white and pale chartreuse *Rhododendron Dalhousiae* (now *R. dalhousiae*, see Plate 7), with its four and a half inch flowers, which often smell of lemon. Rhododendrons could be so rich in fragrance as to fill an entire conservatory with sweetness, conjuring dreams of 'peaks of frosted silver'.

Hooker was as captivated by the Himalayan flowers as he was with their sublime surroundings. The tropical latitude allowed alpines, European woodland flowers, rhododendrons and tropical orchids to thrive within a relatively short distance of each other, separated only by altitude. In the tropical forest below, against the backdrop of real snow there were vast trees clothed for yards with white orchids in 'a continuous garment . . . whitening their trunks like snow.' Armchair collectors reeled at images of luxuriantly thick rhododendron bushes up to eighty feet high, heavy with flower clusters bigger than a man's head – pastel or deep-coloured, but always delicate in contrast to the leathery leaves. One rhododendron Hooker

**Figure 6.5** Sublime mountain scenery and its attendant mishaps. (From *Facts from the World of Nature* by Jane Loudon)

spoke of as 'the most lovely thing you can imagine', another as 'a most noble white rhododendron, whose truly enormous and delicious lemon-scented blossoms strewed the ground'. He described and sketched 43 types – 36 different species, 28 of them new to science.

Towering above the myriad variations on the rhododendron theme in white, pinks, lavender, scarlet and crimson, there were purple magnolias and conifers threaded by tumbling stony currents, while hovering above the clouds glittering snow peaks completed a spectacle which was mimicked in rhododendron woodlands all over Britain. The pattern of plants from the high mountain habitat was transported to tamer waterfalls overhung with trees and contrived rocks, where the low sun of northern summer evenings could focus on the bright violets and purples of primulas and spotlight crisp, pale lilies against dramatic dark shadows, capturing a whisper of their Himalayan origins. Sunlit in dazzling colours or glistening and dripping rain drops in 'banks of hazy vapour', the rhododendrons and all that went with them fitted in well with the British climate as well as the indigenous woodland trees and the many North American pines introduced by David Douglas. (The tenderness of the wild Himalayan species was rectified by hybridisation with a hardy American species.) By the late 1870s the pendulum of garden fashion was swinging away from Italianate terraces and formal parterres filled with

**Plate 8** (above) The conservatory, Broughton Hall, Yorkshire

**Plate 9** (left) A Rhododendron Garden

Pl. 13.

CATTLEYA SKINNERI.

Pub.d by J. Ridgway & Sons 169. Piccadilly. Feb.y 1.st 1838.

Printed by C. Hullmandel, Limited Walk 9 of 12.

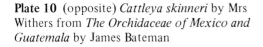

Plate 13 (below) *Abutilon darwinii*, illustrated by Walter Hood Fitch in *Curtis's Botanical Magazine*, Volume 97, 1871
By permission of Bath Reference Library

**Plate 10** (opposite) *Cattleya skinneri* by Mrs Withers from *The Orchidaceae of Mexico and Guatemala* by James Bateman

**Plate 11** (above left) Dendrobium devonianum
By permission of Bath Reference Library

**Plate 12** (above right) 'The Glittering Life of the Tropics'

**Plate 14** (above left) *Tulipa greigii,* from
Turkestan

**Plate 15** (above right) Woody Nightshade (*Solanum
dulcamara*
Photograph by John Presland

**Plate 16** (below left) Detail of sweet pea: a tiny
brush near the tip of the style which sweeps pollen
out of a small hole between the petals

**Plate 17** (below right) Broom, with its spring
released

**Figure 6.6** 'The tangled luxuriance and dismal grandeur of . . . Tropical America. What rich and redundant vegetation! What an endless profusion of climbers and twiners, epiphytes and parasites, *et id genus omne*!! And, then, what a strange variety of animated beings!!! . . . The happy pair in the foreground . . . betray, we fear . . . a less primitive taste, as they evidently are not confining themselves to a *vegetable* diet. That *Epidendrum* [orchid] on the trunk of the prostrate tree must be a fine thing, and we are only sorry to see the lady turn her back upon it.' Vignette from *Orchidaceae of Mexico and Guatemala* by James Bateman. (By permission of Cambridge University Library)

tender exotics towards the wild garden, championed by William Robinson. In 1870 he explained the wild garden as: 'Our groves and shrubberies made beautiful by the naturalization of hardy exotic plants', as well as by British wild flowers. Another strong influence directing public taste towards this more relaxed style was Gertrude Jekyll in the 1890s (see Figure 3.6). Hooker's rhododendrons and their associated flora had an undeniable charisma ideally suited to the 'natural' garden of the late nineteenth century and the twentieth century (see Plate 9). His images of them and their amazing habitat had to suffice Victorian gardeners who tried to recreate them, as it was fifty years before anyone else penetrated the flowering mountains of Sikkim.

## The Jungle

The glorious spectacle of tropical wilderness held its own potent lure for armchair plant collectors. 'The narratives of travellers' delighted their readers who longed 'to behold the luxuriance of animal and vegetable life' (see Figure 6.6). Alive with spontaneous enthusiasm and wonder, these journals marvelled at the vivid equatorial light and described the ostentatious, almost pulsating presence of plants and animals, so different from the quiet orderly countryside of northern climes. They enthused over the 'denizens of a happier climate' and flowers of amazing tropical loveliness and baffling complex structure. Humboldt's descriptions of the tropics, the Canaries in particular, so inspired the young Charles Darwin in 1830 that he immediately started planning a journey: he travelled to London to find out the cost of a passage, started learning Spanish and talked of nothing else but the glories of Tenerife and a famous dragon tree (*Dracaena draco*) of immense proportions.

Like Japan and the Himalayas, the Amazon wilderness had been closed to foreigners but with the end of the Napoleonic Wars the shutters on this dazzling world were lifted and among the first to arrive were Allan Cunningham and James Bowie, sent by Sir Joseph Banks in 1814. They brought back the gloxinia, a flower which was very popular with the Victorians. David Douglas passed through on his travels and was 'particularly delighted' by the 'varied and endless forms' of tropical orchids. Walking in a tropical forest was likened to 'sauntering amid the columns of an empty cathedral, whilst the service is being celebrated aloft on the blazing roof'. Lizards 'of a dark coppery colour, some with backs of the most brilliant silky green and blue . . . seem to enjoy every moment of their existence, basking in the hot sun with the most indolent satisfaction, then scampering off as if every ray had lent vivacity and vigour to their chilly constitutions'. Such evocative images from Kingsley and others fired the imagination and lured young men to 'break through the trammels of business and the ties of home, and start for:

"Some far land where endless summer
  reigns." '

The young man bent on seeing for himself was Alfred Russel Wallace, famous for his ideas on evolution which were simultaneous with Darwin's. In his turn, Wallace must have inspired others with his descriptions of 'the sparkling life of the tropics' in South America, where:

Bright flowers and green foliage combine their charms, and climbers with their flowery festoons cover over the bare and decaying stems . . . most striking of all are the passion flowers, which are abundant on the skirts of the forest . . . – purple, scarlet, or pale pink: the purple ones have an exquisite perfume.

The greatest tropical thrill for any traveller, Victorian or latterday, is to enter a rain forest for the first time. Charles Darwin was not afraid to admit his subjective feelings in his diary:

Delight itself, however, is a weak term to express the feelings of a naturalist who, for the first time, has wandered by himself in a Brazilian forest . . . in these fertile climates, teeming with life, the attractions are so numerous, that [one] . . . is scarcely able to walk at all. . . It is easy to specify the individual objects of admiration in these grand scenes; but it is not possible to give an adequate idea of the higher feelings of wonder, astonishment, and devotion, which fill and elevate the mind.

Henry Walter Bates shared Darwin's contemplative response:

There is something in a tropical forest akin to the ocean in its effects on the mind. Man feels so completely his insignificance there, and the vastness of nature. A naturalist cannot help reflecting on the vegetable forces manifested on so grand a scale round him.

Charles Darwin described the tropical forest magnificently, but even as he tried to fix it all in his mind, he knew 'the thousand beauties which unite these into one perfect scene must fade away; yet they will leave, like a tale heard in childhood, a picture full of indistinct, but most beautiful figures'. Today there are few virgin forests and most plant enthusiasts must be content with a second-hand journey via a screen conscious of time and presentation. As Darwin, Wallace and his friend, Bates, stood for the first time amazed in the forest, time and artistry were irrelevant to their descriptions. Impressions and details bombarded their minds, compelling them to communicate place and experience in their journals. The vivid mental images Bates and Wallace both create bring a three-dimensional panorama to the mind's eye:

. . . the forest-trees, their trunks rising frequently for sixty or eighty feet without a branch . . . tree trunks were only seen partially here and there, nearly the whole frontage from ground to summit being covered with a diversified drapery of creeping plants, all of the most vivid shades of green . . . the huge creepers, which climb about . . . them, sometimes stretching obliquely from their summits like the stays of a mast, sometimes winding about their trunks like immense serpents waiting for their prey . . . they form tangled festoons . . . others, again, were of zigzag shape, or indented like the steps of a staircase, sweeping from the ground to a giddy height. . . The leafy crown of the trees, scarcely two of which could be seen together of the same kind, were now far above us, in another world as it were. We could only see at times, where there was a break above, the tracery of . . . a hundred forms [of] . . . foliage against the clear blue sky . . . [and] the whole illuminated by a glowing vertical sun, and reeking with moisture . . . over the whole fluttered . . . brilliantly-coloured butterflies . . . bright moving flakes of colour.

Tropical jungle was an exotic Victorian dream which could be recreated, given enough wealth. In many ways, greenhouse imitations were better for the flower lover than the real rain forest, where orchid and bromeliad flowers tended to be dispersed in a high green canopy out of sight. In the new glass-houses these could flower in profusion in driftwood and, amongst glistening arum and pepper leaves and humid groupings of tropical ferns, they could transcend their mundane surroundings into shadowy echoes of their distant origins in a past rain forest.

## Creating the Tropical Dream

A tropical forest under glass became the escapist dream for those seeking to impress on a grand scale. J.C. Loudon imagined the possibilities of conservatories 150 feet high to accommodate the tallest forest trees complete with monkeys and the brilliant colours of tropical birds. In the realisation of the dream, caged canaries and nightingales substituted for the vibrating wings of romantically named purple-crowned fairies, blue-throated sylphs, orange-throated sun-angels, and blue-tailed emerald humming birds. (Regrettably vast numbers of these enchanting creatures were still part of the Victorian idea of beauty – but as stuffed items of female jewellery and glass-domed ornaments.) Tropical trees and large shrubs in hothouses were not new: many had been grown in Sir Joseph Banks's day, for example cashew, banana, custard apple, guava, mango, breadfruit, pink frangipani, poinciana, coffee, palm; and in Plate 12 hibiscus (*Hibiscus rosa-sinensis*), sweetsop (*Anona* sp.), the soursop (*Anona muricata*) and cocoa (*Theobroma cacao*). The wealth of the tropic's fruits brought comment from David Douglas, in Madeira, and Charles Darwin on his visit to Tahiti. Before the ebullient extravagances of the Victorians, the emphasis can be seen to have been very much on economic food plants. Exotic fruits were by no means forsaken in the nineteenth-century dream, for as well as featuring in the fantasy landscape, potted fruit trees and shrubs were frequently transported from greenhouses to form an integral part of the decoration and menu at banquets and balls. Peaches, nectarines and oranges were plucked direct from the trees by the guests in the manner of the 'noble savage' (see Figure 6.6).

The realities of glass-house jungles were smaller than Loudon's dream forest but no less imaginative. The 'elegant grace' of tree ferns captured the essence of the jungle paradise – ferns which had a:

> feathery diadem of leaves . . . so magnified that the crown of out-curving fronds shaded an area of twenty feet in diameter, and yet preserving all the voluptuous lightness and minute subdivision which are so characteristic. . . to stand under the beautiful arch and gaze upwards on the filigree-fretted fronds that formed a great umbrella of verdure, – this was most charming, and never to be forgotten.
> (Philip Henry Gosse, *The Romance of Natural History*)

In contrast to the fine-leaved ferns there were the large glossy leaves of tropical climbers such as *Monstera deliciosa*, an appropriate clothing for the grand pillars of these hothouses. Bright passion flowers, bougainvilleas (see Plate 12), and the strange-flowered aristolochias entwined across the faceted skies. By night, the heady intoxication of a dream turning to reality was conjured up in the evocative scent of angel's trumpets (*Datura candida*), with ghostly white flowers, ten inches long, hanging from high branches. By day, their ethereal beauty was matched by the perfume of frangipani, perfect unfurling stars of white or pink, golden-centred, on bare, grey, tree-trunk stems. A brash contrast among the tree tops were trees capable of a profusion of bright red blossoms. These were the claw-like petals of the coral trees (*Erythrina* spp.), reports of which in the gardens of Madeira had long tantalised British gardeners.

Besides such obvious appeal there were trees and flowers which were botanical curiosities of the eighteenth century, such as Francis Masson's *Strelitzia reginae* from Africa and the *Acacia verticillata* from Australia. Australian acacias (wattles, see Figure 7.1) brought a multitude of fluffy yellow flowers and delicate shades of blue-green and grey 'leaves' (technically they are not leaves). According to the *English Cyclopaedia* few plants were considered 'more worthy of a permanent station in a good conservatory' than the fragrant acacia, with the downy acacia as a close second as 'one of the most beautiful' of greenhouse plants. Similar in flower form but a brilliant colour contrast was the red bottlebrush-tree (*Callistemon* sp.). Other 'New Holland' plants were the tall eucalypts, epacris and grevilleas, some fashionably included for seemingly little more than their distinguishing characteristic of 'small dry leaves, that have often a shrivelled appearance' (*Conversations on Botany*). The plants of Botany Bay still retained something of an aura of novelty – Sydney had only been founded in 1788 – and among the collectors of plants of 'that remarkable country', nurserymen Lee and Kennedy had immediately adopted Australian flora as their speciality. New plants, particularly orchids, were still being discovered during the nineteenth century as the interior of the immense continent began to be explored – exploration and plant discovery combining in the extraordinary expeditions (see page 129) of Allan Cunningham who was collecting for Kew between 1817 and 1838.

Even excluding the 'shrivelled' leaves, many of the curiosities were not the type of plants which today's exotics enthusiast would choose. One long-standing attraction of acacias was the sensitive leaves of some species, described romantically in John Lindley's *Botanical Register* of 1841:

> Every evening they rose up and lifted themselves from the blossoms to expose them to the dew . . . but as the day advances, the leaves gradually drooped. . . Who can imagine the gorgeousness of an equinoctial forest at midnight, with the veils thus lifted off myriads of flowers of every form and hue. . .

More novelties were displayed on the contrived jungle floor: coloured bracts of aroids had the waxy appeal of the artificial and foliage plants such as *Begonia rex*, introduced from Assam in 1857, brought a contrast of living metallic sheen to the brash paintbox colours of crotons (see Plate 12), caladiums and coleus. The texture and colour of foliage plants became another passion with the Victorians. Amongst them tropical flowers grew in naturalistic settings of heated pools fed by waterfalls with carefully contrived rockwork and dazzling crystalline minerals. Creeping plants, exotic ferns and orchids mim-

icked nature, encrusting the wet rocks and strategically positioned tree trunks.

*The Great Conservatory, Chatsworth*

One of the most famous indoor tropical landscapes was the Great Conservatory created by Sir Joseph Paxton at Chatsworth (see Figure 6.7). In 1852 it was described as a fairy-tale garden planted in the most excellent taste. In the *Illustrated London News* of 3 May 1851, the King of Saxony was quoted as having 'graphically' compared it to 'a tropical scene with a glass sky'. Queen Victoria and Prince Albert viewed it from a carriage (three of which could be driven through the conservatory simultaneously). For those lower down the social scale there were railway excursions and nearly 50,000 people visited the Great Conservatory each year. The Chatsworth landscape boasted the largest, the most and the first of almost every horticultural novelty. The foundation stone of the giant greenhouse was laid in 1836 and it was ready for the first plants in 1839. Five hundred people were involved in building it and establishing the plants in a layout dictated by their natural conditions and requirements.

Entering at the north gate, there was a main avenue flanked on one side by glossy-leafed orange trees and the century plant (*Agave americana*), with its stiff leaves, three feet and more, edged with sharp teeth. In dramatic contrast were the showy shrubs scarlet archania (*Malvaviscus* sp.) from Jamaica and the very delicate, transient white flowers of *Sparmannia africana* each with its central cluster of sensitive red stamens like ornamented antennae which moved at the slightest touch. Lower down, pink and crimson spikes of changeable starpheta blended with the white flowers and bright red berries of dwarf ardisia. Overhead was the magnificent tiered symmetry of the Norfolk Island pine (*Araucaria excelsa*), a favourite since its introduction in 1793 by Sir Joseph Banks and coveted by many who were unable to keep it because of its great height. (Later on it was grown in Kew's Temperate House.) A tall date palm (*Phoenix dactilifera*) and a dracaena lifted more radial symmetry high into the glass sky.

There was a large piece of rockwork planted with traditional eighteenth-century fruits: two species of guavas, including the purple guava (*Psidium cattleyanum* [*P. variabile*]), more oranges,

**Figure 6.7** Inside the Great Conservatory at Chatsworth. Unfortunately it was necessary to demolish it after the First World War, although the low walls supporting the glass arches remain. (By permission of the Trustees of the Chatsworth Settlement)

ferns, dracaena, the India-rubber tree (*Ficus elastica*), and another large sharp-leafed rosette, *Doryanthes excelsa*, from New South Wales. At the foot of the rocks was a pool with all the atmosphere of a mysterious cave surrounded by stalactites. Crystals brought from India and Siberia and an opalised tree trunk from Australia were strategically placed to glimmer and show off opalescent petals. Around this magical pool grew brightly variegated leaves of various caladiums and the old favourite, the vivid flowered canna. Across the whole wafted the strong scent of hedychium, a delicate flower of the Ginger family. The pool was richly spangled with water-lilies, including the sacred lotus (*Nelumbo nucifera* [*Nelumbium speciosum*]), while at its margins the Egyptian papyrus (*Cyperus papyrus*) evoked yet more romance of the Ancients. Two smaller rockwork creations were covered with low-growing cycads, taller tree ferns – *Cycas revoluta* and the sago palm (*C. circinalis*) – and a 24-foot (7.4-m) European fan palm (*Chamaerops humilis*).

Bisecting the main avenue, a smaller path was flanked on each side by two species of banana, one 30 feet (9.2 m) high – 'among the most elegant denizens of the torrid zone'. From the same family there was the traveller's tree (also called traveller's palm, *Urania speciosa*, [*Ravenala madagascariensis*]), like a vast stalked feather fan. Another grouping included some true palms and a very dramatic and famous novelty: a group of pitcher plants (*Nepenthes distillatoria*, see Figure 9.1), with fifty lurid, lidded pitchers each five inches (13 cm) in circumference, suspended in the air. (The difficulty of transporting and acclimatising pitcher plants, regardless of their insect-catching habits, added to their great attraction.) More appealing to modern eyes were the vivid orange and blue flowers of the bird-of-paradise flower and blue-flowered justicia (*Eranthemum* sp.). Nearby the bluebird vine (*Petrea volubilis*) added hanging sprays of prolific blue and mauve stars, while overhead was the rather rare tree rose of Venezuela (*Brownea grandiceps*), with wonderful orange balls of rhododendron-like flowers. (Kew's tree produced no less than fifty flowering bunches in 1880.)

Further down the walk one came to the brilliant leaves of croton (see Plate 12), and yet more palms including the kittul palm (*Caryota urens*), and the wierd screw-pine (*Pandanus odoratissimus*), with its stilt-like roots and spiky tufts of long narrow leaves growing in twisted lines at the tips of its branches. There were more exotic flowering trees, a cream magnolia from Java and two shrubs introduced by Nathaniel Wallich: Wallich's astrapaea with heavy pink clusters of flowers and Mr Sabine's strobilanthes (*Ruellia* sp.), a delicate mixture of bluish flowers, pink-tipped calyces and purple-backed leaves. Offering sweetness rather than colour was the pawpaw (*Carica papaya*) and sugar cane (*Saccharum officinarum*).

Lastly, in the south-west wooded area, was Sir Joseph Paxton's pride – the strong trunks of the 'Dwarf Cavendish' banana, which Paxton knew as *Musa Cavendishii* although it is now considered to be a cultivar of *Musa acuminata*. Paxton was the first to fruit this new banana, which when exhibited at the Horticultural Society Show in 1836 created a sensation and won him a medal. At a time when any hothouse banana was a rare luxury, this small tree held great promise as not only was the fruit delicately flavoured but the tree fruited profusely – in 1842 one of the Chatsworth plants produced about three hundred bananas. The *Musa Cavendishii* (see Plate 6) became the subject of a delightful legend. It was said that Paxton was captivated by an unknown dwarf banana painted on a Chinese wallpaper in a bedroom at Chatsworth. Convinced that such a banana must exist he sent a collector to China to find it and bring it to Chatsworth where it flourished. The legend became firmly established enough to be taken as fact by many but earlier this century the story was cast into doubt as the banana could not be found on the Chinese wallpapers. It was only following rearrangement of the room that the banana was rediscovered behind a four-poster bed and it seemed that the legend was true after all. For there was no doubt that the real *Musa Cavendishii* was Chinese and thriving amongst bamboos in the Great Conservatory just as it was in the wallpaper, which had been hung between 1823 and 1830, before the Conservatory was built. However the romantic quest was, sadly, found to be mere fantasy, for the banana in fact came to the Great Conservatory by the orthodox and mundane route of purchase from a nurseryman. It had been imported from China via Mauritius in 1829 to adorn a fine garden, and after the owner's death the only two banana plants were sold to the nurseryman – one went abroad and the other, the only plant in England, was bought by Paxton. The link was pure coincidence but no doubt the resemblance between the two had much to do with the tale.[1]

Another 'first' for the Great Conservatory was the long awaited flowering of *Bougainvillea spectabilis*: its copious clusters of brilliant purple were seen 'for the first time, we believe, in England' in 1844 (*Curtis's Botanical Magazine*). From Calcutta's Botanic Garden came another 'first', by courtesy of Nathaniel Wallich (and Dr Ward's very new plant travel case), the Duke of Devonshire's *pièce de résistance* – the graceful pendulous tree, *Amherstia nobilis*. Having seen the flower illustrated in Wallich's breathtaking three-volume work on rare Asian plants, the Duke had despatched one of his gardeners East in 1835 to acquire one, together with as many orchids as he could find. John Gibson had arrived at the Calcutta Botanic Garden as the amherstia's buds were opening for the first time under cultivation. Like the popular frangipani it brought the romance of oriental temple offerings into a greenhouse. Disappointingly, it never displayed its clustered pink butterfly-shaped flowers at Chatsworth. It continued to retain something of its elusive quality: after its discovery it was not seen again for forty years after which it disappeared for a further fifty years before being rediscovered in the wild in 1927.

The massive hoard of orchids brought back by Gibson (p. 115), some eighty species, fared better; for example, the *Dendrobium* sp. (see Plate 11) named after the Duke of Devonshire, a cream flower exquisitely marked with an unusual combination of orange, grey and dusky pink, did well. It was in the words of *Curtis's Botanical Magazine* 'assuredly one of the most delicate and most lovely of all orchidaceous plants, and worthy to bear the name of that distinguished nobleman, the Duke of Devonshire, who has done so much to encourage Horticulture and Botany!'

The whole creation of the Great Conservatory was a masterpiece of escapism, 'a new world' whether seen from below or from above, where even a bird's-eye view was provided. The design of Paxton's plant-encrusted rockwork concealed a stairway which visitors could climb to view the tropical spectacle.

1. It is interesting that the exquisitely painted wallpaper has other features of the Victorian dream conservatory – exotic birds among the trees and intricate rockwork.

From below, looking up through the intricate tracery of fronds, vines, leaves, fruits and blossoms, they could imagine the rain forest, assisted by the Victorian muses:

Oh! to behold ye in your native homes,
Ye strange and glorious creations! There,
Springing 'mong giant trees, whose soaring
   tops
Are roofed by the o'er-arching sky, ye climb,
And bloom, and flourish in uncultured pride,
Gorgeously beautiful.
       (Louisa Anne Twamley, *The Romance of
       Nature*)

### The Palm House, Kew

It was Sir Joseph Paxton's dream that after the Great Exhibition of 1851, the Crystal Palace would become another great greenhouse park, similar to Chatsworth, run by the Government. In the depths of a London winter he envisaged the covered park with a controlled climate inside, a place where people could ride, walk or relax among scented trees and bask in the warmth of Southern Italy, while high above them the structural girders would be disguised with luxuriant creepers. Londoners were never given this indoor escape to the Mediterranean but the vision of Sir William Jackson Hooker gave them the Palm House at Kew – 362 feet (111 m) long, 100 feet (31m) wide and 63 feet (19 m) high excluding its lantern (see Figure 6.8). In his *Wanderings through the Conservatories at Kew*, Philip Henry Gosse begged the accompaniment of his readers on a conducted tour of the Palm House as it was in 1857, nine years after its completion:

> . . . thither, to pay our addresses to the Court of Flowers . . . PROCEEDING up the charmingly-arranged grand promenade, on each side of which lie a profusion of beds of incense-breathing flowers, decked in raiment fairer than the attire of princes, we catch sight of that noble stove, which is perhaps the most magnificent structure of the kind in the world – the Palm-stove. Truly . . . worthy . . . of the delightful science the interests of which it is so eminently calculated to advance . . . A door, and the length of a couple of yards, conducts us from the temperate to the torrid zone. Without was a pleasant genial English summer day, within is the damp and oppres-

**Figure 6.8** The Palm House at Kew in September 1848, two months after the first palms were moved in. There were 64,000 visitors to Kew in 1847 and double that number were expected for the following year.

(From *The Illustrated London News*, 1848: by permission of Avon County Library (Bath Reference Library))

sive heat of Hindostan. Into what noble society are we now introduced? What regal forms are these which stand bathing their green crowns in such an atmosphere of moisture, warmth and light? These are the princes of vegetation, the royal tribe of palms. A crowd of Singular Sensations occupies the mind as we are thus ushered into the vegetable court . . . and arrayed around the peers and commoners of the court, stand grisly old trees with looks so fierce and arms so horrid with spines, that we are by fancy led to believe them to be none other than the warriors and great fighting ones of the army of Queen Flora.

The escapist landscape was largely made up of Australian and Antipodean flora with some African species, such as the African tulip tree (excluded from many hothouses because of its height and the high position of its vivid flower clusters). The effect was obviously a success as Henry Walter Bates found himself recalling it in order to describe a jungle scene in *The Naturalist on the Amazons* in 1863. Such authenticity was made possible by transporting cacti twice as tall

as a man and mature trees in pots into the new Palm Stove (a difficult task as one weighed seventeen tons), and by careful camouflage or distant removal of the hot water piping and machinery on which the warm climate maintained in the Palm House depended. The idea of completely divorcing the mundane from the display was new and was also in evidence at Chatsworth. The mechanics involved, still new and exciting achievements, fascinated the Victorian penchant of 'practical men and utilitarian ladies' for 'devoting their attention to . . . new wonders of mechanical and manufacturing skill [which] astonish them at every turn'. True to his time, Gosse in his *Wanderings through the Conservatories at Kew* gloried in the practicalities of 'the Great Palm House', the chimney arrangements of which were appropriate to the concept and scale of the plants within:

That no chimney might interfere with the *coup d'oeil* of the building, the smoke is conveyed to . . . [the] Water Tower, a shaft of much architectural beauty . . . [along] a distance of nearly 500ft., by a flue contained within an underground tunnel of brickwork seven feet high. This tunnel encloses also a railway for the purposes of bringing coals to the furnaces at the Palm House, which are all underground, and of bringing away the ashes.

In fact the pipes and tunnels to the tower were affected by flooding problems so the Palm House eventually had its own small chimneys.

If this eccentric fantasy was to be complete, there were other mundane realities to be hidden from view, such as the large numbers of gardeners necessary to tend the plants. The gardeners had their own hidden entrance to a grand greenhouse and there was even an idea for a foliage screen behind which a gardener and his tools could quickly disappear and thence descend via a trapdoor, well out of sight of approaching persons admiring the wild, untended splendour about them.

**The Race to Name First and Flower First**

It was on the 1st January, 1837 . . . [we were] contending with the difficulties which, in various forms, Nature interposed to bar our progress . . . [when] lo! a vegetable wonder! All disasters were forgotten. [The water lily had] gigantic leaves, five to six feet across, flat, with a deep rim, light green above and vivid crimson below, floating upon the water; while in keeping with this astonishing foliage I beheld luxuriant flowers . . . [of many petals passing] from pure white to rose pink . . . [with] sweet scent . . . as I rowed from one to another, I always found something new to examine.

(Sir Robert Schomburgk, via *Victoria regia* by
W.J. Hooker)

Another adventurer, Thomas Bridges, was similarly dazzled by the sight of more than fifty flowers: 'Fain would I have plunged into the lake to obtain specimens of the splendid flowers and foliage; but the knowledge that these waters abounded with alligators, and the advice of my guide, deterred me.' Sir Robert Schomburgk's 1837 sighting of the royal water-lily (Victoria water-lily *Victoria regia*, now *V. amazonica* Figure 6.10), with its eighteen-inch (46-cm) flower aroused every competitive aspect of Victorian flower-collecting. The intensity of feeling over

such impressive novelties acquired finally, regardless of alligators, difficulty of terrain and distance, is illustrated by the controversy over naming the plant and the 1849 race to be the first to flower the water-lily in captivity.

As in the Georgian era (see page 5), personality clashes manifested themselves openly over such emotive issues as a plant christening, particularly in the case of 'the noblest flower ever discovered, worthy to bear the name of England's Queen'. In the traditions of such controversies, the old-school botanists were incensed at anything but the purest Latin and Greek familiar to all gentlemen from a classical background. The 1837 discoverer, Schomburgk, who had been sent to South America by the Royal Geographical Society, wanted the lily named *Nymphaea Victoria* after the Queen but on closer examination it was found not to belong to the genus *Nymphaea*. Simultaneously two great men named it – with different names: one named it *Victoria regia* and the other called it *Victoria regina* which precipitated an argument on classical grammar. The first published account of the plant further clouded the issue by using one name in the text and the other in the index. Neither man would step down and accept the other's name.

It then transpired that the 1837 sighting was not the first but the fourth, and the lily had already been christened *Euryale amazonica*. This could have conveniently settled the issue of Latin grammar but for the unfortunate fact that under closer scrutiny the lily fitted no better into the genus *Euryale* than *Nymphaea*. Thus botanical accuracy and the diplomatic gesture towards the Queen could at last be honoured in a new generic name of *Victoria*, but the species named *amazonica* already allocated was immutable. With a name like *Victoria amazonica*, gentlemen of the botanical Establishment faced the unfortunate association of the Queen's name with a sturdy masculine female rather than with the river, as intended. Such an unseemly association was unthinkable in the context of a British Queen, so for her benefit and for the nation the lily lived for fifty years under the misnomer of *V. regia*, while the true scientific name of *V. amazonica* was cloaked in a conspiracy of silence until after the Queen's death. The real name has only recently come into regular use.

*V. regia*'s seeds, no bigger than peas, were brought into Britain by Sir Robert Schomburgk

**109**

**Figure 6.9** The water-lily fashion spread even to glassware. A collection on display at the Great Exhibition in 1851. (By permission of Avon County Library (Bath Reference Library))

but were unfit for growth by the time they arrived. The next batch was collected by Thomas Bridges (in spite of his reticence over alligators) and bought by Kew in August 1846, but four months later they were dead. In 1848 roots were transported in a sealed Wardian case but these were dead on arrival. At last on 28 February 1849, at Kew's instigation, seeds arrived, cocooned in a phial of pure water, and they were alive. Sir William Jackson Hooker gave one of the three resulting plants to Sir Joseph Paxton who created a special greenhouse 61 feet (19 m) by 46 feet (14 m) with a water tank of over thirty feet (9 m) in diameter. It was then a race between the plant at Chatsworth, the plant at Kew and the third given to the Duke of Northumberland at Syon. The public attention roused by the competition heralded the expensive fashion for growing water-lilies in the 1850s; the water-lily fashion even appeared in the design of glassware (see Figure 6.9) and other items.

Paxton's efforts were rewarded by the first flower bud early in November 1849. It opened at 2 p.m. in the afternoon, pure white and emitting a strong fruity smell; during the following day

towards evening the petals fully expanded and the centre gradually flushed with pink. By 10 o'clock at night it was fully expanded with an erect pink centre but without its scent (see Figure 6.10). Then all the petals turned pink as the flower fell flaccid on its side continuing to close throughout the next day until by the third evening it dipped once more beneath the water.

On the first anniversary of its first flowers, Paxton noted: 'it had produced one hundred and fifty leaves and one hundred and twenty-six flowers!' Syon's plant was next to flower and Kew's flowered last in 1850, when the beautiful flowers were shown to an enthralled London public. (Later the plant was put on show in the Crystal Palace.) Although Kew had lost the race, it was Sir William Jackson Hooker who had germinated the seed. Loath to leave all the glory to Paxton and Chatsworth, Hooker immortalised himself in the company of *Victoria regia* in a magnificent book which was published in 1851 with hand-coloured lithographs of the Syon plant drawn by Kew's draughtsman, Walter Hood Fitch.

It was the temperature of the water which had

**Figure 6.10** The royal water-lily (*V. regia*, now *V. amazonica*). An illustration from *Curtis's Botanical Magazine*, 1847, prepared by Sir William Jackson Hooker. (By permission of Avon County Library (Bath Reference Library))

been the problem at Kew: a high temperature is critical to flowering of the water-lily, as well as a high light intensity. English sun, even filtered though the new type of glass roofing, made a poor comparison to the brilliant light of the lily's natural Amazonian setting, described vividly by Henry Walter Bates. His description of a lily pool created little short of a paradise picture to be treasured or recreated in extravagant Victorian stove-houses. For modern readers it is an antique memory tinged with regret in the face of today's dwindling Amazon wilderness. The forest:

opened on a broad placid pool, whose banks, clothed with grass of the softest green hue, sloped gently from the water's edge to the compact wall of forest which encompassed the whole. The pool swarmed with water-fowl; snowy egrets, dark-coloured striped herons, and storks of various species standing in rows around its margins. Small flocks of Macaws were stirring about the topmost branches of the trees. Long-legged . . . [birds] stalked over the water-plants on the surface of the pool, and in the bushes on its margin were great numbers of a kind of canary . . . of a greenish-yellow colour. . . Passing towards the farther end of the pool I saw, resting on the surface of the water, a number of large round

leaves, turned up at their edges; they belonged to the Victoria water-lily. The leaves were just beginning to expand (December 3rd) . . . Luco paddled me amongst the noble plants to search for flowers. . .

Amidst such idyllic surroundings it was little wonder that the flower reduced its first discoverer to his knees 'in a transport of admiration', expressing aloud 'his sense of the power and magnificence of the Creator in his works'.

The romance of the lily's habitat did not fail to catch the attention of the rapidly growing numbers of enthusiasts seeking to have water-lily houses of their own. Jungle ponds were appropriate in the artificial rain forests under glass and the timing of the flower could not have been more appropriate for the Victorian love of fantasy creations: the pools soon reflected the soft lights of coloured lanterns. Some pools were conveniently combined with aquaria. As well as the royal water-lilies, there were pale yellow, pink and white ones from India and the evocative lotus of the East, with its delicate wavy-edged leaves standing out of the water like stalked bowls and its crisp-curled petals. Beneath them flimsy blossoms of lavender-blue water hyacinths wafted across the water. Surrounded by tropical bamboos, weird anthuriums, arums, tall

**111**

osmunda ferns (see Figure 5.14), abutilons (see Plate 13) and pitcher plants (see Figure 9.1), the Victorian water-lily pools must have been a magnificent sight.

Sir Joseph Paxton's dream jungle (see Figure 6.7) surpassed them all and was a national pride, but he was also an immensely practical man. The giant size of the leaves of the water-lily, their great weight and the fact that they rested on the surface as flat as solid wooden trays presented a stimulating example of structural design in nature which as a constructional engineer Paxton was quick to recognise and investigate. When the water-lily was first sighted it had been noticed that local natives used the giant leaves as convenient places to put their children, and so as soon as the Chatsworth leaves had grown large enough the Duke of Devonshire had Paxton's little daughter dressed up as a fairy and placed sedately in the centre of a leaf. Paxton's description of his strength tests on the leaves, recorded in Sir William Jackson Hooker's *Victoria regia* were rather more functional, omitting any fanciful details. He used leaves measuring four foot two inches and four foot nine inches (1.3 m and 1.5 m); his eight-year-old daughter weighed forty-two pounds, so 'a copper-lid, weighing fifteen pounds, being the readiest thing that presented itself, was first placed upon it, in order to equalise the pressure, making together fifty-seven pounds'. The leaf supported such a weight in spite of its surface being so delicate as to be pierced by a straw dropped from a few feet. The key to their strength lay in the structure of the leaf's underside (see Figure 6.10) which consisted of 'deep thick ribs which form the foundation of the blade', criss-crossed with a network of veins, such that the whole had 'the appearance of a spider's web . . . beset with prickles'. The pockets of air caught between the leaf's 'girders' gave it buoyancy.

When Paxton was working on the design of the Great Exhibition building, the lily's leaf structure, and the recently built greenhouse which housed it, contributed to his conception of the Crystal Palace. He borrowed the lily leaf's design of longitudinal and transverse supports to give great strength. The first design met with difficulties but as *The Illustrated London News* for 3 May 1851 reported in retrospect:

> On the morning of the 18th of June, whilst presiding at a railway committee, he sketched upon a sheet of blotting paper his idea for the great Industrial Building. He sat up all that night, until he had worked out the design to his satisfaction; and the elevations, sections, working details and specifications were completed in ten days.

He took the design and a water-lily leaf to show the Fine Arts Commission. It was to be the largest building ever erected, being 1,800 feet (554 m) long, and was a prefabricated structure based on 24-foot (7.4-m) units.

Paxton's novel plans for the construction of the Crystal Palace prompted forecasts of its downfall on many counts: in addition to the obvious fears of it falling down, there were strange notions of people being scorched by the sun's heat through the glass, of the glass panes breaking in the first wind, of the reappearance of the Black Death and of Divine retribution on account of its revolutionary and thus ungodly design. The unique structure was conceived and successfully completed in an incredibly short time, and before the first module was finished, the Crystal Palace, seen from every angle and in every light, appeared and reappeared in the Press throughout 1851 (see Figure 6.11). All classes flocked to pay homage to this temple of Victorian technology born of a greenhouse and a lily leaf. The artisan, Joseph Gutteridge, called it:

> a building to which history offers no parallel, either in the past or the present. Whether we consider the noble and humanizing purposes to which the building is consecrated, the apppropriateness, the elegance, the vastness, and the beauty of the design, or its simple but most admirable novelty.

He had a week's holiday in order to see it and its extraordinary exhibits which included botanical novelties. Like many other working men it was his first sight of the exotic plants of the middle and upper classes. He wrote:

> However much the wonderful structure of glass and iron in which the exhibition was contained might have been admired – it seemed almost a realisation of one of the gorgeous pictures of the Arabian Nights – the treasures it contained interested me most. They surpassed anything previously conceived or read about, and they kept my mind in a state of

**Figure 6.11** 'A man whose name will hererafter stand enrolled among those whose works have done honour to their time and country. Mr. Paxton . . . has acquired a reputation as wide as the civilised world, by the conception of the great idea of the "Crystal Palace" . . . we must acknowledge Mr. Paxton's high claims to the grateful appreciation of his contemporaries, and to that enduring place in the national annals which is the best reward of all true greatness in any and every department of public usefulness.' (*The Illustrated London News*, 1851: by permission of Avon County Library (Bath Reference Library))

continual excitement for some time . . . the peculiarly grotesque forms and strange colouring of orchids, the airy lightness and wondrous frondage of ferns, some of which were so large as to afford shelter to the wayfarer.

It was a pity that the tree ferns could not remain as part of Paxton's dream of a permanent 'indoor park' so as to inspire the ordinary working people in years to come. However, given the immense size of the building and the mundane problems of heating, the idea of the Crystal Palace as a warm southern microcosm in the cold of British winter was destined to remain merely a delightful notion. Paxton's influence on greenhouses has lasted, although the plant fashions and fanaticisms which inspired his garden designs passed as soon as the next novelty was sighted – and the passion for possession, the competition and even the secrecy started all over again.

## Collecting the Biggest and the Most

The royal water-lily provided collectors with 'the biggest', but orchids tempted them with yet more extraordinary superlatives. As Joseph Gutteridge said (see above), their weird forms and bizarre colouring frequently bordered on the grotesque (see Figure 8.12); sometimes these strange attributes coexisted with the most subtle and exquisite – all within the same flower. Charlotte M. Yonge in *The Herb of the Field* marvelled at greenhouse orchids that were like:

a whole shower of pale purple and white butterflies, coming down from a bough . . .

there are many more that are grown in the same manner in England, and that a few lucky people are able to go and admire . . . Their forms are beyond everything astonishing. The monkey, the mosquito, the ant, are only a few of them; there are hovering birds and every wondrous shape, so that travellers declare that the life-time of an artist would be too short to give pictures of all the kinds [of orchids] that inhabit the valleys of Peru alone.

In keeping with mid-Victorian fashion, the orchid blooms were ostentatious, whether in conservatories or a lady's corsage. One species of *Cattleya* had blooms eleven inches (28 cm) across, while another orchid had a spur a foot (36 cm) long (Figure 8.13). Many were exceedingly rare and provided a delightfully obvious symbol of wealth – an unusual plant could fetch £1,000.

They carried the obligatory aura of a wild paradise as portrayed by the old-school naturalists such as Philip Henry Gosse:

From the almost insufferable glare of the vertical sunshine, a few steps took me into a scene where the gloom was so sombre, – heightened doubtless by the sudden contrast, – as to cast a kind of awe over the spirit. Yet it was a beauteous gloom, – rather a subdued and softened light, like that which prevails in some old pillared cathedral when the sun's rays struggle through the many-stained glass of a painted window. Choice plants that I had been used to see fostered and tended in pots in our stove-houses at home, were there in wild and *riant* luxuriance . . . wild pines, ferns, orchids, cactuses . . . – were clustering in noble profusion of vegetable life. . .

(*The Romance of Natural History*)

There was the thrill of danger in acquiring and transporting orchids, and always the element of the unexpected. Who could remain unmoved by an immense orchid plant (*Cattleya skinneri*, see Plate 10), seven feet (2.7 m) in diameter, six feet (1.8 m) high and bearing 1,500 flowers, which had travelled hundreds of miles through Costa Rican jungle and across the Atlantic, having been bought, with difficulty, from a native tribe who almost worshipped it? This amazing specimen, the largest ever discovered, captivated an enthralled Victorian public who flocked to pay their own rather different form of homage.

For the more serious collector, orchids had an overpowering fragrance (the immense *Cattleya* from Costa Rica scented the air for several hundred yards around), and their growth form and foliage were frequently very unusual. The strange extremes of flower structure seen in orchids presented an unparalleled challenge to naturalists: Charles Darwin wrote what is still considered to be a classic work on orchid pollination mechanisms and John Lindley, an orchid expert, made a historic collection of dried orchids which is still preserved at Kew.

In the Victorian era, it was not unusual for a fanatical collector to have 18,000 orchids, and the varying requirements of the plants as well as their sheer numbers and size often demanded more than six greenhouses. The specific conditions required for flowering orchids were initially an obstacle to their successful cultivation. The first tropical orchid (from New Providence Island in the Bahamas) arrived in Britain in 1731, but it was another (from China) which flowered first some years later; orchid plants were few and flowers were infrequent. In these first days of orchid cultivation and in the early nineteenth century when they were very rare, they were treated in the same way as other exotic plants and potted in soil – a state which bore no resemblance to their usual tropical habit of growing attached to trees and creepers. At first sight these orchids growing in the wild would appear to be parasites but this was an early misconception of some naturalists and collectors. In 1818 Kew's collector Allan Cunningham, familiar with terrestrial orchids of Britain and the dry arid conditions of Australia, described tropical orchids growing in mid-air as 'some little parasitical plants . . . adhering to the bark of the trees'. In fact these epiphytic types merely anchor themselves to the tree with their main roots, while other specialised roots develop for the absorption of water and nutriment from the air or from humus collecting in the crevices around the base of the plant. It was not until the 1820s that orchids arrived in this natural growing state complete with attached tree trunks. At about the same time various orchid growers and the Horticultural Society were testing different conditions, and in 1823 a Kew gardener successfully grew some Australian orchids in a turfy soil, more closely approximating humus and interspersed with tree trunks.

There had been another obstacle to earlier success – excessive heat. Unwittingly, Cunningham had found the vital, unrecognised clue in 1818. He had marvelled at the 'great exuberance' of the wild orchids, 'wonderfully promoted by the perpetual humidity that exists in these deep woods, where the solar ray never has any direct chance to exhaust . . .'. It is this humidity which feeds them, and it had been greenhouse practice to place the orchid pots high in the greenhouse just under the excessively hot glass; in addition, the flues gave a very dry heat. A damper, more natural heat only became available after the invention of heating via natural circulation of hot water through pipes. Alternatively, and with more authenticity, humidity could be introduced from a warm waterfall fed from hot pipes, the falling stream being caught by rough stonework and sprayed into many tiny rills. This delightful solution to the problem was used by John Dillwyn Llewelyn, the photographic pioneer (see Table 5.1 and Figure 5.7), who was inspired by Sir Robert Schomburgk's description of the falls at Berbice and Essequibo. His orchids thrived: he presented four species to Kew in 1842. In 1843 he wrote in a letter to his father: 'The Orchid House in especial delights me and the plants in the damp atmosphere of the fall seem to forget their captivity and spread out their roots in all directions to drink the misty air.'

With practical barriers overcome, at last there was the possibility of orchids flowering consistently and in profusion, and nurserymen such as John Gould Veitch took up orchid culture seriously. The wealthy were now seized by a craze for orchid flowers. The mood of the time was captured by James Bateman in his classic book, *Orchidaceae of Mexico and Guatemala*, in which he said: 'an inexhaustible fund of novelty seems to be in store for us . . . the *annus mirabilis* of Orchis-importatum was 1837. In addition to the spoils brought by Mr. GIBSON from the Nipalise Hills [Plate 11], . . . Mr. SKINNER poured into our stoves the richest treasures . . . of Guatemala'. The orchid fanatics had 'humbly craved' Skinner's assistance in obtaining *Cattleya skinneri* (see Plate 10), specimens of which were tantalisingly out of reach in forests 'exclusively in the warm parts of Guatemala', behind a language barrier, and along the shores of the Pacific. *Cattleya skinneri* was named in Skinner's honour in recognition of his having:

> laboured almost incessantly to drag . . . forest treasures . . . from their hiding places . . .

and transfer them to the stoves of his native land. In pursuit of this object, there is scarcely a sacrifice which he has not made, or a danger or hardship which he has not braved. In sickness or in health, amid the calls of business or the perils of war, whether detained in quarantine on the shores of the Atlantic or shipwrecked on the rocks of the Pacific, he has never suffered an opportunity to escape him of adding to the long array of his botanical discoveries.

> (James Bateman, *Orchidaceae of Mexico and Guatemala*)

Bateman himself boasted an eccentric garden which combined orchid stoves, an Egyptian court and a Cheshire cottage (at Biddulph Grange, Staffordshire). He was a leading exponent of the orchid craze, as was the Duke of Bedford, who in 1843 presented Queen Victoria with a large collection which was duly passed on to Kew. Another enthusiastic aristocrat was the Duke of Devonshire at Chatsworth, eager to fill his planned Great Conservatory with dazzling flower discoveries. It was he and Sir Joseph Paxton who had sent John Gibson to Bengal and Assam to bring back 'the spoils . . . from the Nipalise Hills'.

All new introductions, particularly fashionable ones with artistic potential, immediately became candidates for beautiful pictorial folios and books in the vein of *The Temple of Flora*. The immense proportions and extravagant illustration of these volumes was not out of proportion for an aristocratic craze when one considers that the first half of the century fell within the zenith of flower-painting and fine book production. Even the abundant practical gardening books and registers of flowering plants had hand-coloured plates, engraved after originals by the finest artists, and hand-coloured lithographs. James Bateman's eulogy on orchids, the 'chosen ornaments of royalty', surpassed them all. Published between 1837 and 1843, *Orchidaceae of Mexico and Guatemala* was the biggest book ever produced (measuring $20\frac{1}{2}$ inches (55 cm) by $27\frac{1}{2}$ inches (71 cm)). Dedicated to Queen Adelaide, its list of subscribers was headed by various European royalty, Dukes – including the passionate collectors, Devonshire, Bedford and Northumberland – and so on down the social scale with due decorum. The exquisite brushwork of Mrs Withers (see Plate 10) and Miss Drake made the illustrations a superlative in quality as well. They had the art of capturing the three-dimensional form and textured sheen of living plants and of painting the minutiae of floral colouring and structure which seem to lie almost out of reach of the human eye. Every orchid illustrated had flowered in an English greenhouse. Armchair escape into the world of orchids was made complete with vignettes of exotic habitats (see Figure 6.6) and local scenes. Such volumes of course only further intensified the demand for orchid plants and the quest for new ones.

Novelties could, by then, be created by artificially crossing species to give hybrids. The artificial fertilisation of flowers was first regularly practised in the eighteenth century by 'the ingenious Mr. Lee of Hammersmith', one of the most famous firms of nurserymen dealing with greenhouse exotics from the 1750s through until 1899. James Lee I was no ordinary nurseryman, gaining fame in publishing the first English exposition of Linnaeus's new system (*An Introduction to the Science of Botany*) and for putting Linnaeus's 'sexual botany' to pratical use. He observed that 'for want of insects to further the nuptials of plants' or 'favouring breezes', exotics rarely set seed, so he performed 'artificial impregnation . . . which always secured an increase, and proves the practical value of science'. Orchids were special candidates for such treatment. Attempts were made in 1853 by the head gardener at the firm of Veitch and the first orchid hybrids were cultivated by him in 1856. Towards the end of the nineteenth century, there were thousands of hybrid variations derived from relatively few original wild species.

Wild species from faraway places had far more charisma and in the middle of the century orchid fanciers could choose from an extraordinary number of these. Species in their thousands were gleaned at great cost − in natural terms rather than financial ones, although the latter were by no means small. In seeking orchids new to science and collecting botanical specimens with serious intent the way was also opened and even signposted for unscrupulous collectors only motivated by the promise of high returns as the orchid craze gained momentum. One such unwitting directive came from that most scrupulous of collectors, Kew. Sir Joseph Dalton Hooker was entranced by the desirable blue vanda orchid (*V. caerulea*, see Figure 6.12), growing in the Khasia Hills. It had been discovered in Assam in 1837 and the desire for a blue orchid became a passion as intense as the modern-day search for the blue rose.

The flora in the Khasia Hills was different. It was 'the richest in India, and probably in all Asia . . . of Malayan character'. Figs abounded in 'hot gulleys, where the property of their roots, which inosculate and form natural grafts, is taken advantage of in bridging streams, and in constructing what are called living bridges, of the most picturesque forms'. In this exotic setting, within a ten-mile radius, Hooker collected over

**Figure 6.12** The elusive blue vanda orchid (*Vanda caerulea*). Its beautiful azure blue gave it the charisma of the blue rose. Overcollecting precipitated conservation efforts by the Assam and Burmese governments.

2,000 flowering plants, 150 ferns and a profusion of the lower plant orders. Most enticing for Victorian collectors were the 250 species of orchids clothing trees, rocks, damp woodland floors and grassy slopes. In his *Himalayan Journals* Hooker described *Vanda caerulea* growing 'in profusion' in woods of 'small, gnarled, and very sparingly leafy oaks'. These exceptional epiphytic orchids were fully exposed 'to fresh air and the winds of heaven . . . winter's cold, summer's heat, and autumn's drought'. Carelessly 'waving its panicles of azure flowers in the wind' almost like blue butterflies, the orchid was growing in conditions completely at variance with the recently developed British methods of cultivation which assiduously excluded winds and extremes, mimicking airless tropical forests dripping with moisture. This discrepancy, noted by Hooker, accounted for the extreme difficulty in growing the vanda in Britain which, together with its high price and beauty, was responsible for it attracting great attention amongst fanciers. In October 1850 in its natural conditions this azure *pièce de résistance* was prolific: Hooker picked '360 panicles, each composed of from six to twenty-one broad pale-blue tasselated flowers, three and a half to four inches across'. They were for transportation and preservation for botanical purposes and made 'three piles on the floor of the verandah, each a yard high;— what would we not have given to have been able to transport a single panicle to a Chiswick fête!'

In his journal, Hooker also entered a small, rather unfortunate footnote:

> We have collected seven men's loads of this superb plant for the Royal Gardens at Kew, but owing to unavoidable accidents and difficulties, few specimens reached England alive. A gentleman, who sent his gardener with us to be shown the locality, was more successful: he sent one man's load to England on commission, and though it arrived in a very poor state, it sold for £300. . . Had all arrived alive, they would have cleared £1,000. An active collector, with the facilities I possessed, might easily clear from £2,000 to £3,000 in one season, by the sale of Khasia orchids.

Such recommendation brought about export attempts by businessmen on such a large scale that even in those times of little conservation awareness, it became necessary for the govern-ments of Assam and Burma to intervene or the forests would have been denuded. The short-sightedness of overcollecting was all too frequently clouded by the euphoria of short-term gain, for on more than one occasion ignorant or careless cultivation in England caused the loss of a specimen which was then irreplaceable. Despite the official intervention, one highly valued species of Himalayan orchid was lost for fifty years in spite of a £1,000 reward being offered.

The orchids of South American rain forests were so thoroughly collected that even large-scale collectors complained of 'ransacking'. In 1891 Albert Millican bemoaned the fact that the natural orchid habitats were bare due to plants being removed in their thousands, while at the same time he wrote: 'I provided my natives with axes and started them on the work of cutting down all the trees containing valuable orchids . . . [they] would bring to our camp several hundred of plants each night.' After two months he was proud of having accumulated 10,000 plants from 4,000 felled trees, which amounted to eight tons of orchids (mostly *Odontoglossum crispum*), in one shipment. At the outset of the orchid craze one plant could apparently fetch 1,000 guineas. He recounted his exploits in a book entitled *The Travels and Adventures of an Orchid Hunter*, a title which reflected his attitude towards the flowers and all that surrounded them. In contrast to the joy and wonder that emanated from Darwin, Bates, Wallace and Gosse, readers of Millican's book were treated to the compulsory melodrama befalling all such adventurers – a jaguar about to tear its claws into a man but for the novel-styled hero shooting at the beast. Other very Victorian stances were captured on film: the intrepid explorer 'Ready to enter the forest' and 'Native Dinner-Time' (see Figure 6.13).

The home market for orchid plants imported from such romanticised places was insatiable, with a disregard for price equal to the desire to acquire. By 1894 one firm of nurserymen alone had twenty collectors abroad hunting for exotics in competition with their rivals. Many, like Lee and Veitch, were old family firms which had thrived for four generations. There was a long tradition of rivalry between such nurserymen. They would go to any lengths to obtain information, as was illustrated by 'the ingenious Mr. Lee of Hammersmith'. Philip Miller, Curator of the Chelsea Physic Garden (where the first exotic orchid had flowered in Britain), and author of the

**117**

**Figure 6.13** 'Native Dinner Time' during an orchid-collecting expedition on the grand scale. The camp moved forward week by week as all the trees were felled and the plant wealth was exhausted. (From *The* *Travels and Adventures of an Orchid Hunter* by Albert Millican, 1891: by permission of Cambridge University Library)

famous *The Gardener's Dictionary* of 1731 had:

> concealed the names of his valuable collection in the Chelsea Gardens; and the papers, which contained his foreign seeds, were industriously thrown into the Thames; and such is the ardour of Botany, although the acquisition was often to be swam for, these were fished for up again, and the names of the new plants, then introduced, were thus known to Mr. LEE, and others, in a way which greatly surprised the author of the Gardener's Dictionary.

Mr Lee's son carried on the Hammersmith nursery in the midst of even greater botanical ardour: besides commercial nurserymen there were free-lance adventurers and naturalists, like Gosse, Bates and Wallace, collectors representing Kew (such as Sir Joseph Dalton Hooker), collectors from the Horticultural Society (such as Robert Fortune), and wealthy enthusiasts and aristocrats. The large number of collectors in the field created great pressure both on sites abundant with orchids and on rare and coveted species.

In some areas every plant was systematically removed. At its worst the competitive element was manifested in ill-conceived attempts by some collectors at keeping orchid sites secret, which amounted to collecting all that one could and destroying any that were left. This was also a reprehensible ploy to create an artificial rarity and increase the selling price.

Comercial collecting was now a far cry from the relatively blameless orchid-collecting of men like Wallace and Gosse, who both described collecting at its most innocent and joyous level. Gosse, captivated 'by the charming orchids, with most fantastic flowers', captured the excitement of collecting:

> A fine epiphyte orchid scents the air with fragrance, and it is discovered far up in the fork of some vast tree; then there is the palpitation of hope and fear as we discuss the possibility of getting it down; then come the contrivances and efforts, – pole after pole is cut and tied together with the cords which the forest-climbers afford. At length the plant is

reached, and pushed off, and triumphantly bagged; but lo! while examining it, some elegant twisted shell is discovered, with its tenant snail, crawling on the leaves. Scarcely is this boxed, when a glorious butterfly rushes out of the gloom into the sunny glade, and is in a moment seen to be a novelty; then comes the excitement of pursuit. . .

(*The Romance of Natural History*)

Alfred Russel Wallace was another whose loving description of collecting from a natural orchid grove materialised a distant daydream for those creating their own miniaturised jungle under glass:

São Jeronymo, July 1851. . . . it was a complete natural orchid-house. In an hour's ramble, I noticed about thirty different species; – some, minute plants scarcely larger than mosses, and one large semi-terrestrial species, which grew in clumps eight or ten feet high. . . One day . . . I was much delighted to come suddenly upon a magnificent flower: growing out of a rotten stem of a tree . . . a bunch of five or six blossoms, which were three inches in diameter, nearly round, and varying from a pale delicate straw-colour to a rich deep yellow. . . How exquisitely beautiful did it appear, in that wild, sandy, barren spot! . . . The sight of these determined me to try and send some to England, as from such a distant and unexplored locality there would probably be many new species. I accordingly began bringing a few home every day, and, packing them in empty farinha-baskets, placed them under a rough stage, with some plantain-leaves to defend them from the heat of the sun, till we should be ready to embark. . .

This orchid-collecting episode, so different from Hooker's highly organised affair to the Khasia Hills, had a disappointing ending, however, as Wallace wrote in 1853: '. . . all the notes made during two years, with the greater part of my collections and sketches were lost by the burning of the ship on my homeward voyage.'

Thus, little by little, in innocence, short-sightedness and greed, some wild orchid species were lost for ever. There was the complete loss of a species on an island which fifty years previously had been the most prolific source of plants ever found, and there were other less dramatic losses, as well as complete habitats of particularly fine orchids being left barren as if ravaged by a massive forest fire. However, before passing judgement on Victorian collectors and floral financiers one should pause and recall today's vast-scale destruction of the orchids' habitats, at unprecedented speed – a far greater and more final step.

# Chapter 7
# REALITIES

At first sight today's Victorian villas hold little reminder of the great floral passions that took possession of the Victorians; beyond the grand mansion, few conservatories retain their profusion of orchids or towering tree ferns. In order to see the royal water-lily or a mimic jungle under a glass sky the curious observer must still travel to Chatsworth (today, a new greenhouse – the Great Conservatory has long since gone, alas), Kew or one of the other great botanical gardens such as Edinburgh where the largest and strangest flowers retain their exoticism still. More accessible mementoes of past glories remain but are now barely recognisable, for as essential status symbols at every social level of Victorian gardening, their popularity has made them commonplace. They are the ageing custodians of old suburban gardens – cedars, flowering currant, monkey puzzles, clumps of pampas, shrubberies with weigela, forsythia, winter jasmine and kerria, rhododendron collections and bamboo groves.

In dark arboreta and pineta the crushed needles of sitka spruce, Douglas fir (the common fir of North America), the sugar pine (*Pinus lambertiana*, see Figure 7.3), and the giant, noble and silver firs once conjured up the distant towering forests of the North American wilderness, Red Indian 'savages' and the thrilling adventures of their collector, David Douglas. He was the most prolific of all British collectors before or since and, as foreigners, his immense numbers of trees were accorded the height of approval – a place in the limelight near the house, at the expense of the indigenous species banished to be distant silhouettes at the periphery, as was exemplified at the royal residence at Osborne, Isle of Wight. (According to John Claudius Loudon, no garden could even be considered as a candidate for 'good taste' if all the trees and shrubs were not foreign or at least 'improved varieties' of indigenous ones.) Thanks to Douglas, entire formal flower-beds of the mid-nineteenth century could vividly brag about their distant sunny origins: they sported Californian poppies, clarkias, antirrhinums, penstemons, lupins, evening primroses and mallows – all still popular today. Strongly juxtaposed were mystic scents of flowers from Japan, China and the Himalayan foothills planted in Italianate terraces and shrubberies, which abound still in Loudon's 'first', 'second' and 'third class' gardens, and in 'wild' woodland glades. Here and there less common Victorian plants linger with unexpected echoes of historical events, such as a fern 'gathered . . . during Captain Cook's voyage', or another plant merely from 'two travellers' – a reminder of time's anonymity which overtook so many diligent collectors, even professional ones.

It was the tales told by the collectors and explorers themselves which brought foreign plants to life, indeed made them larger than life. These delightful journals were peppered with personal details and comments that are now distinguishing marks of a time when faraway places still meant danger and wild spectacle. Some of these men were spurred by adventure; others, like Alfred Russel Wallace and Henry Walter Bates, were driven by a consuming passion for the wonder of the natural world. They simply cut home-ties and went. Others, like Philip Henry Gosse, were abroad on their own account, mineral-prospecting, whaling, teaching or preaching, and they whiled away their leisure hours in remote parts of the world where there was little else to do other than to observe their surroundings, by collecting. Amateurs or professionals (like Sir Joseph Dalton Hooker, Robert Fortune, Allan Cunningham or David Douglas), their everyday jottings also brought reality to the pleasures of the garden: they showed the real world of collecting, with its irritations, risks and sacrifices.

## Matters of Secondary Importance

For many collectors, particularly those exploring new geographical and botanical frontiers under the auspices of Kew or the Horticultural Society, the financial gain was negligible. Little had changed since Francis Masson's anxious plea to George III (see page 22) concerning his future finances in old age. Masson died at 65, still collecting and in an adverse climate. The first collector to be sent from Kew in 1772, he was paid £100 p.a. salary, payable on his return, with a maximum of £200 expenses per annum. In 1861 Kew sent out its last official collector, Richard Oldham, who was unbelievably paid the same salary with less expenses. Oldham was collecting in Japan at the same time as Robert Fortune who was employed by the Horticultural Society on the same salary. On one of his expeditions he complained that his payment was inadequate: the curt reply was that money should only be a secondary consideration.

In Australia, the King's botanist's finances were assisted by 'indulgences' at a personal level from Governor Macquarie in the form of a weekly ration of beef and wheat, official instructions being 'in the most common and general terms'. Returning with massive collections of hard-won plants from the harsh outback or long sea journeys around the west and north coasts and Timor, Allan Cunningham might have expected a clear passage for the plants on to the last lap of their journey from the wilderness to Kew, but even limited assistance of loaned horse, cart and a spare pack-saddle was slow. On 10 October 1818 he wrote:

> There appearing no favourable direct opportunities likely to offer for transporting my collections . . . to England, I was under the necessity, for the safety of the bulbs . . . to unpack the case and plant them in the garden of a friend, trusting a future eligible conveyance would present itself, enabling me to transmit them home when they would bear removal.

Even with his Kew connections, Sir Joseph Dalton Hooker wrote of his lack of money to adequately pack and forward his specimens from Sikkim to England.

Lack of adequate finance accentuated the uphill struggle of collecting and brought several collectors to a tragic end. William Kerr, who introduced the tiger lily from China, was so destitute that he was unable to mix with people influential in the field of plant-collecting. He was driven to bad company and, apparently, opium, and died at his next post in Ceylon in 1814. Adding insult to injury, the credit for the large numbers of plants and seeds he sent back to Kew went to others, including the East India Company. The immortality he achieved with his popular *Kerria japonica* which appeared in most Victorian gardens was little compensation.

Such brusque treatment, running even to misdirected animosity, in the face of diligent and successful collecting on a financial shoestring seemed to be the tradition for many collectors. Even Allan Cunningham, who introduced so many Australian plants to Kew, and was generally acknowledged to be flawless, received unsympathetic treatment. His request to return home in 1828 was not acknowledged with assent until the end of 1830 when it was more a matter of financial expediency than granting his request. Robbery of instruments, provisions and possessions was another occupational hazard of collecting, with replacement having to come from the collector's meagre salary rather than from the authority employing him.

Much of the trouble and wrongful accusation stemmed from the social stigma of class and status both on board ship and abroad – matters of prime import to the Victorians. A collector was frequently a mere gardener, not desirable company for ships' officers, but on the other hand not conveniently delegated to his actual lowly status as he could not then command any authority over his precious plant cargo. Ashore, the idea of a gardener being promoted to the means or status of a gentleman was unthinkable, although to achieve results within the constraints of Japan and China it was essential to mix with diplomats and wealthy foreign residents interested in plants – as William Kerr had found by bitter experience.

On his victorious return to London in 1827, David Douglas, who began his career as a gardener's boy at the age of eleven, found himself in the potentially difficult position of being lionised by scientists and nobility. When the initial euphoria had passed and no further foreign collecting seemed imminent his difficulty became part of a discontent, exacerbated by the realisation that he was actually paid less than the Horticultural Society's porter. This was in spite of his immense achievements under extreme privations and at such little financial cost – less than £400 covered his entire expedition of two years' collecting, including his salary, and the instant success (for the Society) of his flowering currant alone had covered the whole amount.

Many of those collecting on their own account fared no better. Henry Walter Bates and Alfred Russel Wallace jointly set out to the Amazon with very little money hoping to pay their expenses by means of their collecting. Bates's profit for his eleven years' labour and privations was only £800.

## The British Abroad

Against this background of financial stringency there was an occasional glimpse of Jane Loudon's dignified European gentleman borne aloft on the backs of doting natives. The most familiar painting of Sir Joseph Dalton Hooker portrays him surrounded by natives kneeling to present the floral treasures of the Himalayas. Although ostentatiously glamorised in the Victorian idiom it was not totally removed from the reality. The local people put great faith in Hooker's healing powers and medicines, and at Changachelling they even included him in a new temple fresco, complete with oriental clothes, spectacles and notebook. In Japan, the picture of the European plant collector and explorer was more classical: Robert Fortune, who thought all Orientals were inferior, bartered with temple priests, trading pages of *Punch* and the *Illustrated London News* for tree seeds.

By contrast, the Australian aborigines were often frightening, and may have lacked the beauteous aspect of savagery attributed to the primitive life by some safely distant philosophers. Curious, the natives frequently came to observe the white explorers and Allan Cunningham was at times protected while collecting, as at the most westerly human habitation beyond Bathurst on 26 April 1817: 'Having previously repapered my specimens and hung them out to dry, accompanied by a soldier (armed) I made an excursion down the river.' There was aggression but it was an unusual entry in his brief journal and the more typical interaction was the traditional patronage of trinkets and items to better themselves: 'We decorated their persons with beads, and the reflection of their frizzled visages in a glass created much laughter among them.' Typical presentations consisted of an axe, 'some old rusty nails, files, sharpened chisels', and quick instruction as to their use – frequently received with indifference.

Expeditions in the grand manner were few and far between. Sir Joseph Dalton Hooker's was one of these and it included a military guard, trained plant collectors and obscure sounding personnel such as bird and animal shooters. At Cherrapunji, in the Khasia, where there was over 500 inches of rain during their seven-month stay, he even hired 'a large and good bungalow, in which three immense coal fires were kept up for drying plants and papers, and fifteen men were always employed . . . from morning till night.'

With the notable exception of the various attempts of corrupt politicians to starve Hooker to a halt, victualling and accommodation was usually as befitted an English gentleman, within the severe limits of the hostile unexplored terrain. In his *Himalayan Journals* he described a quiet mountain evening which is positively enviable:

. . . as evening advanced . . . mists . . . below me . . . spread out like a heaving and rolling sea, leaving nothing above their surface but the ridges and spurs of the adjacent mountains. These rose like capes, promontories, and islands, of the darkest leaden hue, bristling with pines, and advancing boldly into the snowy white ocean . . . As darkness came on, and the stars arose . . . I quitted with reluctance one of the most impressive and magic scenes I ever beheld.

Returning to my tent . . . I wandered amongst my followers in the darkness, and watched unseen their operations . . . My tent

meat, rice, biscuits and tea, and his customary
cigar.

However sometimes politics and terrain made
the menu and shelter less predictable and cosy.
For a month, while searching along the River
Lachen near Tibet, they survived on wild mush-
rooms, wild leeks, nettles and other herbs to eke
out their limited provisions of a kid and a
smattering of flour and potatoes. The appease-
ment gift of much needed 'provisions' sent to
Hooker on his return by the Rajah consisted of
sweetmeats and embroidered silks – as inappropriate as his own 'private stock of provisions'
used on another lean occasion. Describing this
meal, he noted in his journal that:

> of four remaining two-pound cases, provided
> as meat, three contained prunes, and one
> '*dindon aux truffes*'! Never did luxuries come
> more inopportunely; however the greasy
> French viand served for many a future meal as
> sauce to help me to bolt my rice, and accord-
> ing to the theory of chemists, to supply animal
> heat in these frigid regions.

The idea of transporting gourmet meals to high
Himalayan mountains was obviously one that
died hard, as the 1922 Everest expedition carried
similar French fare.

Imported cuisine was out of the question for
Allan Cunningham's travels with Oxley's expedition into the Australian unknown. Living off
the land except for flour and salt pork and
frequently reduced to merely surviving, their
tastes were catholic to the point of indiscrimina-
tion. At Cunningham's suggestion (a botanist
was always useful for identifying the edible): 'our
people gathered a quantity of the young leaves of
the . . . [saltbush], which they boiled and found
them to be an excellent substitute for a better
vegetable, which, with the emu made us an
excellent dinner'. Besides emus the expedition's
dogs provided the table with dingoes and occasionally kangaroo-rats. Any new creature was
tried, including 'strange birds . . . with beautiful
red breasts', which turned out to be 'hard and
rancid' – they were galahs.

> Economy and necessity had taught us to turn
> every accident to some account. The flesh of
> our deceased horse afforded our faithful but
> famishing dogs some tolerable meals, and the
> skins furnished our people with materials for
> mocassins or shoes, which they divided

**Figure 7.1** The varnished acacia (*Acacia verniciflua*)
'was discovered by MR. ALLAN CUNNINGHAM,
during MR. OXLEY'S Expedition in 1817, in the
country around Bathurst, where it flowered through
the winter . . . With us (at Kew, whence the specimen
here figured was sent by MR. AITON) it blossoms in
the spring . . . It was first raised at Kew from seeds
sent from the Colony in the year 1823.' (From
*Curtis's Botanical Magazine*, 1833: By permission of
Avon County Library (Bath Reference Library))

was made of a blanket thrown over the limb of
a tree . . . one half was occupied by my
bedstead . . . The barometer hung in the most
out-of-the-way corner, and my other instruments all around. A small candle was burning
in a glass shade, to keep the draught and insects
from the light, and I had the comfort of seeing
the knife, fork, and spoon laid on a white
napkin.

The food that followed was cooked by his
servant. His meals rarely erred from stewed

equally with mathematical niceness.

(Hooker's white table napkin was missing but the menials for gathering food still featured.)

David Douglas had to eat his own horse on several occasions: he travelled light almost to the point of courting disaster, depending entirely on shooting, fishing and gathering edible plants although weather and terrain frequently rendered this impossible. In extreme conditions he was driven to eating the dried skins of animal specimens he had intended to send back to English scientists. He also bartered nails, knives, beads and tobacco for food from the Indians. They were frequently troublesome to the Hudson's Bay Company, but amid these times of violence and upheaval Douglas coped well with them, being the first to journey into one area without an armed guard and the first to receive Indian hospitality from some tribes. His fame and expertise at shooting birds on the wing seemed a particularly useful ploy for impressing any opposition. One tribe, at first terrified by his spectacles, came to understand his natural history quest and christened him the 'Grass Man' (his interest was very much at one with their own knowledge of local flora and fauna and the natural cycles). Some of his most miserable hungry times were shared with Indians. On one desperate journey from Fort Vancouver on the Columbia to Gray's Harbor he and they survived for about six days on a few berries and roots and, while it lasted, a little chocolate. The journey seemed ill-fated from the outset. He set out with a large abscess on his knee joint and an inflamed leg, and early on his canoe split from end to end. Crossing the mouth of the Columbia their food was washed overboard and they had to drag the canoe through four miles of forest (at a place aptly named Cape Disappointment), which turned out to be a mere prelude to being stormbound for two days and having to face a further trek of 16 miles. Fatigued and starving, Douglas managed to crawl out of his shelter of pine branches when the weather abated. He shot five ducks – but as soon as he saw them fall 'my appetite fled'. One Indian did not even wait to pluck the bird. Recuperating in an Indian village he continued botanising regardless, returning to his point of departure after 25 days of misery – but still with a touch of the intrepid, as he sailed back along the Columbia using his blanket and coat as sails.

Travelling without supplies made such distress more common than exceptional and accentuated any clash of personalities. He and two white companions passed a wet fortnight on one meal a day and soup made of pounded roots which made Douglas physically sick. They argued over their whereabouts and as Douglas wrote in his journal:

> The fact plainly this: all hungry and no means of cooking a little of our stock; travelled thirty-three miles, drenched and bleached with rain and sleet, chilled with a piercing north wind; and then to finish the day experienced the cooling, comfortless consolation of lying down wet without supper or fire. On such occasions I am very liable to become fretful.

It was little wonder that his food expenses during his three years among the Indians amounted to a mere £61 – a point of great rejoicing with his employers on his return.

James Harry Veitch's stately strolls around the public and botanic gardens of Ceylon, India, Java, Singapore and Japan in 1891 – belonged to a totally different world. He was the eldest son of John Gould Veitch who had collected 30 years before in Japan. His journals entertained his readers to details of bandstands rather than surviving in desperate conditions. This nurseryman–collector managed not to even touch a wild flower for the first six months of his world travels – such was the contrast of place and time and the demeanour of a more orthodox Englishman abroad.

## Local Encounters

Large expeditions brought their own difficulties, in particular the provision of large quantities of food. Hooker was continually worried about the problem, which was cunningly used as a weapon by the corrupt politicians set against his explorations. By treating the ailments of local people in exchange for food he could obtain enough for himself but not for his large number of helpers. Threats of no food supplies in such a hostile environment posed an uncompromising dilemma. As he pointed out: 'To remain in these mountains without a supply was impossible' as was the delay in sending elsewhere, and not for the first time he 'lay long awake occupied in arranging measures'. Retaining the hard-won food in transit was another problem of a large organisation: the 'plundering' of his provisions by the expeditions' coolies was frequent. Dismissing and replacing them was not always an expedient solution, as when he 'was relieved by their making off of their own accord . . . as it was impossible to procure men on the top of a mountain 10,000 feet high, or to proceed . . .' The dilemma was – as he put it – 'awkward'.

Hooker's journeys were further complicated by corrupt officialdom concocting difficulties such as forbidding repairs to bridges and tracks lost in landslides, which sometimes descended

for 3,000 feet. The party was forced to cross difficult debris somehow: 'the whole face of the mountain appeared more or less torn up for fully a mile, presenting a confused mass of white micaceous clay, full of angular masses of rock'. Villagers were instructed to misinform him of geographical features, even the whereabouts of the Tibetan border. Shooting game for food was stopped by devious stories of gun shots bringing rain. Parties of soldiers frequently harassed the expedition, finally arresting Hooker's friend and fellow traveller, Dr Campbell, as a hostage on 7 November 1849. Hooker opted to remain with his friend, quietly continuing to collect rhodo-

**Figure 7.2** The golden-rayed lily of Japan (*Lilium auratum*), introduced by Robert Fortune (and others independently). He remarked that in Japan he usually saw it four feet high with up to five large flowers on a stem. (From *Curtis's Botanical Magazine*, 1862: by permission of Avon County Library (Bath Reference Library))

dendron seeds by the wayside during the less than enjoyable travelling that followed. The two were lost to civilisation for nearly two months and then a diplomatic situation erupted after Hooker had eventually been allowed by his captors to write to Lord Dalhousie. He named *Rhododendron dalhousiae* (see Plate 7) which he collected in October 1849 after Lady Dalhousie.

The lone collector may not have faced these sort of difficulties but he was often confronted with equally fierce ones. In Japan, the first wave of collectors in 1860 and 1861 faced the fanatical violence of traditional aristocrats and their retainers against all foreigners whose presence in their country was politically official but was not yet approved by their spiritual ruler, the Mikado. In the meantime these over-patriotic warriors regarded it as their duty to kill any foreigner without question. While in Tokyo, Robert Fortune and John Gould Veitch stayed with the British Legation behind high fences and had to be accompanied by armed guards whenever they ventured outside its confines. Later Fortune and his Chinese assistant were able to take over a vacated temple in Kanagawa, somewhat solitary accommodation which caused Fortune some apprehension. One night while he was there the British Legation itself was attacked. However, in spite of Fortune's fears, these Japanese experiences were tame by his own standards. While travelling in China, under similar constraints, he had risen from his sick bed in the manner of a Victorian novel and, waiting until his target approached to twenty yards, had opened fire and warded off a fleet of five pirate junks single-handed. Three days later, when six more appeared, he once more rose from his bed with aplomb, delivered an impeccable repeat performance, despatching all of them with his double-barrelled gun before retiring to bed once more.

Victorians at home could thrill to the equally swashbuckling encounters of David Douglas. His tales of adventure had the added attraction of being passed on by hearsay from elegant dinner parties and scientific gatherings. (Some years later, selections from his travel journal were published in 1836, two years after his death, but the entire journal did not appear until 1914.) As he reached the culmination of his long-drawn-out quest for the sugar pine (*Pinus lambertiana*) and its seeds, he saw cones only in the upper heights of the trees, which were usually without branches for two-thirds of their 200-foot length:

**Figure 7.3** The cone of the sugar pine (*Pinus lambertiana*) nearly cost David Douglas his life.

I took my gun and was busy clipping them from the branches with ball when eight Indians came at the report of my gun. They were all painted with red earth, armed with bows, arrows, spears of bone, and flint knives, and seemed to be anything but friendly. I endeavoured to explain to them what I wanted and they seemed satisfied and sat down to smoke, but had no sooner done so than I perceived one string his bow and another sharpen his flint knife with a pair of wooden pincers and hang it on the wrist of the right hand, which gave me ample testimony of their inclination. To save myself I could not do by flight, and without any hesitation I went backwards six paces and cocked my gun, and then pulled from my belt one of my pistols, which I held in my left hand. I was determined to fight for life. As I as much as possible endeavoured to preserve my coolness and perhaps did so, I stood eight or ten minutes looking at them and they at me without a word passing. . .

His tactics worked, the Indians went after demanding tobacco, and he was able to retreat to his camp by dusk, where he took up his pen '. . . constantly in expectation of an attack, and the position I am now in is lying on the grass with my gun beside me, writing by the light of my Columbian candle – namely a piece of wood containing rosin.' And thus he recorded in his *Journal* the events and the pine's botanical details, '. . . lest I should never see my friends to tell them verbally of this most beautiful and immensely large tree'. Next morning he awoke to find three grizzly bears, he paid his guide with one of the carcasses, then dealt with the crisis of his horse getting caught in a river and proceeded back to his base to find that it was under threat from a party of Indians.

## Disease and Other Hazards

In spite of the joys of discovery and the revelations of beautiful wildernesses, nineteenth-century collecting and exploring involved difficulties and privations which the twentieth century has forgotten. Plastics and man-made fibres have dispatched with the problem of achieving a watertight covering for both living specimens and the collector, while insect repellants, inoculations and drugs have removed many of the tropical hazards for today's adventurers. The matter-of-fact tone of the naturalists' descriptions of their travels emphasises the extent of their achievements.

In tropical temperatures the 'incredible profusion' of insects and leeches kept the collector in 'a constant state of irritation'. In Sikkim at the end of each day the plant hunters returned 'streaming with blood, and mottled with the bites of peepsas, gnats, midges, and mosquitoes, besides being infested with ticks'. Hooker wrote how leeches swarming from bushes and long grass 'got into my hair, hung on my eyelids, and crawled up my legs and down my back. I repeatedly took upwards of a hundred from my legs, where the small ones used to collect in clusters on the instep'. The sores took five months to heal and their scars remained for years. Sikkim had the most magical landscape and flora but also provided 'the most insufferable torment' – and ironically the smallest in size – an insatiable midge. The glories of the royal water-lily in the Amazon were also accompanied by the

attentions of a minute creature, the 'Pium', which replaced the nocturnal mosquitoes punctually at sunrise. Swarms were as dense as thin smoke clouds and several hundred bites a day were normal. 'Their abdomens soon become distended and red with blood, and then, their thirst satisfied, they slowly move off, sometimes so stupified with their potations that they can scarcely fly.' With true Victorian spirit, personal discomfort was cast aside by Henry Walter Bates in the quest for detailed knowledge: 'I took the trouble to dissect specimens to ascertain the way in which the little pests operate.' Later while on the Upper Amazon he wrote how after a week he became habituated to the Piums, 'all the exposed parts of my body, by that time, being so closely covered with black punctures that the little bloodsuckers could not very easily find an unoccupied place to operate on'.

Such pests were as hazardous for specimens as they were for collectors. In the jungle:

Cages for drying specimens were suspended from the rafters by cords well anointed, to prevent ants from descending, with a bitter vegetable oil: rats and mice were kept from them by inverted cuyas, placed half-way down the cords.

The ants were so voracious that during half an hour's conversation the valuable contents of an insect collecting box were dismembered and scattered as 'a delicious repast'.

Biting pests brought diseases with them – the more insidious diseases lasted for life if not treated. In the early 1840s, Charles Darwin started to suffer from ill health – nausea, great lassitude and internal pains – for which doctors could find no cause. This was to have a dominant effect on his whole life. In fact his symptoms and later heart attacks corresponded exactly with a disease (Chaga's disease) carried by 'the black bug of the pampas' and while in Argentina he was severely bitten and taken ill. Unfortunately, the obscure path of the disease was not elucidated until after his death. The disease is similar to malaria and sleeping sickness in that as the insect bites it injects the micro-organism causing the disease and this then travels in the blood system, sometimes making its presence felt only intermittently, thus further confounding diagnosis. With no apparent cause for his life-long illness, Darwin was branded a hypochondriac. (There are other theories on Darwin's illness: see Biographical Notes in the Appendix on page 185.)

Debilitating tropical fevers and epidemics of smallpox and yellow fever were regularly faced without proper medication and with a *naïveté* and determination that makes twentieth-century travellers blanch. There was a certain Victorian austerity in the treatment and after-care of such ills. While waiting for medicines he had ordered from a nearby town, Henry Walter Bates, ill with yellow fever, wrapped himself in a blanket and 'walked sharply to and fro along the verandah', drinking herb tea at intervals. Such measures were at least more useful than those taken by the desperate government, which took 'all the sanitary precautions that could be thought of; amongst the rest was the singular one of firing cannon at the street corners, to purify the air'. As soon as a fever abated, it was standard practice among the collectors to return forthwith to the hardships of collecting, spurning any concessions and frequently falling seriously ill as a result.

Extremes of climate posed other threats; mountain habitats offered 'the insidious piercing night-wind that descended from northern glaciers' while the arid lands brought thirst and dehydrating heat. The two in quick succession created immense physical distress, experienced several times by David Douglas in North America. The pretty lilac-coloured *Clarkia pulchella*, and the bright mariposa lily were his prize and compensation after one such experience in 1825. In lower Columbia, it took an hour each night to dry his blanket before sleep and the incessant rain spoilt most of his collections. Shortage of food reduced him to advanced fatigue and journeying on into the arid interior, he walked 19 miles with feet burning and blistered across a barren plain without a drop of water, in a temperature of 97 °F in the shade. It was here that he found the *Clarkia*. A year later his eyes began to trouble him: the reflection of the blazing sun on the bare desert and the blowing sand had made them inflamed and he could scarcely distinguish objects that were ten yards away. Within a week he was in another extreme of climate in snowy mountains, suffering from snow-blindness. Eight years later his eye problems had progressed to the total loss of sight in one eye.

The stress of the continuous threat of drought can best be appreciated from a few of Allan Cunningham's diary entries each day written in hope and ignorance of what the next day would bring. He was collecting (and prolifically) in central New South Wales, Australia, while discovering a new landscape where no white man had been before:

May 19, 1817 Our journey was unavoidably lengthened in hopes of finding water; we had travelled 12 miles and found none or the appearance of any! We managed 2 miles farther and encamped . . . Having pitched the tents and unladen our poor horses, who felt the privation infinitely more than ourselves, we sent our people in several directions in quest of water. . .

20th The whole of us went out in search of water as usual; after some time expended in a fruitless search one of our people procured some miserable filthy water by digging a hole on some low damp ground.

21st . . . this morning . . . we learnt to appreciate the value of good water, which like other great blessings are only estimated by the loss of them. All the water we could procure, which we brought from distant corrupted holes, was very foul and muddy and filled with animalcules, to destroy which we boiled and strained the water.

Later in the day they found water in a swamp. The thirst of the fourteen animals travelling with the expedition presented further problems. During the night of 25 May the horses, 'much fatigued' after battling through bushwood dense enough to drag their loads from their saddles, strayed away from the camp looking for water and were lost for five days.

During this time Cunningham had been 'seized with a violent ague (originating in a cold), which increased this day and obliged me to remain at rest'. With horses finally returned, the expedition was ready to proceed with all possible speed:

Although not sufficiently strong and scarcely recovered of my late attack, still I was unwilling to become the instrument of further delay and as the whole of us walk, all our horses being very heavily laden, I had no other resource or alternative but to walk likewise.

Soon they were again in dire straits:

> June 2  Our horses were so much enfeebled and debilitated by the late severe exercise and want of water that it was considered advisable to remain the whole of this day under the range . . . We searched in vain for water; all the creeks are dry now. We returned to our tent at dusk. One of our horses from debility, and in an attempt to rise up under his load, having fallen down was so strained as to be rendered useless which obliged us to shoot him. Our lat. is 34°08′08″S., and long. 146°42′25″E. . . . Our people made shoes of the skin of the horse.

Getting lost, without food and water supplies, was another hazard of extremely arid terrain, and this was a particular danger in the Australian bush with its vast distances of grey-green uniformity. In his early journals Cunningham continually used the word 'same' and it does capture the essence of the bush scenery. He aptly described one species as 'a drooping melancholy shrub'. (Darwin was likewise impressed with the uniformity of the vegetation when he went to Bathurst in 1836.) The bush plants are all stamped with the hallmark of desperate measures to counteract dehydration – mean small leaves, even reduced to needles, thick outer skin, protecting matted hairs – a dull shrivelled look as dank and waterless as dehydration itself. As greenhouse exotics for the fashionable, their foliage was more novel than beautiful. Cunningham described the bush landscape as 'a greyish gloominess in consequence of the great numbers of *Acacia pendula*' and saltbush. The plains were like 'a gloomy desert with stunted trees and dry wiry . . . grass . . . a sterile and dreary aspect . . . with small timbers of *Eucalyptus micrantha* and small cypress'.

With each landmark the same as the last, it was a fatal risk to take the bush at its face value. The thirteen people of Cunningham's expedition became separated and lost several times, resorting to firing guns to indicate their situations. Cunningham's younger brother, Richard, who more or less took over on Allan's return to England, unfortunately did not share his brother's good sense. Over-zealous botanising took him away from his party in 1835: he became lost, his horse died of exhaustion and he was eventually found by friendly aborigines. He was probably in a state of delirium as he became violent in the night and they panicked and killed him.

Setting out on one's own into the wilderness was always a risky business. David Douglas survived attacks from aggressive Red Indians and grizzly bears and all the outsize hazards of stalking giant trees in the Rocky Mountains. Having lived through so many near-misses of drowning in sea and river torrent and survived starvation, cold and hunger, he met a sudden hideous death by being gored by a wild bull caught in a pit trap in Hawaii. Because of various inconsistencies of evidence and events, his death is still something of a mystery. Some believe it was murder for a purse of gold, the body flung into the pit afterwards.

The Duke of Devonshire and Sir Joseph Paxton joined a syndicate to send two young gardeners to Canada and North America to collect plants in Douglas's footsteps. Before collecting a single plant the two gardeners drowned just below Death Rapids (Dalles des Morts, beyond Upper Arrow Lake in Columbia), where only eleven years before Douglas had manoeuvred a boat and a back pack with prolonged effort and anxiety. Death among collectors was frequently caused by violent accident or gruelling illness. Tropical orchids alone claimed eight British collectors.

## A Naturalist's Occupation

Day-to-day life in between the excursions and crises was disciplined and busy but relatively mundane, involving identification and the 'housewifery' of specimen-collecting – much the same routine as that of today's field worker. The journal of Henry Walter Bates, *The Naturalist on the Amazons*, gives a vivid picture of a 'naturalist's occupation'.

Home from excursions on foot and by canoe, Bates led 'a quiet uneventful life' in a 'rude' dwelling in a settlement:

> following my pursuit in the same peaceful, regular way as a Naturalist might do in a European village. . . I rose generally with the sun, when the grassy streets were wet with dew, and walked down to the river to bathe. . . Alligators were rather troublesome. . .

In the dry season there were usually one or two alligators to watch out for. Bates swam with the natives with his eye:

fixed on that of the monster, which stares with a disgusting leer along the surface of the water. . . When a little motion was perceived in the water behind the reptile's tail, bathers were obliged to beat a quick retreat. . . Five or six hours of every morning were spent in collecting in the forest, whose borders lay only five minutes' walk from my house: the hot hours of the afternoon . . . and the rainy days, were occupied in preparing and ticketing the specimens, making notes, dissecting and drawings.

Solitude, frequently without word or succour from the outside world, was an occupational hazard for the naturalist. On one occasion, a period of isolation coincided with a yellow fever attack:

I was worst off in the first year, 1850, when twelve months elapsed without letters or remittances. Towards the end of this time my clothes had worn to rags; I was barefoot, a great inconvenience in tropical forests . . . my servant ran away, and I was robbed of nearly all my copper money.

Towards the latter part of his stay Bates suffered from ill health arising from bad and insufficient food. The want of intellectual society and of the varied excitement of European life was also felt most acutely and this, instead of becoming deadened by time, increased until it became almost insupportable:

I was obliged at last, to come to the conclusion that the contemplation of Nature alone is not sufficient to fill the human heart and mind. I got on pretty well when I received a parcel from England by steamer once in two or four months. I used to be very economical with my stock of reading lest it should be finished before the next arrival and leave me utterly destitute. I went over the periodicals . . . with great deliberation, going through every number three times; the first time devouring the more interesting articles, the second, the whole of the remainder; and the third, reading all the advertisements from beginning to end.

Douglas used a similar technique to combat loneliness. He wrote in his journal:

To console myself for the want of friends of a kindred feeling in this distant land, for an exchange of sympathy or advice, I vary my amusements; by day it is a barren place that does not afford me a blade of grass; a bird, or a rock, before unnoticed, from which I derive inexpressible delight, while during the stillness of a cloudless night their localities are determined, altitudes measured, the climate they breathed analyzed. Thank God my heart feels gladness in these operations; without such to pass away an hour, my time would be blank.

At times Douglas had felt the pressure of solitude, never more than when he was experiencing difficulties and achieving little. Three days after returning from a miserable and fairly fruitless trip he found that he had no letters in the yearly batch of mail. Six weeks later on New Year's Day, 1826, when his knee (p. 125) was still troubling him and his thoughts were forlorn, he wrote:

Commencing a year in such a far removed corner of the earth, where I am nearly destitute of civilized society, there is some scope for reflection. In 1824, I was on the Atlantic on my way to England; 1825, between the island of Juan Fernandez and the Galapagos in the Pacific; I am now here, and God only knows where I may be next. In all probability, if a change does not take place, I will shortly be consigned to the tomb. I can die satisfied with myself. I never have given cause for remonstrance or pain to an individual on earth. I am in my twenty-seventh year.

## Why?

Why did they do it? All of the collectors' privations so often ended in loss. During collecting there were disappointments like David Douglas's loss of 'the labour of fifty-four days of fatigue and anxiety' in a river crossing. Worse still was loss at a later stage; for example when, having traversed jungle and river, been sorted, identified and meticulously packed, South American plants perished at sea in faulty Wardian cases. All over the world sacrificial efforts came to nought because of customs officials, shipwrecks or just freak cold weather. There was also the disappointment of neglect once the risky business of introduction was complete or only limited success in a new climate – both of which Robert Fortune experienced after carefully introducing Chinese tea to India. Douglas had the horror of actually discovering specimens he had carefully packed and sent in 1825 not even unpacked in 1828, largely destroyed by moths and rendered indescribable. Worst of all was the disappointment of having to break up one's own hard-won collection because of financial pressures, as happened to Henry Walter Bates. (This loss was particularly tragic as scientific information on now extinct species was irretrievably lost.) Sacrifice was essential for even the chance of initial success and hope for a final successful outcome was slight.

There are some people who almost seem to have been born with a passion to see plants and to grow them. Allan Cunningham was one of these. In order to spread colour and influence the minds of the children destined to live and possibly plant gardens in the Australian wilderness, he freely distributed seeds of English wild flowers. Like Robert Dick, he not only collected plants, he planted them. He did this with two thoughts in mind. One was practical and the other was romantic. He planted fruit seeds and acorns in the hope of 'providing a meal for some famished European or some hungry black fellow' but he also hoped to pose an unexpected query for future travellers. Even at the most arduous moments of exploration he was thinking of planting, as after crossing a swollen river on an improvised raft, miraculously without misadventure:

> our raft being waterlogged, and when laden was several inches under water, independently of the rapid whirls of the stream against which we had to contend. We encamped on the rising grounds of the north bank. I sowed some peach stones and quince seeds.

In common with bird- and insect-watching, collecting has always had the element of the unexpected: it was, and still is, a gamble. There is always the promise of another better day and the possibility of a first sighting like the royal water-lily, particularly in the tropics, so 'prodigal in variety and beauty'. The severities of a terrain were always recompensed by the sight of its flowers. Sometimes collectors' dreams materialised: on one glorious day in October 1849

above Choongtam village in the Himalayas, Sir Joseph Dalton Hooker collected seeds of no less than six 'superb rhododendrons'; the four white flowered ones (including *R. dalhousiae*, see Plate 7) in his opinion excelled all others in their delicacy and beauty. The most enviable luck beyond even dreams also materialised in the unexpected appearance of seeds of a Victorian favourite – on a plate, literally. In the 1790s nuts from the monkey puzzle tree were served as a dessert at an official Chilean dinner; one of the guests simply slipped some into his pocket.

There was the hope of being served with edible seeds or finding an overnight success like David Douglas's flowering currant or the gamble of finding the biggest and the first. Many collectors probably persuaded themselves that their motivation was thoughts of such success but at heart they were actually romantic adventurers. Others had an overriding Victorian sense of duty to their employer or patron, even though their payment was pitiful and treatment frequently scandalous. From their writing it would seem that the most potent driving force was frequently the elusive magic of a unique spectacle. Philip Henry Gosse sums it up in his lyrical description of one sight which made all his discomforts worthwhile. His descriptions, regardless of their Victorian idiosyncrasies, have one outstanding quality which modern scientific writing has almost wholly lost – a burning love of the natural order of things, and an awareness of beauty, without which respect for living things can be lost in factual details. Like so many of the collectors, he seems never to have lost his sense of wonder, as in the beauty of swarming butterflies gathered:

> around a blossoming tree at sunrise . . . one of the most gorgeously beautiful of butterflies . . . arrayed in a dress of rich velvet black and emerald green, arranged in transverse bands, with a broad disk of ruddy gold, the whole sparkling with a peculiar radiance, like powdered gems. . . As the approaching sun is casting a glow over the eastern sky, one after another begins to come, and by the time the glorious orb emerges from the horizon, the lovely living gems are fluttering by scores, or even by hundreds. . . The level sunbeams, glancing on their sparkling wings, give them a lustre which the eye can scarcely look upon; and, as they dance in their joyousness over the

fragrant blooms, engage in the evolution of playful combats, or mount up on the wing to a height of several hundred feet above the tree, they constitute, in that brief hour of morning, a spectacle which has seemed to me worth years of toil to see.

(*The Romance of Natural History*)

## Chapter 8
# THE PASSION FOR DETAIL

### 'So Many Microscopical Wonders'

The tiny intricacies of plants had been a source of fascination since the invention of the first compound microscopes (microscopes with several lenses). The first was made about 1600 and in 1664 one of the earliest microscopists, Robert Hooke, described the plant cells of cork. In his book *Micrographia*, published in 1665, he marvelled over other parts of the plant which he managed to magnify 270 times. Everything from the minutest of flowers – the 'flowery ornament' of grasses – to leaf hairs excited him. Writing about thyme seeds, it was as if nature 'would, from the ornaments wherewith she has deckt these Cabinets, hint to us, that in them she has laid up her Jewels and Masterpieces . . . The Grain affords a very pretty Object for the Microscope, namely, a Dish of Lemmons plac'd in a very little room'. The other father of microscopy, a Dutchman called Antoni van Leeuwenhoek,[1] wrote with equally infectious excitement. He used a simple single lens microscope and revealed the contents of split apple seeds and the cotton seed with its incredibly advanced embryo plant within, complete with veins and glands with contents of 'the most beautiful light green colour that one's eyes could contemplate'. In 1682 Nehemiah Grew opened up the 'New World' of plant structure, method-

ically but still joyously, travelling with his microscope from root to bud (and, incidentally, becoming the first to recognise and state the existence of sex in flowers).

The Victorians recaptured this early delight in the revelation of the minutiae of plants (see Figure 8.1). A favourite subject was the orderly patterns, distinctive shapes and intricate sculpturing of pollen grains (see Figure 8.2). Different genera have their own diagnostic shapes: in the bloody or blood-red cranesbill (*Geranium sanguineum*), the pollen grains are 'like a perforated globe of fire' while in the passion flower they are marked with three rings 'as though they had been formed with a turner's lathe'. The passage of 160 years had not altered the descriptions of some pollen: the 'Holland Cheese' was a standard likeness for certain pollen grains and the supposed similarity between the pollen grains of mallow (Figure 8.2) and various spiked weaponry still stood. Grew had written of the pollen grains of mallow as being 'beset round about with little Thornes; whereby each looks like the seed-Ball of Roman Nettle, or like the Fruit of Thorn-Apple . . . or the Fish called *Pisces orbis minor*, or the Murices used antiently [sic] in wars'. In his very Victorian book *Half-Hours with the Microscope*, Edwin Lankester described mallow as 'covered all over with little sharp-pointed projections, like a hand-grenade'.

Most Victorians did not share Grew's curiosity as to the purpose of all this unsuspected detail and diversity. Popular Victorian writers such as the Rev. J.G. Wood and Edwin Lankester avoided the embarrassment of query and explanation. Their books were merely providing

1. Leeuwenhoek even measured his objects, using his own unbelievable scale of 'standard measurement' which included the 'eye of a louse', the 'thread from the cocoon of a silkworm', the diameter of fine sand grains and hairs from his beard.

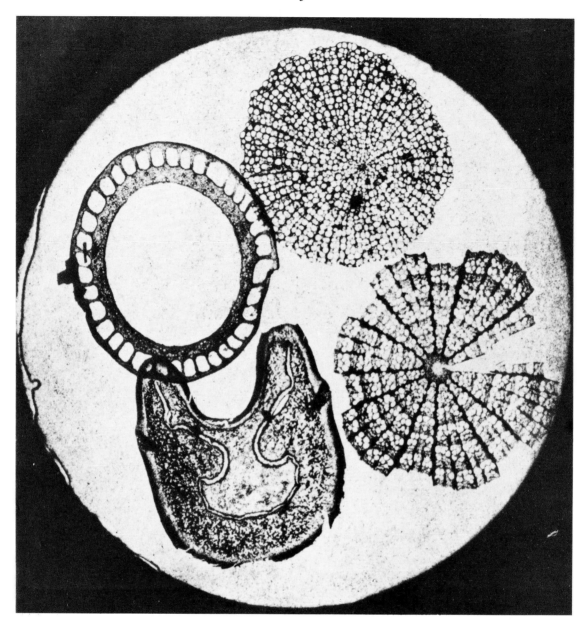

**Figure 8.1** One of the early 'Sun Pictures' or 'Photogenic Drawings' made by William Henry Fox Talbot in the 1830s. He used objects to cast well-defined shadows on sensitised paper placed in the sun and thus made a negative. He discovered a means of preserving the image and used the negative as the object to be copied in order to create a second image – with light and dark the correct way round. In this picture of sections of plant material he used a solar microscope fixed at the window to focus the sunlight on plant sections and on the paper. (From the Lacock Abbey Collection, Fox Talbot Museum, The National Trust)

**Figure 8.2** The dilettante microscopists of the 1860s were delighted with pollen texture and its resemblance to various imaginary objects: for example, 'wheels with teeth'. Shown here (not to scale) is the pollen grain of mallow (on the left) and a poppy seed.

amusement for the home: recommending close inspection of poppy seeds (see Figure 8.2), sections of wood and potato, hairs of the tobacco plant, cotton fibres, petal of geranium and pollen of lily, sunflower and passion flower. The living plants of the drawing room provided convenient specimens such as the tentacles of the insectivorous sundew (see Figure 8.18), the glands of the Venus' fly-trap (see Figure 8.3), and, in season, fern spores. Interest in microscopes coincided with interest in ferns: the minute details of ferns were very much a part of their fascination: 'No one that has not tried can tell the pleasure there is in searching out the beauty of forms of one piece of shield-fern', wrote Charlotte M. Yonge, 'Yes, honour to the shield-fern [*Polystichum* sp.]. . .' From dried collections came the wing scales and antennae of butterflies and moths.

For those with more courage, the living denizens of the aquarium provided specimens such as 'Foot of Male Water-Beetle' and 'Foot of Frog, showing circulation'. The sea and fresh water aquaria and garden ponds were ideal material for the squeamish who could follow in Leeuwenhoek's footsteps and simply take a drop of water and marvel at the miniature kaleidoscope of living creatures and plants within. (Aquarium writers recommended their readers to acquire a microscope.) There was the thrill of anticipation and the unexpected as these normally invisible organisms materialised into focus – attached by a 'foot' to pond weed (see Figure 8.4), or drifting and darting about the field of vision.

The structures of these organisms added to the excitement – there was disbelief that there could be such minutiae and that they could be actually doing something: Victorians watched in fascination as single-celled organisms were propelled along by whip-like hairs or bands of short ones (cilia) beating in synchrony. There was even an opportunity for the spectator sports: watching tentacles capturing prey which was then slowly devoured – not by carnivorous plants this time but by micro-organisms (see Figure 8.4). Quite different in appeal were the 'exquisitely-fashioned' diatoms and foraminifers of fresh and sea water. Their geometric and symmetrical shapes covered in finely sculptured latticework made pollen grains look almost shabby; some could only be compared to stylised filigree snowflakes. The diatoms and foraminifers were favourites of the composer Elgar, who kept three microscopes on his billiard table. In fact, their breathtaking symmetry and pattern and the beautiful translucence of light passing through living specimens probably helped the interest in microscopes to reach mild craze proportions by the end of the 1860s. By then those in fashionable dining circles ended the meal by turning their attention from the dinner table to the microscope for a little light entertainment. Presumably inspection of any remains of fine Stilton cheese was discreetly avoided.

The serious investigators, on the other hand, would probably have seized the opportunity to study the mould in Stilton. The circumstances surrounding the birth of the Microscopical Society in 1839 would have allowed them ample opportunity. This learned society (now the Royal Microscopial Society) grew out of a sociable habit of Dr Nathaniel Bagshaw Ward, who was a microscope enthuasiast as well as inventor of the Wardian case. He held a weekly open-house *conversazione* and refreshments for anyone who cared to come along. Such events, reminiscent of the eighteenth-century hostesses, were customary among some naturalists and were announced in the specialist journals. Local microscopical societies sprang up all over the country for those with a serious interest who looked askance at what one of their number called 'the "curious bauble" style of Soiree'. Doctors and Admirals and frequently ladies numbered among their members. As well as peering at the same natural oddities as the amusement seekers, they ventured into the realms of the less easily obtainable: sections of coal, crystals, a diseased lung teamed with human eyebrow and tongue, flea's gizzards, ant's

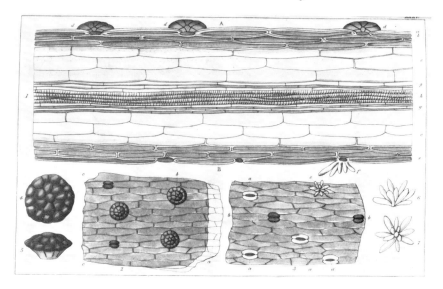

**Figure 8.3** Anatomy of a leaf of the Venus' fly-trap seen through the microscope, from *Ladies' Botany* by John Lindley. 1 A highly magnified view of a slice of the leaf (d = glands; f = hair tufts) 2 Looking at the leaf from above 3 Looking at the leaf from below 4 & 5 A very highly magnified gland.

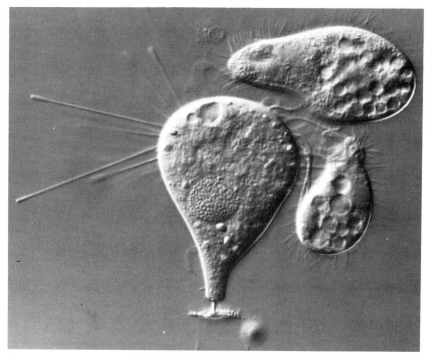

**Figure 8.4** Garden ponds and freshwater aquaria provided water plants and attached animal life for microscopic scrutiny. A common organism in such environments is *Tokophrya* (pear-shaped and with a stalk for attachment to pondweed), which uses its tentacles to capture and feed on other micro-organisms, *Tetrahymena*. They are seen here through an electron microscope, magnification × 1000. Charles Darwin's first compound microscope, made in 1846, also magnified up to × 1000, although not with great clarity by modern standards. (Robert Hooke's microscope magnified × 270.) (By courtesy of Dr J.B. Tucker, St Andrews University)

tongues, moss capsules and the tongue of a butterfly (to check the count of 74 suckers thereon).

Microscopes cost two or three guineas each, from which one might expect that only the wealthy and well-to-do were able to explore this romantic miniature world. But as with collecting, those with a will to see and to understand nature somehow achieved their goal. Robert Dick spent the small profit he made from baking almost exclusively on learning. After years of saving he eventually bought his microscope through his flour supplier. This unusual merchant was by then practised in purchasing by proxy for Dick and packing valuable items like books in bags of flour to ensure a safe passage to Thurso from Leith; the microscope was similarly cushioned on its voyage. Joseph Gutteridge who was frequently in financial distress during fluctuations in the silk ribbon trade 'put up a small work bench, and with the rude tools I possessed made better ones', making a plane, a small tenon saw from a steel brush, and chisels 'out of watchmakers' worn-out flat files'. He learnt the art of lens-grinding from the watchmakers in his district, and 'buying nothing but the raw material from which to construct it', he made his microscope. The marvels he hoped to see were at first disappointingly indistinct, but:

> By dint of perseverence and under many difficulties . . . I at last succeeded in making a powerful achromatic microscope. I think of it now with much pleasure as the greatest triumph I ever achieved towards helping me to understand the various phases of matter . . . It opened up a new world. It passed the utmost stretch of imagination. . . It was a great joy to contemplate these wonderful and exquisitely beautiful structures concealed from the normal powers of vision. . .

(His homemade microscope was displayed 'in a carved oak case, imitating gothic architecture' and exhibited at the Exhibition commemorating the opening of Coventry Market Hall in 1867.) It was necessary for a man like Gutteridge to go to these lengths to learn such things because museums only came into being after the Great Exhibition in 1851 – the Natural History Museum in London only being opened in 1881 – and natural history was not taught in schools until the 1880s. Thus, understanding of common-

place natural events could only be gained from first-hand observation or from books and magazines. As has been seen, the popular volumes often tended to obscure accuracy with moralising, sentimentality or a deluge of irrelevant facts while some were simply inaccurate and perpetuated old misunderstandings. For more accuracy and detail, and in the absence of school textbooks, enthusiasts were forced to go to the other extreme and turn to the scholarly volumes that were 'the life studies' of the foremost researchers of the time such as Charles Darwin.

## The Pollination of Flowers

The revelation of the means of pollination of flowers by the microscope was particularly exciting for horticultural enthusiasts and those caught up in the latest flower craze. It was not unusual for ladies eager to create new hybrid varieties to go to the expense of acquiring a nosegay of a desirable geranium and hang it hopefully above their own plants to promote cross-fertilisation. Others sent their geraniums to nurserymen, somewhat like a horse going to the stud. There was the thrill of involvement in seeing it all under their microscopes: the delicate translucence of the sensitive stigma and the tiny patterns on pollen and seeds. Joseph Gutteridge habitually created his own hybrids, and for him, seeing the pollen grains growing down into the stigma was a personal discovery: 'The study of plants had always been a source of delight . . . but [I] could never conceive the processes involved until the microscope revealed the secret.' Darwin also made this discovery for himself. As a student at Cambridge he observed details of pollen grains and on first seeing some with the pollen tube emerging he rushed excitedly to Henslow, Professor of Botany, to communicate his 'discovery'.

Even with the aid of the microscope the secrets of pollination had evaded naturalists for some time. The elucidation of flowers by the Victorians can only be fully appreciated when one looks at the strange mixture of fact and misconceptions they inherited from the eighteenth century.

### The Eighteenth-century Inheritance

During the eighteenth century the purpose of the

**Figure 8.5** Common mallow. A flower is in the male phase on the left, with sticky pollen grains adhering together and making balls around the anthers. On the right, in the older flower, the pollen is spent and the stamens bend back away from the splayed receptive female stigmas. (Photograph Dorset, June)

beautifully patterned grains of pollen had only been finally accepted after a long and bitter struggle. The protagonists had fallen into two camps. On the one hand there were those who attacked any concept of maleness and femaleness entering into the innocent beauty of flowers 'with all the arms . . . [they] could muster, both sacred and profane'. For them pollen was 'accumulated by chance' or from the 'dryness' of the anthers or was just an ornament. A less attractive view was that pollen was an excrement of the anthers which 'did the office of kidneys, purging the several parts of the plant from all such particles as were not fit for its nourishment'. The possibility of it being 'noxious' was believed to be amply demonstrated in nigella (love-in-a-mist), where the 'constantly elevated' position of the female stigmas kept them well above the pollen-bearing anthers 'lest they be hurt by the odious powder'. One author was driven to botanical despair: 'Perhaps it may be produced for the sake of insects – for of what service the powder is to the plant . . . does not appear, nor perhaps will it ever appear.' In the other camp were those 'curious philosophers' who found

'nobler Uses for this Dust' – namely, fertilisation of the ovule to produce a seed.

Towards the end of the century when the pollen controversy had been settled there was still a general misunderstanding as to how pollen reached the stigmas and the question of the flower–insect relationship. In spite of studies showing the importance of insects in pollination in the 1730s and 1750s, the idea continued to circulate that self-pollination was the rule, with a flower's stamens dropping pollen on to its own stigma, or as Erasmus Darwin thought in 1800, the one positively seeking the other. They had a 'sensibility to the passion of reproduction . . . by what means are the anthers in many flowers, and stigmas in other flowers, directed to find their paramours? . . . by mechanic attraction, or by the sensation of love'. These 'vegetable amourettes' found each other by another organ of sense, 'one probably analogous to our sense of smell'. From ideas of floral sensations and actions, it was but a short step to choice, including the wrong one. The exchange of pollen between male and female in separate flowers was viewed by Erasmus Darwin and others as an exceptional act of infidelity: some 'mistake the males . . . of the neighbouring flowers for their own husbands; and bending into contact with them become guilty of adultery'. It had to follow that the flower's nectar was produced by the flower for its own nourishment. All insects were therefore thieves, plundering the floral larder.

The exact purpose of the nectar was uncertain. Some thought that, when it was reabsorbed, it might 'conveniently serve the same purpose as the white of egg', or that it was 'that balsam which the seeds imbibe, to make them keep and preserve their vegetable quality longer'. Another view was that nectar was a lubricant for the 'vegetable uterus'. Erasmus Darwin felt that flowers fed on nectar in order to mature, or, as he put it, 'become sensible to the passion, and gain the apparatus for the reproduction of their species'. (The parallel with butterflies, and other sexual phases of insects, feeding on nectar was too much for him, and he finally described flowers as akin to insects: 'similar in every respect except their being attached to the tree'. It was then but a small step to the wonderfully bizarre idea of the first insects having been flowers which had 'loosed themselves from the parent plant'.)

The role of nectar in attracting insects and the myriad adaptations of flowers for nectar production, protection and advertisement were eventually stated in a classic work, *The Secret of Nature in the Form and Fertilization of Flowers Discovered* by Christian Konrad Sprengel in 1793. He explained the flower's shape and pattern in terms of attracting the right type of insect for pollination. He pointed out the contrasting lines – honey guides – on petals, like signposts leading the bee towards the centre of the flower, as in the wild pansies in Figure 4.3 and 9.11. He also noted petal spurs (visible in the columbine, Figure 4.5). Petal spurs collect the nectar produced by nectaries: a nectary can be seen in the opened honeysuckle, as in Figure 8.7. Sprengel pointed out nectar protection was also provided by a plant's habit – as in the violet hanging on a thin stalk with its head bent down keeping the nectar well protected from rain – rather a different interpretation from the moralists' view that it was designed to convey the virtue of humility.

Thus Sprengel heralded the nineteenth-century approach to understanding flowers which were no longer defensive and passive towards insects,

but attracting, directing and manoeuvring them from one part of the flower to another in a definite sequence. Sprengel's experiments excluding insects led him to the correct conclusion that if no insects visited the flower it did not set seed. Unfortunately Sprengel's *avant garde* ideas remained generally unnoticed until the mid-nineteenth century when Charles Darwin began checking Sprengel's observations (p. 147) and publishing his own.

## The Nineteenth-century View of Flowers

Scientific flowers are sometimes thought of as efficient but dull botanical machinery – unromantic factual flowers stripped of beauty and mystery. Nothing could be further from the truth. The scientific view of flowers holds the wonder of discovering minute mechanisms for beyond petal beauty is the greater marvel of design for survival, where function creates the beauty. Botanists of the nineteenth century saw in each flower many tiny structures working intricately together in a harmonious way to effect successful pollination and survival of the species. The flowers had, in effect, sophisticated living machinery. Machinery was not an inappropriate term at the time, as many flowers such as sweet pea (Plate 16), broom (see Plate 17 and Figure 8.6), sage (see Figure 9.10) and orchids were found to employ Victorian-style gadgetry: there were petal replicas of pistons, springs (Plate 17), brushes (Plate 16), levers (see Figure 9.10), sprung lids and explosive glue dispensers (see page 64). This new insect-eye-view of flowers allowed understanding of their design for a specific function. The way a flower worked now took on its own fascination and replaced the traditional enthusiasm for merely ordering and classifying.

There was also the element of surprise that the more flowers that were studied, the more their patterns, scent and shapes were revealed as 'so many baits and traps set by nature to entice insects to come to the flowers'. 'Is it not beautiful', continued Arabella Buckley, 'to think that the bright pleasant colours we love so much in flowers, are not only ornamental, but that they are useful and doing their part in keeping up healthy life in our world?' Developing alongside the very Victorian delight in usefulness, there seemed to be an underlying concern that the growing awareness of the functionality of a

**Figure 8.6** Broom (*Sarothamnus scoparius*) delighted Victorians with the intricacy of its hidden spring mechanism within the flower. Here 'press stud' connections between two sets of petals retain a state of tension before release of spring by a visiting bee (see Plate 17). Photograph: Loch Lomond, May.

flower would detract from the sense of its beauty. Charles Darwin reassured his readers in 1878:

> The beauty and poetry of flowers will not be at all lessened to the general observer, by his being led to notice various small, and apparently quite unimportant, details of structure . . . He will, I believe, come to the conclusion that flowers are not only delightful from their beauty and fragrance, but display most wonderful adaptations for various purposes.

And in *Flowers, their origin, shapes, perfumes and colours* John Ellor Taylor rendered the new view of flowers palatable to the amusement seekers:

> What a fund of ingenious amusement may be derived from a more detailed study of the floral structures of our commonest wild flowers. Those who delight in unravelling the enigmas and charades of magazine columns will find in the shapes, tints, streaks, and internal structures of flowers, riddles of the most delightful kind, whose deciphering will not only pass away many a pleasant hour, but leave the student in possession of a mass of actual knowledge!

The sentimentalists were content to be dazzled by Taylor's 'mass of actual knowledge' (as well as its content), and at the great minds deciphering it. Charlotte M. Yonge wrote:

> I was thinking . . . what could be said about the vegetable world in October, when I recollected a story told of one of the most learned men who ever lived. He was sitting one day upon an open common, when he laid down his hand upon a piece of turf, and said that in that small space which he thus covered, there grew so many wonders that their study would occupy the longest life of the greatest philosopher. So I do not think we need despair of finding something marvellous . . .

Marvel followed marvel – for example, the seedling and the microscopic green chloroplasts in its leaves described by Arabella Buckley in *The Fairy-land of Science*: 'How ingeniously it pumped up the water through the cells to its stomach – the leaves! And how marvellously the sun-waves entering there formed the little green granules, and then helped them to make food and living protoplasm!' Such wonders of order and minute mechanism were ideal material for the natural theologians. Citing the different shapes of flower stalks, William Paley wrote: 'How wonderful are these diversities of this apparently trivial part of the plant!' To delight in minutiae was a pious duty according to Charlotte M. Yonge: 'Perhaps it may be some assistance in rendering our thanks for these, His beautiful works, to be led to examine a little into their structure, and the wonderful perfection of their parts.' There were some, however, who refused to pry with the microscope into the secret sex life of flowers – most prominently, John Ruskin. In *Proserpina* he refuted the botanist's premise that the existence of a flower was for the sole purpose of producing seed to ensure continuance of the species:

> And these are the real significances of the flower itself. It is the utmost purification of the plant, and the utmost disciple. Where its tissue is blanched fairest, dyed purest, set in strictest rank, appointed to most chosen office, there – and created by the fact of this purity and function – is the flower. But created, observe, by the purity and order, more than by the function. The flower exists for its own sake, not for the fruit's sake. The production of the fruit is an added honour to it – is a granted consolation to us for its death. But the flower is the end of the seed, – not the seed of the flower. . . It is because of its beauty that its continuance is worth Heaven's while. . . Fasten well in your mind, then, the conception of order, and purity, as the essence of the flower's being, no less than of the crystal's. A ruby is not made bright to scatter round it child-rubies; nor a flower, but in collateral and added honour, to give birth to other flowers.

To achieve the new scientific intimacy with flowers, vast numbers of observations and measurements had to be made. The hallmark of all of the dedicated men of science was their dogged persistence and intense vocation, manifested in the minutest details which they never overlooked. Their writings allow today's reader to share the joy of discovering such intricacies without the tedium of searching. Accumulating quantities of such information demands straightforward discipline and staying power and fortunately these were two staggering qualities of the ideal nineteenth-century man. The great ideal was self-sacrifice in the name of investigation and furthering the frontiers of knowledge. Such a climate nurtured a quest for learning and a thoroughness which possibly only inspire amused disbelief in today's atmosphere of reaction against such ideals of discipline. Hours and days spent watching one flower group to catch a glimpse of a pollinator were taken for granted. Charles Darwin was perhaps the most glittering example of Victorian dedication. His observation inspired others – for example, Hermann and Fritz Müller. The understanding of flowers had

entered its golden age. Joseph Gutteridge paid tribute to those who dedicated themselves:

> All honour to such men having studied . . . for the benefit of the thoughtful and enquiring mind . . . For this and much more we have reason to be thankful that such men have devoted their lives to discover as far as possible the laws governing the lower forms of creation that had hitherto baffled any attempt at elucidation. How much I feel indebted to such men my pen would fail to record. Many a doubt has been removed and many a difficult problem solved through the unwearied labours of these our noblest men of the age.

The 'unwearied labours' of the 'noblest men of the age' were bringing into focus a picture of the miniature world of flowers and their associated insects far more extraordinary and entertaining than Hooke, Leeuwenhoek and Grew could ever have imagined.

### 'The Unwearied Labours of These Our Noblest Men of the Age'

*Hermann Müller*

Hermann Müller must have kept watch on one group of flowers for hour upon hour. He meticulously identified and sexed each insect visitor and made careful measurements of insect tongues and flower dimensions. Charles Darwin described him as having 'indomitable patience'. Darwin wrote the preface to the English edition of Herman Müller's book, *The Fertilisation of Flowers*, which was published in 1883 (the German original was published in 1873). This thick volume was packed with information about the detailed structure, pollination mechanisms and insect visitors of a staggering array of wild and cultivated flowers, familiar and unfamiliar – flower by flower. Victorian enthusiasts were familiar with Müller's work and he also became a source of inspiration for later botanists.

Hermann Müller was born in Thuringia; his father was a minister and his mother was the daughter of a chemist-pharmacist of distinction. Both parents had a very keen interest in natural history which greatly influenced their two boys. Hermann was their second son; Hermann's brother, Fritz (see page 145), who later became the more famous naturalist of the two, was seven years older.

Hermann Müller taught at the Realschule in Lippstadt and was inspired quite late in life by Charles Darwin's classic book on the pollination of orchids (see page 147) and by Darwin's *Origin of Species*. Inspiration from these and other of Darwin's works committed Müller totally to the study of flowers and their pollination. It is the incredible detail of Müller's observations which makes his descriptions of flowers so fascinating. His writings still open one's eyes to seeing flowers anew – as objects of staggering detail and mechanisms. His staunch scientific objectivity does not allow one to know a little of the man as well – his passion for plants is indicated by his careful observation of minute details rather than by his words – but one can at least share his vision of flowers.

A miniature and intricate world of insect and floral survival emerges from Müller's honeysuckle flower. The flower smells most strongly at night and it is then that its nectar is abundant, favouring night-flying moths. The nectar is produced by a thickened area inside the petal tube near its base (see Figure 8.7). The tiny opening of the nectar store is narrowed still further by the spread of stamens at the mouth of the trumpet.

Müller found the tube to be 30 mm long and only 1 or 2 mm wide for most of its length. The width available for insect use is even less – limiting insect visitors to those with accurate tongue aim and co-ordination. Müller found that the flower imposed a further limit. The maximum nectar level only half fills the 30-mm tube, so only moths with tongues longer than 15 mm can reach the nectar.

On one plant, on 27 and 29 May 1868, Müller caught two convolvulus hawkmoths, six privet hawkmoths, seventeen elephant hawkmoths (see Figure 8.8), one small elephant hawkmoth and six related moths. Such numbers and varieties of the hawkmoth family would be a rare occurrence today, alas. Such beauty in abundance makes a delectable daydream for today's insect watchers. A century later, one could only be sure of one of Müller's less exciting finds, the silver-Y moth. Müller meticulously examined his specimens to ascertain the extent to which they had become dusted with pollen during their visit and found that the hairs around the tongue base were 'richly covered with pollen; and in several of the larger species the hairs and scales of the whole of the under side of the body . . . antennae, legs, and

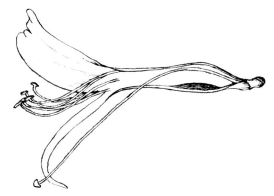

**Figure 8.7** A honeysuckle flower opened to show its nectary – a thickened area of tissue (shaded) near the base of the flower.

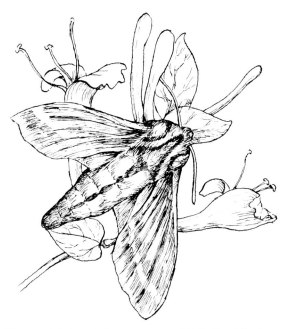

**Figure 8.8** Emulating Hermann Müller's night-long vigil on a honeysuckle plant, one may see the elephant hawkmoth, easily recognisable by its dazzling combination of dark pink and olive-green. The hawkmoths have extremely long tongues and feed while hovering. (Moth drawn from a dead specimen, found in a garden shed)

wings were thickly dusted'. He even measured the tiny dust-like grains of pollen and found them to be 'rounded tetrahedra, 0.047 mm in diameter' covered with small sharp spikes to better adhere to the insects.

*Fritz Müller*

Hermann's brother, Fritz, collected and studied flowers in South America and sent specimens and observations to Hermann and to Charles Darwin. He has been described as 'one of the greatest and original naturalists' of the nineteenth century. His arrival among the exotic flowers of Brazil in 1852 was bizarre; he left Germany under a cloud, not allowed to complete his state medical examinations because of his political allegiances and his refusal to accept orthodox religious views. He first became a farmer, regardless of his glittering qualifications of six languages and a zoology PhD. In 1876 he was appointed travelling naturalist for the Museum of Rio de Janeiro but lost his post and its pension in 1891 over a disagreement. His maverick life ended tragically with imprisonment by rebels and the death of his wife and daughter.

He elucidated many pollination mechanisms of exotic flowers, such as abutilon (see Plate 13), and gave account of sterility in particular species. Darwin frequently referred to his observations. Hermann's occasional references to observations made in Fritz's garden in Itajahay unconsciously created a tantalising, mosaic image, albeit a very incomplete one, of the very jungle paradise that wealthy British enthusiasts were trying to create in their greenhouses. Here he observed among many other plants, various species of passion flowers. The pollination Müller described so objectively must have been a vivid spectacle: many immense star-like flowers of vermilion centred with green, or bright cobalt blue overlaid with mauve stripes and white, and blooms of greens and whites. The humming birds darting and hovering before the flowers vied with their colours for, in Count Buffon's words, they 'of all animated beings' were 'the most elegant in form and the most brilliant in colour. Stones and metals polished by art are not comparable to this gem of nature.' Fritz Müller was extremely observant and noticed the possibility of birds visiting the flowers for the small insects they contained rather than to drink the nectar. The striped filamentous structure at the flower's centre (the 'Crown of Thorns') and 'projecting ledges' seemed to him 'to be of service in detaining small insects in the lowest chamber (which often contains no honey)' and in keeping them 'caged for the humming birds'. In support of this he described a nectarless and odourless species in his garden which was 'diligently visited' by the humming birds while another with abundant nectar was ignored.

*Charles Darwin*

Charles Darwin is not usually thought of as a botanist. However, he carried out detailed experiments and extensive studies of plants and their habits which were (and are still) ranked among the most significant of the nineteenth century. In all Darwin wrote seven major books on plants (all published after the *Origin of Species* of 1859 although he began his botanical enquiries and observations long before that date). Several of them sowed the seed of large areas of modern research. Years of observation, collecting information and experimenting went into each book: *The Effects of Cross- and Self-Fertilisation in the Vegetable Kingdom* (1876) took eleven years. In 1875 his son, Sir Francis Darwin (a medical doctor by training), became his assistant in plant research. Some of the microscopic objects which were mere amusement for many – pollen grains, seeds and sundew tentacles – were for Darwin the subjects of painstaking observation. His first compound microscope (made in 1846) now resides in the Botany Department at Cambridge together with his well-thumbed instruction manual and his own delightful handwritten 'translations' of Messrs. Smith & Beck's technical jargon – 'two turns of this screw'.

Darwin's plant work earned him the unqualified respect of great botanists like Sir Joseph Dalton Hooker. Although Hooker knew much more about identification and orthodox botany (frequently assisting Darwin with these aspects), he nevertheless stood in awe of Darwin's detailed knowledge and discoveries of the factors governing the way plants actually lived, grew and reproduced. Darwin appreciated and intensively studied the significance of the geographical distribution of plant species. On his travels he actually discovered many new species – many were named after him – but no one had the time or expertise to cope with the large number of unknown plants he had collected. Some of his herbarium specimens are still unnamed and are mixed with other collections. He had an immense love of plants, both aesthetically and botanically, which shines through his writing in spite of his objective observations. He also assisted Kew by making large financial contributions to the compiling of the definitive species lists kept by that establishment (these contributions continued for several years after his death, on his instructions).

He was born into a highly intellectual family with wide interests and a strong botanical tradition. He also married into a family with botanical leanings: his wife's uncle was a founder member of the Horticultural Society. His father was a keen gardener and also reared birds, particularly pigeons (the breeding of domestic pigeons later became significant to his evolutionary theory). His elder brother, Erasmus, gave him what he later considered to be his best grounding for a future in experimental science – in the garden tool-house which Erasmus converted into a laboratory while he was still at school. When Erasmus went up to Cambridge in 1822 Charles was left in charge of their experiments.

Charles was brought up on Gilbert White's *Natural History of Selborne* which set him bird-watching, and he read poetic favourites such as James Thomson's *Seasons*. The family library also reflected the interests of Charles's grandfather, Erasmus Darwin, and included the great natural history volumes of the seventeenth and eighteenth centuries. He began identifying plants according to Linnaeus's system from an English version published in 1783 by his grandfather. Erasmus's brother, Robert Waring Darwin (bearing the same name as Charles' father), wrote *Principia Botanica* in 1787. Besides these there were Erasmus's own extraordinary works including the science-poem, *The Botanic Garden*, which portrayed Linnaeus's classification of many wild and exotic plants. Another book by Erasmus which Charles closely studied and marked with notes and queries were *Phytologia, or the Philosophy of Agriculture and Gardening*. He investigated many of his grandfather's pet topics and species.

For the modern reader, Darwin's unravelling of each floral enigma reveals fascinating miniature details previously unnoticed and invokes immense admiration for the patience and staying power of a man utterly devoted to fathoming the natural world. In his own words, he had a 'love of science, unbounded patience in long reflecting over any subject, industry in observing and collecting facts, and a fair share of invention as well as of common sense'. The accuracy of his assessment is exemplified in all his writings. His other outstanding attribute was objectivity and self-criticism: 'I have steadily endeavoured to keep my mind free so as to give up any hypothesis, however much beloved (and I cannot resist forming one on every subject), as soon as facts are shown to be opposed to it.'

Darwin's researches were not purely of an academic nature, of theoretical interest only to other plant fanatics. Many of his investigations were of an utterly practical nature, communicated through the practical horticultural journal, the *Gardeners' Chronicle*, read then, as now, by nurserymen and professional gardeners. His thoughts and experiments on such subjects as the vitality of seeds, double flowers, manures and bumble bees stealing by cutting holes in nectar spurs, rubbed shoulders with horticultural chit-chat and ornate advertisements for items like the 'Galvanised Iron Tub Garden Engine' and the masterpieces of cogs, pulleys, levers and fluted pillar legs which were 'Improved Chaff Machines'. He described his studies on the fertilisation of the scarlet runner (kidney) beans in detail:

> I have this year covered up between three and four feet in length of a row of Kidney Beans, just before the flowers opened, in a tail bag of very thin net; nothing in the appearance of the plants would lead me to suppose that this was in any way injurious to their fertilisation.

And always self-critical and seeking possible flaws in his own experiments, he continued:

> and I think this conclusion may be trusted, for some of the flowers which I moved in the same way as the bees do produced pods quite as fine as could be found in the uncovered rows. The result was that the covered up plants had produced by August 13th only 35 pods . . . whereas the adjoining uncovered rows were crowded with clusters of pods . . . The Kidney Bean is largely frequented by the thrips [thunder fly or thunder bug], and as I have with some other plants actually seen a thrips which was dusted with pollen leave several granules on the stigma, it is quite possible that the fertilisation of the covered-up flowers might have been thus aided.[1]

1. Darwin's thoroughness in investigating the efficiency of bees pollinating the scarlet runner bean even extended to

Interested in the effects of natural crossings of bean varieties by insects, Darwin requested further information from the magazine readership, some of whom provided observations from their vegetable gardens 'in the most obliging manner'. One such detailed reply from a Mr Farrer on the scarlet runner bean was, in his own words, 'made by one who has not the slightest pretence to scientific knowledge, [and] would never have been sent to the press, but for the kind suggestion of Mr. Charles Darwin'. He ended with an appreciation of Darwin's approach and experiments (this sort of appreciation was obviously a common feeling among many practical gardeners reading the *Gardener's Chronicle* if one judges by the letters written on Darwin's death):

> To an amateur, dismayed by the difficulties of botanical classification, perplexed by his own incapacity for microscopical dissection, and disgusted by the mere cataloguing of species, Mr. Darwin's suggestion . . . [on cross-pollination] is a ray of light which opens out an endless field of interesting observation. And to those who look in science for wider speculations, the grand generalisation contained in these and other papers of Mr. Darwin's . . . with all its consequences, affords endless matter for thought, whilst it receives life and reality from the minute observations of details in which his papers abound, and of which they set such wonderful and stimulating examples.

## Plant Enigmas and Darwin

### Solving the Orchids

The most complex and baffling of all floral minutiae existed in the orchids. As Darwin said in his book *On the Various Contrivances by which British and Foreign Orchids are Fertilised*: 'an examination of their many beautiful contrivances will exalt the whole vegetable kingdom in most person's estimation'. John Ellor Taylor regarded Darwin's descriptions of orchid machinery as reading 'like a fairytale'.

timing hive bees sucking nectar in an orthodox manner from the front of the flower versus those taking advantage of holes bitten through the petals by bumble bees. He found that the short cut enabled the bees to visit twice as many flowers in the same time scale.

Orchids had all the extremes. Nectar was sometimes to be found in petals exaggerated beyond recognition or it could be hidden, almost humorously, in an unexpected place making a mockery of an empty nectar spur. Christian Konrad Sprengel had been bewildered by the perpetually dry nectary spurs of some of the Northern European orchids such as the marsh orchid (also called fen orchid and southern marsh orchid, *Dactylorhiza praetermissa*, see Figure 8.10), and the green-winged orchid (*Orchis morio*). In these and the spotted orchid (*Dactylorhiza fuchsii*, see Figure 8.10), there were prominent spurs but apparently no nectar; he accordingly interpreted them as an elaborate pretence and declared them 'sham-nectar-producers' (*Scheinsaftblumen*), perpetuating their existence by 'an organised system of deception' of insect pollinators. Charles Darwin could not believe in 'so gigantic an imposture'. He declared: 'He who believes in this doctrine must rank very low in the instinctive knowledge of many kinds of moths.' Also he had watched insects repeatedly drinking at the flowers on 'Orchis Bank' – an orchid-covered slope half a mile from Darwin's home and affectionately so named by the Darwin family. He determined to solve the riddle.

Once set on a problem, Darwin's methods were the definition of thorough scientific investigation. The only way to discover new facts then, as now, was to sit and watch closely, ignoring the balminess of the sun, the discomfort of the rain and the temptation of an unusual natural episode nearby. Indoors there is the dogged perserverence to follow each query and possibility to its conclusion: the flower's world becomes the centre of existence – and it was such for Darwin until he had answered every possible query. Darwin first tested 'the intellect of moths' by removing nectar spurs from some flowers and found that less pollen was removed than from the intact flowers which seemed to indicate that 'moths do not go to work in a quite senseless manner'.

*Hidden Nectar.* With typical thoroughness Darwin checked every possibility which could explain the spotted orchid's apparently dry nectary – examining not one flower, nor several flowers from a group, but eleven flowers taken from the most favourable position on each of different plants growing in different districts. He still found no nectar in their spur petals. Not satisfied, he:

> looked at them after hot sunshine, after rain, and at all hours: I kept the spikes in water, and examined them at midnight, and early the next morning: I irritated the nectaries with a bristle, and exposed them to irritating vapours . . . but the nectary was invariably quite dry.

By comparison with these dry spotted orchids, there were other species, such as the butterfly orchid (*Plantanthera chlorantha*, see Figure 8.9) and the sweet-scented or fragrant orchid (*Gymnadenia conopsea*), which had spurs always half full of nectar. There was another apparently inconsequential difference between the two groups which Darwin noticed: the dry orchids had a large gap between the inner and outer skin of the petal spur whereas the nectar orchids had no such space. Also it was easy to penetrate this slack inner membrane. The ability of moths and other insects in this direction was largely unknown but Darwin suspected that they were puncturing the inner skin and sucking the copious fluid between the two petal layers. Why should a flower create such a diversionary challenge for its pollinators? In effect insects were being forced to take longer to feed from the spotted orchid than from the butterfly orchid – why?

In order to see the relevance of such detail in a delicately controlled sequence, it is necessary to look first at the structures above the nectary, at the centre of the orchid, which turns out to be 'more like a conjuror's box' as Arabella Buckley described it. Nowhere is there any resemblance to the anthers and filaments, stigma, style and ovary, and so on, of the orthodox flowers so far described. The fundamental framework of all orchids consists of unrecognisable remnants of all of them, rearranged, exaggerated and adapted to carry out the most sophisticated mechanisms in the flower world – there are triggers, insect slides, trapdoors and mazes. At the centre of an orchid, sheltered under the arch of petals, are two club-shaped bodies containing the pollen grains (see Figure 8.10). Orchids are unique in that they do not shed pollen as a fine powder to catch among insect hairs. Instead they force the insects to transport the entire pollen-making equipment (somewhat resembling a lollipop), from one flower to another. These *pollinia* are

stuck to the insect's long tongue or the top of its head as it reaches to drink nectar. As the insect withdraws the *pollinia* are wrenched from their anchorage within the flower and the insects fly off with their antennae-like attachments 'projecting up like horns'.

Darwin was fascinated by the extraordinary mechanisms by which the insects release the plant's fast-setting glue from its sac at the entrance of the nectary and by the way the *pollinia* became attached ready for transit. Firstly the insect alights on the large lower petal, the lip, which is spotted in the spotted orchid, long and trailing down like a butterfly's body in the butterfly orchid and resembling the torso and limbs in the man orchid (*Aceras anthropophorum*, see Figure 8.12). It then pushes its head into the mouth of the flower to reach the tip of the nectary; Darwin used 'a sharply-pointed common pencil' as a demonstration (see Figure 8.11): he found that 'owing to the [sac of glue] projecting into the gangway of the nectary, it is scarcely possible that any object can be pushed into it without the . . . [sac] being touched'. When touched, the skin of the sac ruptures along predetermined lines like a lid. In modern parlance the packaging of the glue pads or balls splits along perforated lines, rather like a packet of biscuits. 'So viscid are these balls that whatever they touch they firmly stick to. Moreover the viscid matter has the peculiar chemical quality of setting, like a cement, hard and dry in a few minutes' time.' (This orchid precursor of a modern rapid-setting glue works on exposure to air, hence the need for the glue balls to be enclosed in a sac of fluid until such time as required.) The firmness of the cement attachment is vital to the success of fertilisation which depends on the *pollinia* not falling sideways. Also, insects have frequently been seen to try and scrape off the floral attachments.

Now comes the relevance of some species demanding that insects linger and take their time at the nectar feast, puncturing several points in the double skin of the petal in order to reach the enclosed nectar. Darwin found on looking back through his notes that there was a tiny consistent difference between the five orchids with nectar easily available and the species with it hidden in the petal skin. Orchids with easy nectar had a different type of glue: it was exposed to the air and was already sticky. To make sure of the glue's properties, he removed the glue balls of

**Figure 8.9** The butterfly orchid (*Platanthera chlorantha*). 'The remarkable length of the nectary [shown best on the second bud on the right of this spike] containing much free nectar, the white colour of the conspicuous flowers, and the strong sweet odour emitted by them at night, all show that this plant depends for its fertilisation on the larger nocturnal moths.' (Darwin, 1877) (Photograph taken in Hampshire: June)

149

**Figure 8.10** A spotted orchid hybrid – *Dactylorhiza* species, most probably *D. fuchsii* (common spotted) × *D. praetermissa* (fen orchid or southern marsh orchid).

(Photograph taken in the water meadows of the River Meon, Hampshire: June)

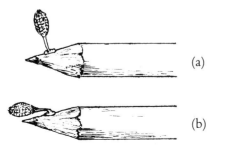

(a)

(b)

**Figure 8.11** 'If you will . . . put a pencil down the tube to represent the head of the bee, you may see the little box open, and two pollen masses cling to the pencil [a]. Then if you draw it out you may see them gradually bend forwards [b], and by thrusting your pencil into the next flower you may see the grains of pollen break away, and you will have followed out the work' of the insect. (Arabella Buckley) (Drawing after Darwin's from *On the Various Contrivances by which British and Foreign Orchids are Fertilised by Insects*)

**Figure 8.12** The man orchid (*Aceras anthropophorum*), was given its name because of a fanciful resemblance of its lip petal to a human figure. (Photograph: Hampshire, June)

the *pollinia* stuck fast to them at the slightest touch. On the other hand, orchids with hidden nectar, like the spotted, had glue which stuck hard only when exposed to air, thus needing total protection in a pouch until needed, and, once released, involving some delay in the hardening process. For these orchids, delaying insects via the difficulty of access to the nectar would have the advantage of allowing the glue to set the *pollinia* firmly in place before the insect moved to another flower.

If accidental, Darwin surmised: 'it is a fortunate accident for the plants. If not accidental, and I cannot believe it to be accidental, what a singular case of adaption!' As Darwin pointed out, such cases 'afford a good lesson of caution with respect to the importance, in other organic beings, of apparently trifling particulars of structure.' He wrote:

> Now let us suppose our insect to fly to another flower, or insert the pencil [see Figure 8.11a], with . . . [its attachments] into another nectary . . . it will be evident that the firmly attached pollinium will be simply pushed against or into its old position . . . How then can the flower be fertilised? This is effected by a beautiful contrivance: though the viscid surface remains immovably affixed, the apparently insignificant and minute disc . . . [at the base of the pollinium] is endowed with a remarkable power of contraction . . . which causes the . . . [whole] to sweep through about 90 degrees . . . in the course, on an average of thirty seconds. . .'

Thus realigned (see Figure 8.11b), the *pollinia* will now strike the female surface of the next flower to be visited by the insect.

Darwin marvelled at these movements – he had never seen anything so beautiful: 'I have shown this little experiment to several persons, and all have expressed the liveliest admiration at the perfection of the contrivance by which this Orchid is fertilised.'

Arabella Buckley, author of *The Fairy-land of Science*, was delighted, for: 'Do not such wonderful contrivances as these make us long to know and understand all the hidden work that is going on around us among the flowers, the insects, and all forms of life?'

Darwin noted every insect he saw which had the encumbrances of *pollinia* stuck to it like strange stiff antennae. One bee bore aloft on its

the butterfly orchid (so exposing surfaces usually covered), but still found the glue to be sticky and ready for instant use after more than 24 hours. Most important of all, this type of glue stuck on impact. There was no advantage to be had in delaying insects visiting the butterfly orchid for

head 16 *pollinia*, while a moth had eleven pairs –
its tongue presenting 'an extraordinary arbores-
cent appearance'. Thus encumbered, the 'unfortunate' moth could hardly have reached the
full depth of the nectary, 'and would soon have
been starved to death'. Such a sight is a rarity
today: a keen flower or insect watcher is fortunate to see a pollinator laden with even one *pollinia*
pair, and in order to carry out the pencil
experiment one must first find an orchid site –
which is not so easy as it was in Darwin's time.
From seed, an orchid plant takes many years to
mature and even in old-established colonies
where their very exacting light and soil requirements are met, flowering is notoriously unpredictable from one year to the next.

*Tropical Extravaganzas.* The nectar arrangements
of the exotic tropical orchids arriving in British
greenhouses and conservatories presented even
more bizarre pollination mechanisms. One of
these was the Madagascan orchid, *Angraecum
sesquipedale*; the first British flowering of this
breathtaking plant was described and illustrated
in the *Gardener's Chronicle*. It was famous as the
flower for which Darwin forecast the discovery
of a moth (and its dimensions) capable of
carrying out pollination. It had the same heady,
penetrating scent as the madonna lily, with
flowers sometimes as long as the plant, which is
two feet high (see Figure 8.13). To see
Madagascan forest with 'trunks of trees loaded
with this prince of Orchideous flowers' as they
were in the 1850s must have been a breathtaking
experience. Darwin likened the seven-inch (18-
cm) diameter flowers to 'stars formed of snow-
white wax . . . a green, whip-like nectary of
astonishing length hangs down beneath . . . In
several flowers sent me by Mr. Bateman I found
the nectaries eleven and a half inches long, with
only the lower inch and a half filled with nectar.
[*Curtis's Botanical Magazine* of 1859 quoted a spur
a foot long.] What can be the use, it may be
asked, of a nectary of such disproportionate
length?' Darwin admitted that it was 'surprising'
that any insect could possibly reach the nectar,
but, he argued, in the forests of Madagascar there
must be moths with tongues capable of extending to between ten and eleven inches. Entomolo-
gists greeted the idea of such a moth even
existing with ridicule, but by the second edition
of Darwin's book on orchids in 1877 an insect of
similar dimensions had been discovered by Fritz

**Figure 8.13** The Madagascan orchid, *Angraecum
sesquipedale*: an exotic orchid with an immensely long
nectary spur. Darwin predicted the dimensions of its
pollinator several years before any such insect was
discovered.

Müller in South Brazil. The tongue of a dried specimen was between ten and eleven inches long and when not in use coiled 'into a spiral of at least twenty windings'. This sphinx-moth was later found to have a Madagascan counterpart – *Xanthopon morgani praedicta* – and its tongue was exactly the right length for the orchid's nectary.

How was Darwin so sure that the tongue would extend to between ten and eleven inches when the first ten inches of the nectary was empty, with nectar only in the inch and a half below? A moth with a tongue the same length as the nectary, or longer, would seem to be a safer prediction. Darwin never used guesswork – he used only investigation and method, and his reasoning is best conveyed in his own words:

I could not for some time understand how the pollinia of this Orchid were removed . . . I passed bristles and needles down the open entrance into the nectary . . . with no result. It then occurred to me that, from the length of the nectary, the flower must be visited by large moths, with a proboscis thick at the base; and that to drain the last drop of nectar, even the largest moth would have to force its proboscis as far down as possible . . . The distance from the outside of the flower to the extremity of the nectary can be thus shortened by about a quarter of an inch. I therefore took a cylindrical rod one-tenth of an inch in diameter, and pushed it down. . . By this means I succeeded every time in withdrawing the pollinia; and it cannot, I think, be doubted that a large moth would thus act; that is, it would drive its proboscis up to the very base . . . so as to reach the extremity of the nectary; and then the pollinia attached to the base of its proboscis would be safely withdrawn. If the Angræcum in its native forests secretes more nectar than did the vigorous plants sent me by Mr. Bateman, so that the nectary ever becomes filled, small moths might obtain their share, but they would not benefit the plant. The pollinia would not be withdrawn until some huge moth, with a wonderfully long proboscis, tried to drain the last drop.

In all Darwin examined fifty tropical genera, sent to him by prominent collectors such as James Bateman, Kew, John Lindley, nurserymen such as the firm of Veitch and the famous explorer Sir Robert Schomburgk (who described

the royal water-lily on the Amazon). These exquisite rarities from the illustrious, the glamorous and the great were not housed in a sumptuous conservatory jungle but in a rather ordinary, small glass lean-to greenhouse behind the kitchen at Down House, Downe in Kent. Here one rather hideous tropical species exploded its *pollinia* with such force that they were ejected into the air and one was liable to be shot in the face. The hazard of losing observations through tropical flowers being 'let off' accidentally by unofficial Kentish insect intruders, was a real and frustrating one. He looked at the beautiful 'flying' swan orchid (*Cycnoches ventricosum*, see Figure 8.14), whose trigger turned out to be an apparently insignificant filament – although having solved that there was the question of its ability to then set seed, as it seemed possible that it had male, female and hermaphrodite forms of the same species. This popular orchid was frequently illustrated, but probably its most unusual portrait was in a delightful cartoon featured in James Bateman's *Orchidaceae of Mexico and Guatemala*.

### Plants 'furnished with a brain'

*Moving Plants.* Darwin's interest was not limited to the structure of flowers, although their aesthetic aspect delighted him. Botany for him was fathoming the workings of the whole living plant in its surroundings. He investigated the value of the climbing habit, discovering such intricacies as the time taken for hops to make a complete revolution in hot weather and the maximum diameter support a twining plant would attempt (thus avoiding climbing into shade). By ingenious experiments he showed how the climber's bending was related to light and hormones and from his study grew today's science of plant growth hormones. He was fascinated by plant movements of all sorts – shoots growing and seeds germinating. His apparatus was very much 'string and sealing-wax'. He and his son kept watch for sixty hours while the tiny root of a cabbage seedling grew from 0.05 to 0.11 of an inch, trailing a tiny bead attached to its tip in a zigzag course across a sheet of smoke-blackened glass.

Darwin's particular interest was the sleep of plants where leaflets fold together and hang down. The wood sorrel (*Oxalis acetosella*) is a familiar example. The similar nightly folding of

**Figure 8.14** The 'tail-piece' of James Bateman's *Orchidaceae of Mexico and Guatemala* contributed by Lady Grey of Groby: 'a most ingenious device, compounded of divers Orchidaceous flowers, which, with very gentle violence', were induced to create the scene. 'The hag came forth, broom and all, from a flower of *Cypripedium insigna* . . . two specimens of *Cycnoches* sail majestically on the globe below.' Other capering orchids included species of *Brassia, Oncidium* and *Epidendrum*. (Darwin investigated them all except *Megaclinium*.) (By permission of Cambridge University Library)

the leaflets of the acacias lay at the heart of their nineteenth-century appeal (so eloquently described by John Lindley, see page 104). The sensitive plant (*Mimosa pudica*, see Figure 8.15) was the most captivating of all for as well as sleeping at night, the leaflets folded and the whole leaf hung down within a few seconds, if the plant was handled or shaken. The delicate appearance and behaviour of the various *Mimosa* species, popularly called the sensitive plants, endeared them to modest moralisers like Rebecca Hey who quoted from the botanical verses of Charles Darwin's grandfather, Erasmus Darwin in *The Botanic Garden*:

Weak with nice sense, the chaste MIMOSA stands,
From each rude touch withdraws her timid hands;
Oft as light clouds o'er pass the summer-glade,
Alarm'd she trembles at the moving shade;
And feels, alive through all her tender form,
The whisper'd murmers of the gathering storm;
Shuts her sweet eye-lids to approaching night,
And hails with freshen'd charms the rising light.

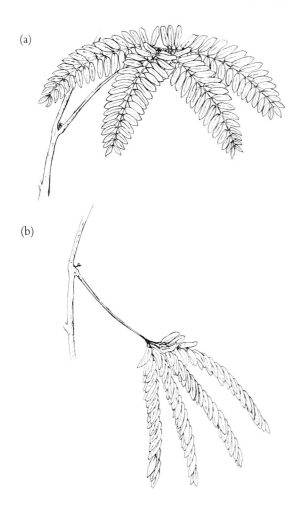

(a)

(b)

**Figure 8.15**(a) *Mimosa pudica*, the sensitive plant.

And it opened its fan-like leaves to the light,
And closed them beneath the kisses of Night.

But none ever trembled and panted with bliss
In the garden, the field, or the wilderness,
Like doe in the noontide with love's sweet want,
As the companionless Sensitive Plant.

(Shelley)

(b) Leaves of the sensitive plant in the sleeping or shocked position. Leaflets fold closely one upon the other: 'the whole leaf is thus rendered very compact'. (Darwin)

Charles Darwin's delight in the same withdrawing movement manifested itself in a bizarre manner: in one of what he called his fool's experiments, his son Francis played the bassoon close to the sensitive leaves. However, his extensive studies and measurements on *The Power of Movements in Plants* (published in 1880) were far from foolish although their concept was unorthodox.

Darwin checked on the genera in Linnaeus's list of sleeping plants which included *Malva* (mallows), *Hibiscus*, *Oenethera* (evening primroses), and *Impatiens*. He investigated 86 genera in all; among them were *Gossypium* (cottons), *Mimosa*, *Acacia*, *Robinia*, *Passiflora* (passionflower), *Nicotiana* (tobaccos), *Euphorbia* (spurges) and *Siegesbeckia*. He made many important and unexpected discoveries, such as a plant's need for a sufficient amount of light during the day. One of the experimental subjects was *Abutilon darwinii* (see Plate 13), and as in so many of his researches the idea and situation of the investigation were homely. Some 'very fine' abutilon plants were growing in his hall in which the only light was daylight through a glass cupola in the ceiling. He noticed that these plants never slept, whereas the leaves of other very young plants 'stood almost horizontally during the day, and hung vertically at night'. In order to sleep at night, leaves had to be fully illuminated by day: accordingly he exposed the plants from the hall to full daylight outside the house after which they 'slept soundly' all night.

The circumstances surrounding this particular plant illustrated the closeness of the Victorian 'botanical family', created by the shared passion for plants. *Abutilon darwinii* had been discovered in Brazil about forty years previously by a Scottish landscape gardener, John Tweedie, for whom Darwin was a hero. Seeds were sent to Darwin from Brazil by Fritz Müller, brother of Hermann (who had discovered and described many pollination mechanisms (see page 145), including the self-sterility of abutilons and their fertilisation by humming birds). Fritz was a frequent correspondent of Darwin's, assisting over the controversial long-tongued moth needed by *Angraecum sesquipedale* (see Figure 8.13), and constantly supplying him with exotic seeds. The flowering specimen illustrated (see Plate 13) was a piece of Darwin's magnificent pot plant which he sent to Sir Joseph Dalton Hooker at Kew in April 1871: Walter Hood Fitch's glowing portrait of it appeared four months later in *Curtis's Botanical Magazine*. The chatty character of Hooker's accompanying notes on the abutilon's location even included reference to

Tweedie's writing and spelling, which were 'equally bad'.

The most spectacular plant movements of all occurred in the carnivorous plants, such as the Venus' fly-trap (*Dionaea muscipula*, see Figure 8.16) from North America and the wild sundew (*Drosera rotundifolia*, Figure 8.17). The whys and wherefores of plants like the Venus' fly-trap were a subject of interest far beyond the confines of the studies of the learned, for they were the centre of attraction in front parlours, conservatories and greenhouses in every suburb. Introducing them to lady botanists, John Lindley recommended that if his readers were not already acquainted with it, they should 'search for it immediately in the nurseries' and secure 'one of the most curious examples of irritability which the vegetable world contains; and which, in some respects, is more striking than even the sensitive plants themselves, for they merely shrink away from the touch, while this plant firmly grasps, with its wonderful leaves, anything that comes within their reach'. He pointed out the 'three delicate almost invisible bristles, uniformly arranged in a triangle' which if touched triggered the collapse of the leaf like 'an iron rabbit-trap when it has closed on its prey'. The boundaries of natural theology limited further enquiry:

**Figure 8.16** The horrific Venus' fly-trap (*Dionaea muscipula*) from America – an insect is being trapped by leaf 'c'. (From *Ladies' Botany* by John Lindley)

**Figure 8.17** The sundew (*Drosera rotundifolia*). Darwin called it 'my beloved Drosera'.

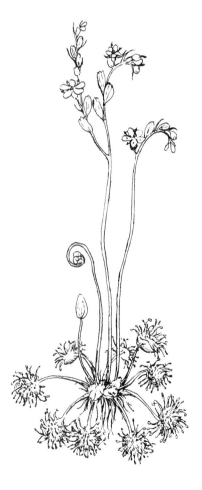

Why it is, or by virtue of what power, the bristles possess the key to the irritability of the *Dionæa* leaf, no one has ever succeeded in discovering. The phenomenon seems to belong to the extensive class of final causes which man is not permitted to explain.

As with moving and sleeping plants, the insect-eating species also extended a shared fascination and challenge of understanding across the generations of the Darwin family. Erasmus failed to notice the acid digestive fluids poured over insects caught up in the Venus' fly-trap and assumed, like his contemporaries, that they were pierced or crushed to death. Without much experiment, he leapt into realms of heady speculation that the 'various motions of peculiar parts of vegetables evince the existence of muscles and nerves in those parts'. He envisaged plants with the sense of:

> taste . . . at the extremities of their roots . . . for the purpose of selecting their proper food . . . To these must be added the indubitable evidence of their passion of love, and of their necessity to sleep; and I think we may truly conclude, that they are furnished with a brain or common sensorium belonging to each bud.

Not surprisingly he interpreted the insect-eating habit as a sophisticated example of plant armament against marauding insects bent on stealing flower nectar – a speculation compatible with his erroneous ideas on the interrelationship of insects and flowers and pollination (see page 140). The concept of the plant actually consuming insect protein evaded him. Charles was critical of his grandfather's 'overpowering tendency to theorise and generalise' regardless of a glaring lack of factual evidence. Seeking 'final causes' which defied easy explanation was his *métier* and he embarked on a detailed and fascinating inquiry into the workings of these unorthodox plants. This was triggered by a chance encounter with the common sundew.

*The Carnivorous Sundew.* Like the Venus' fly-trap, these 'most curious little plants in the world' were recommended for the suburban Wardian case and for the ladies' magnifying glasses by John Lindley in *Ladies' Botany*. He magically transformed the death-dealing tentacles of the sundew's leaf (see Figure 8.18).

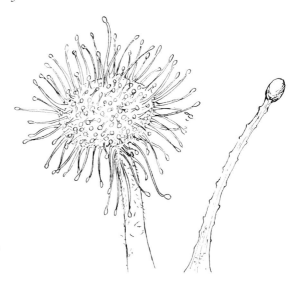

**Figure 8.18** A sundew leaf ready to clasp insects. Detail of one tentacle.

what seemed a little hair with a drop of water at its point, is really a long curved horn, transparent and glittering like glass; delicately studded from top to bottom with sparkling points; beautifully stained with bright green passing into pink, and mellowing into a pale yellow, as if emeralds, rubies, and topazes had been melted, and just run together without mixing; and finally tipped with a large polished oval carbuncle, or ruby of the deepest die [sic] . . . In this there is no exaggeration; for what tints can possibly represent the brilliancy of vegetable colours, except those of the purest and noblest of precious stones?

Erasmus Darwin's descriptive verse in *The Botanic Garden* went even further into the realms of fancy:

> A zone of diamonds trembles round her
>     brows;
> Bright shines the silver halo, as she turns;
> And, as she steps, the living lustre burns.

His lines were quoted incessantly in Victorian books, making the sundew 'rather seem to be a fairy than a plant'. In order to share such delight first-hand readers 'anxious to make acquaintance with *Drosera*' were warned by John Lindley that they had to face the realities of the places of wilderness, for 'her home is the fen and the marsh, the oozy heath and the treacherous morass'. Charles Darwin shared his grandfather's fascination for sundews, but his first encounter with the sundew was tame by comparison. He described it in *Insectivorous Plants*:

> During the summer of 1860, I was surprised by finding how large a number of insects were caught by the leaves of the common sun-dew (Drosera rotundifolia) on a heath in Sussex. I had heard that insects were thus caught, but knew nothing further on the subject. I gathered by chance a dozen plants . . . On one plant all six leaves had caught their prey . . . On one large leaf I found the remains of thirteen distinct insects . . . As this plant is extremely common in some districts, the number of insects thus annually slaughtered must be prodigious. Many plants cause the death of insects, for instance the sticky buds of the horse-chestnut . . . without thereby receiving, as far as we can perceive, any advantage; but it was soon evident that Drosera was excellently adapted for the special purpose of catching insects, so that the subject seemed well worthy of investigation.

Darwin began by timing how long it took for all the tentacles to clasp the insect. It was 'one hour to four or five or more hours . . . An insect, such as a fly, with thin integuments . . . is more efficient in causing prolonged inflection than an insect with a thick coat, such as a beetle', the thinner skin allowing ready passage of animal matter in solution. The largest insect Darwin noted enmeshed by the sundew's tentacles was a small butterfly (although dragonflies have been seen). The most frequent were flies. Darwin, with his increasing regard for living animals, did not apparently share the fashionable predilection for watching the plants do this, and not for the first time admitted to interfering with life's struggle for survival: he rescued a minute gnat which, much to his surprise, had triggered the tentacles with 'its excessively delicate feet'.

Fascinated by the smallness of items stimulating the leaf into action, Darwin had placed 'two particles of the thinner end of a woman's hair, one of these being 18/1,000 of an inch in length', on two glands on opposite sides of the same leaf. In spite of their minuteness, these had bent halfway towards the leaf's centre in just over an

hour, without any other tentacles moving. He wrote 'My surprise was greatly excited . . .' He looked at all types of touch stimuli, from a small camel-hair brush to particles of meat, milk, hard-boiled egg, dead flies, dried moss, sponge, cinders, glass, wood and pieces of paper.

The practicalities of Darwin's experiments were often delightfully homely:

> My experiments were begun in June 1867, when the plants were collected and planted in six ordinary soup-plates. Each plate was divided by a low partition into two sets, and the *least* flourishing half of each culture was selected to be 'fed', while the rest of the plants were destined to be 'starved'. The plants were prevented from catching insects for themselves by means of a covering of fine gauze, so that the only animal food which they obtained was supplied in very minute pieces of roast meat given to the 'fed' plants. [(With Darwin's relations in mind, it is an endearing thought that the plates in question were possibly choice Wedgwood!)]

After ten days the 'fed' plants were 'brighter green and the tentacles of a more lively red'. Two months later, Darwin found that the 'fed' plants had more flower stems, seed capsules and seed than the 'starved' plants and also their non-flowering parts weighed more. With offspring numbers and species survival in mind, he wrote: 'It is of interest to note that the most striking difference between the two sets of plants is seen in what relates to reproduction – *i.e.* in the flower-stems, the capsules, and the seeds.' He continued his comparison throughout the winter. He cut off the flower stems and allowed the plants to rest without food until early April, 'in order to test (by a comparison of spring-growth) the amounts of reserve material accumulated during the summer'. He found the fed plants were double the weight of the starved ones which proved 'that the fed plants had laid by a far greater store of reserve material in spite of having produced nearly four times as much seed'.

Having shown that the plants used their insect prey so effectively Darwin set himself a detective hunt to find what, besides touch, actually caused the leaf tentacles to act. Darwin found that the sundew's 'awareness' of the chemical constituent of its contrived prey was impressive. As an alternative to offering his plants roast meat, he made 'decoctions of some vegetables known to be rich in nitrogen . . . and these acted like animal fluids'. They included green peas and 'the pale dirty green fluid' from chopped cabbage leaves for which the sundew had as strong a liking as it did for 'a cold, filtered infusion of raw meat'. An even more unexpected tempter on his menu was the connoisseur's delight of bird's-nest soup! He actually had good reason for such extravagant eccentricity as:

> The edible nest of the Chinese swallow is formed of matter secreted by the salivary glands . . . The usual-sized drops [which he carefully practised and measured] were placed on three leaves, and these in 1hr. 30m. were well . . . inflected.

Human saliva also provoked the tentacles and he came to use his own as a sort of fitness test on his plants.

Some people thought that the plants could almost smell the presence of potential food, including human fingers, without having been touched by it. Darwin soon dispelled such vagueness. He sterilised various items (handling them with sterilised instruments), placed them on the glands of several leaves and found the response was exactly the same as for well-handled particles.

> I breathed on some leaves for above a minute, and repeated the act two or three times with my mouth close to them, but this produced no effect . . . pieces of raw meat stuck on needles were fixed as close as possible, without actual contact, to several leaves, but produced no effect whatsoever.

Darwin's careful comparisons to differentiate between fact and fiction beautifully illustrate the idea of controlled conditions. These exclude interference from outside factors and discard the assumptions and vagueness of isolated anecdotes lacking adequate comparisons (which all too often enter into some theories about plant sensitivity and behaviour, even today).

Darwin next looked at the sundew's digestive powers. The leaves as it were salivated over their food: droplets of secretion on the tentacles increased even before they touched the meat. These 'pellucid drops', so 'resembling an earl's coronet', as his grandfather described them,

'completely dissolved albumen, muscle, cartilage, gelatine'. Darwin wrote: 'I have observed the same leaf with tentacles closely inflected over rather indigestible substances . . . pouring forth acid secretion over bits of bone for ten successive days.' Indigestion, it seemed, was also part of the plant's extraordinary repertoire: 'Raw meat, unless in very small bits, and large pieces of albumen . . . injure the leaves, which seem to suffer, like animals, from a surfeit.' The sundew could on occasion switch to a vegetarian diet: Darwin observed them to absorb matter from pollen and fresh leaves. He marvelled at the 'new and wonderful fact in physiology . . . That a plant and an animal should pour forth the same, or nearly the same, complex secretion, adapted for the same purpose of digestion.' Equally staggering were the movements and behaviour of protoplasm inside the tentacle which he observed under his microscope. When the tentacles were stimulated, slowly structures became organised and visible within, like 'muscles' (foreshadowing the array of cell organelles (see Figure 8.4) carrying out different functions revealed by modern microscopy).

The accordance between plant-eating habits and animal-eating habits was indeed amazing. In a wild moment one could imagine the plants as sentient beings, ascribing sundew tentacle movement and even simple petal expansion in the presence of evening moisture (as in the case of catchfly flowers) to cogniscent vegetable strategy. Any isolated contortion of bending growth immediately becomes a matter of meaning and the possibilities are not only endless, but deliciously improbable. As has been seen Darwin's grandfather, a master of extrapolating speculations to their utmost, imbued plants with nerves, muscles and brains, and inevitably with the passion of love.

Charles Darwin, by contrast, had his feet firmly on the ground: for him the process by which all the insect-eating species could have gradually attained 'these remarkable powers' was fascinating enough. He checked the effects of many nerve-paralysing poisons such as morphia, cobra poison, strychnine, and throughout his experiments looked at the activity of the living contents of sundew tentacles. He studied and compared other insectivorous plants and also randomly chosen plants with hairs and glands on their stems and leaves, such as saxifrages (remotely related to the sundew family), marvel of Peru (*Mirabilis longiflora*), tobacco (*Nicotiana tabacum*), pelargoniums and *Primula sinensis* (his son, Francis, counted 35,336 glandular hairs per square inch on the upper leaf surface of this plant, and 30,035 on the lower). The latter two species and the saxifrages showed some signs of the power of absorption. He pointed out the frequent appearance of movement in leaves, flower stalks, tendrils, 'explosive' stamens and so on, and made many comments relating to possibilities, or not, of vegetable brains. One of Darwin's fellow enthusiasts used a galvanometer and showed the existence of an electric current.

Sundews and their kin did have some unexpected animal attributes. They fed like animals, with comparable digestive fluids, and they had the facility of contraction. What was their status? Disappointingly for the romantics, Darwin on many counts delegated the plants as:

inferior even to animals low down in the scale . . . But the greatest inferiority of all is the absence of a central organ, able to receive impressions from all points, to transmit their effects in any definite direction, to store them up and reproduce them.

## Chapter 9
# SCIENTIFIC CONTROVERSY

### 'Design for the Convenience' of Man

*Watering the Weary Traveller*

Before the evolutionary controversy most Victorians, whether of botanical inclination or not, were brought up and convinced in the belief that plants were created for the convenience of man. Plants that were useful were 'good' and natural theology's concept of Design in a man-centred world required that every one, even the macabre insect-catching pitcher plants, offered some benefit. Accordingly some natural history books described 'the benevolent provision of these vegetable fountains for the refreshment of the thirsty traveller in tropical regions'. The aptly named pitcher plants were first discovered in the swampy jungles of the Far East in 1789 and there followed tales of wild animals, particularly monkeys, using this unusual source of water, ready and inviting in conveniently lidded pitchers.

In 1828, the contents of *Nepenthes distillatoria* were described in *Curtis's Botanical Magazine*: when the pitchers were pressed they yielded so much 'sweet, limpid, refreshing liquor' that the contents of half a dozen could quench a man's thirst. This species (see Figure 9.1) was the first to enter the hothouse of the wealthy, remaining for a long time the only one in cultivation – much to the impatience of fanciers who feasted on tales from collectors such as Alfred Russel Wallace who described 'wonderful' and 'elegant' species in Borneo in the 1850s. Popular demand merited the nurseryman Veitch sending a special collector to Borneo on a year's quest in the 1870s

and for special hothouses to be designed for their needs.

By the 1870s the purpose of pitcher plants was less clouded by thoughts of man's benefit and they were realistically described as 'a great provision of nature for decoying and for the destruction of insects', and more vividly: '[insects accumulate] in a seething, filthy, half-dead, half-living mass, within the interior of this diabolically contrived trap – a mere manure heap for the benefit of the plant'. The insects, mostly of the small crawling and clumsy (cockroach) type, are attracted by nectar secreted inside the curved edge of the pitcher, and below is the waxy slippery fall to destruction (so delightfully described by Shirley Hibberd: see page 62). Inside are the digestive juices and accumulated rain water. The specimen illustrated (see Figure 9.1) was described by Sir William Jackson Hooker as having 'rather more than a drachm [$\frac{1}{8}$ fl. oz.] of limpid fluid' before the opening of the lid. The liquid had a 'subacid taste' and on boiling it emitted 'an odour like baked apples'. Modern observers liken the contents to an objectionably odorous soup and describe the pitcher's drink as rather salty: the nature of the beverage probably depends largely on one's choice of pitcher.

Thirsty travellers in Madagascar had a choice of plant reservoirs from which to drink. As well as pitcher plants there was the traveller's tree or palm. The massive leaves of the palm somewhat resemble those of the banana, to which it is related. They stand aloft on a tall stem, splayed out flat just like a feather fan – in fact, the tree could almost be one of the fans traditionally

**Figure 9.1** The pitcher plant (*Nepenthes distillatoria*). High up the stem of the plant the leaves grow long 'and taper into a tendril at the point, from which is suspended a long funnel-shaped, green cup, often as large as a three ounce vial, covered by a lid, and sometimes containing water'. (From *Ladies' Botany* by John Lindley) (Illustration from *Curtis's Botanical Magazine*, 1828: by permission of Avon County Library (Bath Reference Library))

wafting slowly behind the oriental potentate in a story-book. The large hollow stalks of the leaves are packed symmetrically one on another at the 'fan's' base, making receptacles in which rain water collects. Each can store a quart of water – sure proof of the tree's supposed Design with man in mind.

Most convenient of all was the drink which was easily transportable – the orange. According to Charlotte Yonge 'our Father's gracious Providence' had created 'such as can be spread over the whole earth'. Inside the orange the juice was distributed throughout the pulp in 'very small bags, or bottles' for a good reason:

with the orange, its juice, if it was all together, would soon be spoilt by the heat, but in these separate bottles it is safely secured, a little in one and a little in the other, and kept good till we want it . . . proof of the wisdom of the Hand that made the orange, such that it may be carried long distances, and brought to be the refreshment of thirsty lips, so many miles from the sun that ripens it . . . Another arrangement, to fit the orange for travelling long distances, is the oil in the little dots in the peel, which keeps it fresh, though separated from the tree, as well as the thick, strong, yellow coat, lined with white, so much less tender than the covering of apples, pears, plums, or such fruits as are eaten on the spot.

The orange, seen through the eyes of Charlotte M. Yonge in 1853, had one last trump card for the traditionalists: 'but does it not show that oranges were made for our especial benefit, that there should be so many without pips, so as to be of no use at all, excepting for food?' Faced with such delightfully devious interpretations, it is almost a disappointment to consider the mundane alternatives of wild fruits and seed dispersal by animals and the changes produced during a long history of cultivation by artificial selection and breeding.

*Uses of Plants*

The orange could also be regarded as food and, as William Paley reminded his readers, such fruits 'with little aid of art, yield our chief luxuries'. Most Victorians listed the delicacies on nature's menu before the essentials. A typical list comprised two hundred species 'variously used for food' – which is pitifully low compared to the total of 2,897 listed by the American Dr E. Lewis Sturtevant, in 1892. The discrepancy reflects the scrupulous exclusion of uncivilised foods, eaten by uncivilised peoples who lacked the discerning palate of the Victorian gentleman: 'The New Sealander [sic] and Tasmanian derive some sustenance from the subterranean stems of a fern . . . and the natives of Northern Europe sometimes use the ground bark of a pine . . . to eke out their scanty meal.' (Dr M'Cosh, *Typical Forms and Special Ends in Creation.*) These foods were too sparse and too barbaric to be counted as part of the Design. They were just the kind of items which were noted by Sturtevant who listed the red petals of the hothouse exotic, the hibiscus (see Plate 12), as the basis of a kind of pickle in China and India. Devout Victorian followers of William Paley would not have countenanced such a possibility:

Whether from veneration of the lovely form which is destined to produce the fruit, or from finding it less adapted to the grosser purposes of life, mankind seems by common consent to abstain from applying the expanded flower to the purposes of food. The blossom of the nasturtium and the marigold are too rarely in use to be worth notice as exceptions.

(Paley was obviously blissfully unaware of the 'grosser purposes' served by the beautiful hibiscus flower which being extremely mucilaginous was used for polishing shoes in the West Indies, reflected in its alternative name of 'shoe flower'.)

The poorer classes of early nineteenth-century society used some unexpected plants for 'the grosser purposes of life'. The wild orchids, relatively unusual or rare today, were favourites of London's 'coalheavers, porters and other hard-working men' – not for the flowers, but the tubers, an ounce of which would apparently sustain a man for a day. Beech leaves were used for stuffing mattresses while soap was made from rolling bracken ash with clay in the Forest of Dean. An unexpected use of plant dyes (see Figure 9.2) was the purple colour upon playing cards, prepared from privet (*Ligustrum vulgare*) berries. Probably one of the most bizarre com-

**Figure 9.2** The traditional uses of plants still existed in the Victorian era. For example, some plants were used to make dyes: lichens, pasque flower (*Pulsatilla vulgaris*) for marbling eggs and privet berries. Yellow flag (*Iris pseudacorus*) was also used: the flowers producing yellow and the root giving black. (Photograph: Caithness, July)

ments on the exclusive right of man to plant usefulness was made in *Cassell's Household Guide* of 1875 concerning the use of moss to fill the spaces between the rafters of the suburban summer-house; it was:

a source of overpowering temptation to the birds, who look upon it as specially adapted to their own architectural requirements, and appropriate it in the most unscrupulous manner, much to the disadvantage of the human race to which it properly belongs.

### Plants for Healing

It was also a firm belief that one of the divinely appointed functions of plants was to provide against man's ills. The old Herbals were based on this premiss: plant details and instruction were seen as messages from God, in much the same manner as the morals conveyed by flowers (see Chapter 4). The influence of the Herbals was by no means dead by the nineteenth century: the products of centuries of practice, repetition and, more potently, philosophy and religious belief lingered, faded and then enjoyed a resurgence of interest in the 1890s. The traditional recognition of a herb's intended healing properties is explained by William Coles in *Adam in Eden, or The Paradise of Plants*, 1657: plants were 'stamped' with 'legible Characters' or specific signatures which held the message or clue to their intended use. For example, the 'bloody colour' of roots of bistort was the divine stamp recommending its use to stay bleeding, while 'the writhed or twisted form . . . of the Root, is a sign that [it] is good against the bitings of Serpents, or Snakes'.

Jaundice was frequently identified with yellow plants such as mouse ear, broom, gorse (*Ulex europaeus*), groundsel (*Senecio vulgaris*), the yellow berries of ivy (*Hedera helix*) and the yellow roots of a species of dock (*Rumex*). Nicholas Culpeper's instructions on these jaundice cures, dating from 1652, continued to be the popular guide to herbal medicine and his book, *The English Physician Enlarg'd*, was still published through the nineteenth century. His theory involved the judicious use of herbs under the same or opposite planets to that supposedly governing the disease. Mullein (*Verbascum thapsus*, see Figure 9.3) was under the dominion of Saturn, lesser celandine or pilewort (*Ranunculus ficaria*) was under Mars. He also subscribed to the old doctrine of signatures, as in the lesser celandine:

. . . behold here another verification of the learning of the ancients, viz. that the virtue of an herb may be known by its signature, as plainly appears in this; for if you dig up the root of it, you shall perceive the perfect image of the disease which they commonly call the piles.

In all, about ten editions and reprints of Culpeper's books, *The English Physician Enlarg'd*, *Complete Herbal*, and *London Dispensatory* appeared between 1802 and 1840. There was a lull until 1880, when there was once more a spate of books on the subject, such as *Herbal Simples* and *Golden Recipes for the use of all ages* by various authors.

Gradually the plant 'simples' (i.e. used as they occur naturally, not mixed with other substances) came under critical scrutiny and 'much rubbish' was cleared from the 'Augaean Stable'. With text books of *materia medica* now containing carefully selected herbs, 'all became clearness and precision'. Details of the plant's active properties, preparations of crude drugs which could be extracted and compounded from them, were gradually added and formed elaborate treatises such as Pereira's *Elements of Materia Medica*, 1839, which continued into later editions for many years. William Paley had called the attention of his readers to the blessing of 274 plants used in 'the modern practice of medicine' and many remain in today's pharmacopoeia lists. But as the foundations of natural theology came under attack from Darwin's theory half a century later, it was the intention behind the drugs from plants which became a matter of opinion – Divine Providence or evolutionary accident?

### Nature's Good Housekeeping

Last in the catalogue of plant usefulness the Victorians considered the natural balance between all living things, explained by George William Francis:

Plants, too, are of the highest importance in purifying the atmosphere, and in tempering the climate of the world; by the shelter they afford, the rain which they assist in producing, the moisture which evaporates from their

**Figure 9.3** Common mullein (*Verbascum thapsus*) with its 'many fair, large, woolly white leaves, lying next the ground . . . pointed at the end, as it were dented about the edges'. Nicholas Culpeper's first instructions (*The English Physician Enlarg'd* 1652) on the use of mullein leaves for treating cramp, warts, splinters and boils, and on the use of many more healing herbs were still being published during the nineteenth century. (Photograph: Hampshire, April)

leaves, the noxious gases which they absorb, and the purer ones which they give in return.

Even here, though, the plants were working away doing their bit for the benefit of man – as was explained by Arabella Buckley in *The Fairyland of Science*:

Think sometimes when you walk in the woods, how hard at work the little plants and big trees are, all around you. You breathe in the nice fresh oxygen they have been throwing out, and little think that it is they who are making the country so fresh and pleasant, and that while they look as if they were doing nothing but enjoying the bright sunshine, they are really fulfilling their part in the world by the help of this sunshine; earning their food from the gound . . . putting out their flowers and making their seeds, and all the while smiling so pleasantly in quiet nooks and sunny dells that it makes us glad to see them.

At the cellular level, the busy activity of 'active grains' moving about doing the plant's 'useful work in the world' could be seen under the microscope.

The interaction between living beings presented more tangible and immediate benefit for the practically minded. Blackbirds and thrushes existed to rid their shrubberies of snails, others 'inspected' orchard trees for destructive caterpillars and their eggs while those taking insects on the wing had been 'commissioned' to do so lest clouds of insects infested houses and destroyed the just rewards ready to be reaped from the fields. Birds gathering nest-building materials were considered to be keeping the environment tidy: 'beautifying' it by gathering up withered sticks and removing dry grass from fields in order that they might look greener. The plants themselves helped here by competing to produce the finest flowers. (Not to be outdone, birds migrated so that they could be enjoyed by people in distant lands in turn.) The many species of grasses had been created so that man could 'be in good hope a keeper of herds and a tiller of the ground'.

*Inconvenient Plants*

Inevitably there were plants which apparently provided nothing towards man's welfare or, worse still, actually seemed to have been created to positively detract from it. Why did a useless weed like a dandelion have such an elaborate and efficient mechanism of seed dispersal? The traditional reply was that the riddle surely served to underline man's ignorance, as the mere fact of its abundance was proof enough that it was required in the great scheme of things.

The existence of poisonous plants was a frequent bone of contention in the ideological battle: the traditionalists saw the existence of poisonous plants such as the nightshade family (see, for example, Plate 15), as a punishment to man from God. As has been seen their view was of a benign and beautiful world which had undergone a great change at the Fall of Man: poisons, thorns, prickles, weeds and difficulties of culivation then suddenly appeared as both punishment and as a reminder to Adam and his descendants. Charlotte M. Yonge's verdict on poisonous fungi reflected the other interpretation open to traditional thinkers: 'I do not think we have a right to call any of the works of the Creator nasty. I am sure we should not, if we once looked well into them.' In a world where 'civilised man' stood almost on a pinnacle of perfection above nature's chattels, the survival value of poisons and prickles against the effects of overgrazing (or poisons as an incidental by-product of a plant's living processes) was an anathema.

## The Controversy of Timescale – and its Casualties

One of the evolutionary controversies causing the most outraged reaction was that of timescale. The comfortable man-centred view of the creation had envisaged the appearance of each plant, fruit and flower as having been carefully synchronised to coincide with the finer faculties and skills of men through the ages and across the globe. Dr M'Cosh explains in 1856: 'There were . . . long preparations made . . . for the support of man, who appears when all is prepared for him.' The 'evidence' supporting this view was that ornamental flowers were thought to have appeared at the same time as man and:

as to the plants which clothed the earth before man was called into being, we cannot but remark the almost total absence of families whose products minister to his wants and comfort . . . no species yielding 'cinnamon, and odours, and frankincense, and wine, and oil, and fine flour and wheat' . . . Doubtless the earth formerly yielded Ferns, Firs, Cycases, and Palms . . . some of the human family can, by a troublesome process, extract nourishing matter from the stems or seeds of a Cycas . . . but how small a part, after all, of the millions of men in our world do the foresaid plants support, and that part is the least civilised and intellectual!

This cosy viewpoint of a creation timed for civilised man not only followed a predictable sequence of appearances but also a known timescale. This had been computed from the Old Testament by various people with staggering accuracy: in 1856 two calculations put the earth at 5,473 or 8,342 years old, and Victorian slavery to detail even went so far as to quote the date and time as 9 a.m. on Sunday 23 October. The most frequently quoted authority was Archbishop James Ussher who in 1650–4 had added together all the lifespans of the patriarchs quoted in the Bible and had arrived at 4004 BC, making the earth 5,860 years old in 1856 (see Figure 9.4). This was indicative of the limited horizon of the clerical world which was soon to be faced with Darwin's ideas of no special creation and species changing during millions of years. Both Carl Linnaeus and Count Buffon had suspected it was older, but Linnaeus had been steered by biblical

**Figure 9.4** Calling at the Cape Verde Islands on the Beagle voyage, Darwin was impressed by the baobab trees (*Adansonia digitata*), reputedly six thousand years old – about the same age as the earth was thought to be. One was drawn in his notes.

**Figure 9.5** A challenge to the old timescale – a tree trunk (about 150 million years old) turned to stone. Details of growth rings and medullary rays can still be seen. (Fossil found on the Isle of Portland, Dorset)

infallibility and Count Buffon was threatened with excommunication. By the time Darwin's theory became public the riddles and controversy of timescale were already afoot.

Over the centuries there had been many bewildering discoveries which had to be accommodated within the literal interpretation of the Old Testament. For instance, in 1677 Robert Plot was considering the significance of complete trees and strange human relics buried deep in the earth, and while touring the country between 1786 and 1791 the Rev. William Gilpin noted many petrified trees and roots deep beneath the peat of the Scottish Highlands and Cumberland. There were aged and petrified trees (see Figure 9.5) from very different worlds exposed in marshes, among dunes and old shore-lines, all of which presented the picture of lost forests and a changed landscape. The explanation was seen as relatively straightforward: here was evidence of Noah's Flood. These brief glimpses into the world before the Flood were occasional and gentle, exposed largely by natural weathering and domestic activities like peat cutting. By

contrast the canal and railway building of the Victorian age slashed and gouged its way deep into the secrets of the past on a scale which could only be described as immense: whole valleys and landscapes were basically changed. The scale of physical change makes an ironical comparison with the philosophical havoc which indirectly resulted from it – via the dramatic fossil evidences of the distant past which were unwittingly revealed. The earth was opened like Pandora's box and men repeatedly saw layers of different soils and rocks from the past with their encased fossilised remnants of plants and animals.

*Theories and Fossils*

The building of the great network of canals associated with the coalfields gave an unprecedented opportunity to William ('Strata') Smith, the Resident Engineer to the Somerset Coal Canal Company. A self-educated surveyor, he formulated the concept of geological strata, one upon another like 'slices of bread and butter', each with characteristic and identifiable fossils

**167**

**Figure 9.6** While working on a canal to carry coal from the Somerset coalfield around Radstock, William ('Strata') Smith made the discovery that strata had characteristic fossils. The canal was never linked to the main system and was mostly reworked for a railway, leaving only very few short lengths of Smith's cuttings of the 1790s – of which this is one. (The picture shows only the remaining top 20 feet (6 m) of Smith's exposed cliff with its sloping strata, the lower 40 feet (12 m) having been already obliterated by a rubble tip.) (Photograph: January, 1983: Dunkerton to Combe Hay by Peter Scourse)

(see Figure 9.6). His strata of different ages made it impossible to believe in only one great Biblical Flood. The year was 1796, but his disturbing discoveries and his historic geological maps were not made public and were not noticed until 1815. In 1814 and 1821 Mary Anning's famous first Ichthyosaurus and nearly complete Plesiosaurus appeared on the scene. Knowledge of these startling discoveries was not limited to the aristocrats and gentry who bought them. The discovery made ideal copy for Victorian news-papers with the necessary ingredients of senti-ment and morality – the little girl selling her fossils to support her widowed mother. Thus the drama of fossils and their inherent queries suddenly entered the lives of ordinary people who had never heard of William Smith or of the discussions concerning the earth's age and how its life had come to be as it was. The popular natural history books never mentioned such awkward topics.

The potential embarrassments of extinct plants and animals were 'satisfactorily' accommodated by the 'catastrophist' theory which gained wide popularity in the 1830s: there had been not one, but a sequence of catastrophes, such as floods, the most recent being Noah's which being the only one involving man was the only one about which he had been divinely informed. Sir Roderick Murchison (Director-General of the Geological Society who had visited Robert Dick) and many other eminent geologists subscribed to it with relief, followed by a growing number of ordinary Victorians drawn by wonder at the growing number of fossils and curiosity at the intense academic battle of words and ideas. The only problem was that the number of catastro-phes kept multiplying as more strata and fossils were found, and there was a rash of 'lost continents' bobbing up and down across the globe as well.

*A New Timescale and Changing Landscapes*

Between 1830 and 1833 plants, animals and man were dramatically placed in a more distant perspective of geological time and in a landscape which had changed and was still changing. In his *Principles of Geology*, Sir Charles Lyell presented evidence that the earth was changing, land was elevated by earthquakes, soils and rocks were being worn down by rain and waves. Robert Dick wrote: 'The sands are many, it is true, and the boulders and stones innumerable; but the sea, the million handed ocean, that rounded them in his palm, is vastly more extensive. The sea is a work-man that never wearies, never rests, never slumbers!' All of these land-shaping processes were confirmed by Charles Darwin's own observations – regardless of John Stevens Henslow's warning to read Lyell but on no account to believe his ideas. In effect Lyell's observations suggested that there was no definite time of the creation: it was a continuing process of change, over a vast period of time and was sufficient to account for the modern landscape without any recourse to catastrophes. This was the real crisis of faith – when Darwin was still looking at the world afresh, twenty-five years before he finally published equivalent views on the living part of the landscape.

The scriptural age and history of the earth and its life was now under open attack and, as far as the staunch traditionalists were concerned, it was catastrophic. A contributor to Geological Pamphlets calling himself only 'A Military Officer, a pilgrim from the last century' defied exclusion from any portrait of the outraged Victorian Establishment. He wrote of having:

witnessed the attempts to undermine the Book of God, to lessen our confidence in its truth . . . The writers . . . deny the correctness of the date of this world's creation as defined by Moses . . . Destroy the truth of Moses, and the foundation of the only true religion is taken away. No wonder, then, that Satan has worked so hard in the cause! . . . I feel called upon as the head of a family and as a duty to others to record in defence of my Christian Profession thus attacked, the impressions which God has planted in the mind of an old soldier.

Launching into mixed metaphors on rocks from geological sources and 'the only Rock of Ages', the inspired gentleman defended God's rock against Satan's fossils in the traditional style of the natural theologians: 'It is not for man however to affect to know by what processes God produced his creations, or caused His destructions in the earth, which knowledge He has reserved in His "secret things".'

The more scholarly could seek reassurance in the opinions of William Buckland, an eminent geologist, a catastrophist and Dean of West-minster Abbey. In 1836 he wrote a volume on geology in continuation of William Paley's great work, *Natural Theology*, in which he declared that geological findings confirmed the biblical account of the creation. Three years later he went so far as to further interpret God's intention for the Victorian age. A crowd of several thousand gathered to hear a geological lecture in the Dudley Caverns near Birmingham. Pointing to the illuminated rich minerals surrounding them, he pronounced them a demonstration of God's intent: by this gift the British should become the wealthiest and most powerful on earth. Strong in the faith that Providence had indeed directed all things with civilised man in mind, the assembled multitude burst into a thunderous rendering of 'God Save the Queen!' as they emerged into the sunlight and security of old ideas. (Charles Darwin was disdainful of Buckland's dramatic lectures which included a capering imitation of a flying Pterodactyl.)

The details of giant plants of past landscapes and weird extinct creatures now entered the lives of every Victorian. From quarries and cuttings (see Figure 9.6), huge teeth and monstrous bones were accumulating in large numbers and quite out of any known scale. In 1842 Sir Richard Owen coined for them the collective name of Dinosauria or 'Terrible Lizards' – a term and idea which thrilled those of Romantic inclination with its flesh-creeping overtones. Later the Victorian public at large could wonder at them, housed in Sir Richard's brainchild, the Natural History Museum in London, which was almost a shrine to creation.

Fern fronds (see Figure 9.7), roots and sections of giant horsetail stems were being discovered in coalmines – real manifestations of the extinct carboniferous forests which had created the Victorian coal riches. The sublime excitement of these ancient gloomy swamps was recreated by the magical writing of a self-educated stonemason turned geologist, Hugh Miller. His books on 'the natural history of the past' (his apt definition of geology) could be read by all without fear of divine retribution, for Miller was a devout member of the Free Church of Scotland and editor of its newspaper, *Witness*, one of the most influential Scottish newspapers. Much of his geological work was influenced by Genesis; he was more or less a catastrophist, and best of all for the traditionalists, he pretended that Lyell's controversial views and evidences did not even

This alien world captivated the Victorian love of the sublime and exotic landscape; even Thomas Hardy referred to it in describing the ferny Dorset grove (p. 80) in *The Return of the Native*:

> The scene seemed to belong to the ancient world of the carboniferous period, when the forms of plants were few, and of the fern kind; when there was neither bud nor blossom, nothing but a monotonous extent of leafage, amid which no bird sang.

It was Miller's 'living' fossils that fired Robert Dick into his own geological study and researches and after 1845 he provided Miller with many fossils and much information, not all of which accorded with Genesis. Dick differed from Miller in that the inevitable questions did not replace his delight nor plague him for an answer. He wrote: 'A few days since I found myself standing by the sea-shore on the east side of Dunnet Head. I was scanning with delighted soul the overturned strata, and musing on the Past, on the Beginning, on Eternity!' To him, the rocks were a revelation of a past world, when North-east Scotland was covered by sea and then strewn with boulders and boulder clay carried and ground down by advancing glaciers. He saw the present world as part of such a sequence, ultimately to come to a similar fate and to be replaced by a new heaven and earth. He deprecated the idea of trying to explain the formation of the universe and never lost sight of what he saw as the immensity of the concepts and the littleness of the attempted explanations. Miller was concerned about the inexplicable timing of his beautiful fossils – they had existed and disappeared before man who alone could have appreciated their beauty (he was not alone in his worries concerning beauty and its purpose, as will be seen). He decided that the ages previous to man's were trial attempts or dress rehearsals for 'the real thing' that was destined for man's edification. His last book, *The Testimony of the Rocks* (1857), was a desperate attempt to wed geological discoveries and a literal interpretation of Genesis. While this book was in the press, he apparently became unbalanced and committed suicide. It was Dick's belief that Miller's insanity was caused by the dilemma of keeping in line with church dogma which did not correlate with the scientific evidence they had shared. Today's opinion is that he may have been suffering from a

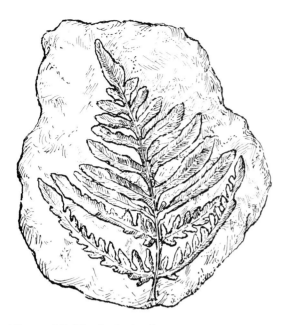

**Figure 9.7** 'The leaf of a fern . . . consigned to the tomb . . . in a block of coal' – *Alethopteris serli* from the Radstock coalmine, Somerset. (Shirley Hibberd, *Brambles and Bay Leaves*)

exist. In *The Old Red Sandstone* (1841), written at Sir Roderick Murchison's suggestion, he brought the realities of the landscape of the Carboniferous Era into every front parlour in America as well as Britain. He vividly described each fossil's detail as if it were alive and he was standing by it: ferns, pines and horsetails (see Figures 9.8 and 9.9).

> We near the coast, and now enter the opening of the stream. A scarce penetrable phalanx of reeds, that attain to the height and well nigh the bulk of forest-trees, is ranged on either hand. The bright and glossy stems seem rodded like Gothic columns; the pointed leaves stand out green at every joint, tier above tier, each tier resembling a coronal wreath or an ancient crown, with the rays turned outwards: and we see atop what may be either large spikes or catkins . . . these gigantic reeds! – are they not mere varieties of the common horse-tail of our bogs and morasses, magnified some sixty or a hundred times? Have we arrived at some such country as the continent visited by Gulliver. . ?

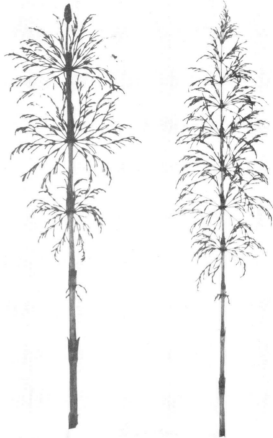

**Figures 9.8 and 9.9** Horsetail (*Equisetum sylvaticum*): the plant growing today in a Caithness ditch and a specimen from Robert Dick's herbarium. The modern horsetail is a humble shadow of its immense predecessor from the swamp forests of the Carboniferous Age, 300 million years ago – was it a product of a catastrophe and a new Creation, or was it a product of gradual change? (Herbarium specimen by permission of Thurso Museum)

mental illness, as throughout his life and writings he had a fixation of death. (With a mind as imaginative as his, fossils and rocks were the very stuff of death.) Dick's own opinion on the geological controversy was that: 'Possibly the business cannot be settled in the present stage of discovery, and friend Hugh had rather too much veneration for sundry great living men, to strike out a new path amid such an entangling forest of conflicting opinions.'

In his background, person, position and writings, Miller had been so popular and influential that when he cut short his own life he also snuffed out the popular enthusiasm for fossils and past worlds. His unhappy end was interpreted as a direct result of his geological researches and involvement; the creation and its timing was obviously not a topic which men should investigate. It was 'reserved in His "secret things" '.

Three years later, Charles Darwin's *Origins of Species* was published and the uproar which followed is now well known history. Darwin had left England on the Beagle in 1831 holding the traditional views of life on earth and its timescale. But by 1835 he had rejected any thoughts of 6,000 (see Figure 9.4) or 8,000 years as the age of the earth and was a disciple of Lyell's, thinking in terms of a grander scale of millions of years. As if to underline such thoughts, 7,000 feet above sea level in the Andes he came upon an extraordinary botanical relic preserved intact in spite of extremes of force and change – a small landscape of trees and more real than any from Miller's talented pen. At first sight it was a bare slope with a group of snow-white columns. They were petrified trees (somewhat like the small fossil in Figure 9.5); eleven were silicified, more than thirty were crystallised lime and they even had branches. They were a fir type, partly like the Norfolk Island pine and partly like yew. Darwin was delighted – here a group of trees had grown on volcanic soil raised above sea level and then with its upright trees this piece of land had sunk into the ocean, only once more to be raised up from the sea bed into a chain of mountains in a timescale inconceivable in the experience of man or his civilisations.

*Churchmen and Evolution*

Finally, in the face of the mass of Darwin's evidence, the officially approved timescale of the earth and its plants and animals was moved backwards by the churchmen. It was then agreed that Archbishop James Ussher's computations of age applied solely to man. Interestingly the geologists remained aloof from the Darwinian part of the controversy: on intellectual grounds, Lyell was cautious, Sir Roderick Murchison was bitterly against Darwin to the grave, as was Sir Richard Owen who was confident of a major chink in the evolutionary armour – until the timely discovery of the first missing link, the half-bird half-reptile Archaeopteryx, in 1862.

The botanists were divided. Sir Joseph Dalton Hooker was one of Darwin's staunch supporters through the affair. In fact, experienced naturalists of the day had been approached for their views and standpoint ahead of the *Origin*'s publication, in anticipation of the adverse reaction it would arouse. By 1857 it had become necessary to stand on one side or the other. Sir Joseph Dalton Hooker, and later Darwin, approached Philip Henry Gosse, the immensely popular writer on aquaria and wanderings around Kew. His son recollected that: 'Every instinct in his intelligence went out at first to greet the new light.' But Gosse was only a biologist second. First and foremost he was an empassioned believer of the

old school, the word of God was his only pleasure and he was convinced that he had exclusive personal knowledge of God's will and divinely inspired interpretation of the Bible (which he knew almost wholly by heart). For Gosse, if Genesis stated six days' creation, then six literal days it was. He decided to have nothing to do with the 'terrible theory'. He wrote a fanatical book seeking to unite science with his own literal interpretation of the scriptures. Geology was the arena in which he chose to bring the turmoil to a close, possibly influenced by the fact that he respected Darwin and Hooker but disliked Lyell, who was about to publish another geological bombshell. Gosse's theory was that in the catastrophic act of creation the world immediately took on a geological appearance of a place where life had existed for many aeons – that there had been no modifications of the earth's crust or its life. The book was scorned both by those for Darwin and those against; Darwin himself remained silent as Gosse fell from favour both with the public and the press. The effect on Gosse was shattering; his religious fanaticism transformed his rejection into a direct punishment sent from God and he tortured himself with searching for the reason.

There were other, less famous and less dramatic casualties of church and evolution. One of these was the prolific plant moralist, John Ellor Taylor, who at the age of eighteen had become a lay preacher of the Wesleyans. He had to face the dilemma of choosing between his scientific opinions, hard won by self-teaching, and becoming a minister. He chose the former and in the historic year of 1858 (when Darwin and Wallace's paper was read at the Linnean Society), at the age of 21, he was a popular lecturer on scientific topics, later touring Australia with his lectures. He was elected to the Geological and Linnean Societies.

There was of course the philosophical casualty of natural theology. It was ironical that the very evidence for Paley's Design was in fact the evidence for Darwin's natural selection. What was even more ironical was that Darwin had been an ardent admirer of Paley; he had been obliged to read Paley's *Evidences of Christianity* and *Moral Philosophy* as a student at Cambridge and, thorough as always, he had learnt them almost by heart. He admired Paley's clear use of words and most of all, the evidences and logic of *Natural Theology*. An utterly convinced traditionalist at the time, he had reckoned these studies to have been the only useful part of his course and was always proud to have had a personal link with Paley at Cambridge – that of occupying the same rooms in College. But in the 1860s the tables were turned: Paley's Design had become Darwin's adaptation to the environment from an alternative viewpoint. As time progressed the doctrine of natural theology died with its old followers.

In 1863 Lyell's geological bombshell dreaded by Gosse exploded. It was *The Antiquity of Man*. It presented evidence which contradicted the Church's redrawn stand on man's creation in 4004 BC. In a past landscape of fossil trees, plants and ancient animal types, there were now signs of man. It was this picture of primitive man which brought the most vehement indignation. The old school thought in terms of human perfection in Eden as opposed to crudely chipped axeheads from a distant savage past. 'Instinct, reason, cherished thoughts of early greatness, start up in alarm and disgust to protest against such an origin of our race . . . [made] a little lower than the angels.' Man's position in the living world was made far too mundane by discoveries of axes and these in vast numbers suggesting an early occupation of trading in such basics. This was no alternative to wandering about Eden's paradise garden, marvelling at its divinely inspired ferneries, as depicted by Shirley Hibberd (see page 85).

Others saw it as part of some sort of plot, manipulated from beyond England's hallowed shores: 'those cock and bull stories about Pre-Adamite horse shoes and other unbelievable curiosities which are now so frequently copied . . . into our English papers, with a view to sensational effect upon the orthodox English mind.' Regardless of their occupation the remains of the men were unarguably associated with a world acknowledged as more than 6,000 years old. At length the Church settled for the special creation of man. By the 1880s the Church took up its final stance: men had evolved physically but his soul was the work of the Creator.

## Evidence from Flowers

The interpretation of flowers as working parts of the plant was a vital part of flower evolution, for the future abundance of a plant species depends on its pollinating success. Darwin's theory of evolution by natural selection was that living things had not been individually created, remaining unchanged since the Creation, but that they had slowly changed and were continuing to do so, by a natural interplay of variation within a species, the changing demands of the environment and competition for resources.

Darwin's detailed studies of flower mechanisms were not published until after the *Origin of Species*, 1859, but he had begun collecting information in earnest as early as 1838. For four years he concentrated on cross-fertilisation by insects, flower structures (see Figure 9.10) and their variability, reading Sprengel's classic work on the form and fertilisation of flowers towards the end of 1841. He made detailed observations on flowers in the gardens at his family home and at the Wedgwood's during the following summer. His insect-eye view of flowers was an integral part of his picture of evolution.

*Minor Variations – the Means of Evolution*

*Orchids.* The study of orchid 'contrivances' provided Darwin with one of the finest test cases of his theory – very few survived from a potential of many:

**Figure 9.10** Flower–insect co-operation: Design or selection pressure? As a bee pushes into the tubular throat of the sage it pushes against the lower pedal extension of the filament, causing the pollen-bearing anther at the other end of the lever to swing down and clamp on the bee's back, dusting it with pollen. (Only one of the two stamens is visible in half-flower.)

It is notorious that Orchids are sparingly distributed. . . In my examination of Orchids, hardly any fact has so much struck me as the endless diversity of structure, – the prodigality of resources, – for gaining the very same end, namely, the fertilisation of one flower by the pollen of another. . . This fact is to a large extent intelligible on the principle of natural selection.

(*On the Various Contrivances by which British and Foreign Orchids are Fertilised*)

He explained the principle in the case of the long-spurred Madagascan orchid, *Angraecum sesquipedale* (see Figure 8.13), and its long-tongued pollinator. The characteristics. of each had become adapted to the other – the spur of the orchid is 11½ inches long with nectar in the bottom 1½ inches, and the moth's tongue is 10 to 11 inches and the pollen is best removed when the creature pushes its tongue hard down into the spur:

If such great moths were to become extinct in Madagascar, assuredly the Angræcum would become extinct. On the other hand, as the nectar, at least in the lower part of the nectary, is stored safe from the depredation of other insects, the extinction of the Angræcum would probably be a serious loss to these moths. We can thus understand how the astonishing length of the nectary had been acquired by successive modifications. As certain moths of Madagascar became larger through natural selection in relation to their general conditions of life . . . those individual plants . . . which had the longest nectaries (and the nectary varies much in length in some Orchids), and which, consequently, compelled the moths to insert their . . .[tongues] up to the very base, would be best fertilised. These plants would yield most seed, and the seedlings would generally inherit long nectaries; and so it would be in successive generations of the plant and of the moth. Thus it would appear that there has been a race in gaining length between the nectary of the Angræcum and the . . . [tongues] of certain moths; but the Angræcum has triumphed, for it flourishes and abounds in the forests of Madagascar, and still troubles each moth to insert its proboscis as deeply as possible in order to drain the last drop of nectar.

Small, apparently insignificant variations within a species such as nectary length and tongue length are the raw material of evolution.

*Pelargoniums and Pansies.* Variations in plants and animals under domestication provided more material for Darwin's theory. He had been collecting every fact he could find on domestic breeds since 1837 – just after his return from the Beagle voyage. He studied all the agricultural and horticultural journals and came to the conclusion that the keystone of domestication was the selection of breeding partners.

In any group of plants or animals there were slight individual differences, and sometimes, quite unexpectedly larger variations occurred which man selected as the raw material for a new breed or variety. The popularity of particular plants such as pelargoniums required that they were cultivated in their thousands by nurserymen which gave ample opportunity for any peculiarities and idiosyncrasies to be noticed – just the material for Darwin's records. For instance, there were the different requirements of some varieties: more water, confinement of root in the pot before flowering, some were 'very impatient of the knife if too greedily used in making cuttings', while the timing of the bloom varied from the beginning to the end of the season. Darwin noted how important such differences could be in the wild state: 'These odd peculiarities would enable a plant in a state of nature to become adapted to widely differing circumstances and climates.' Here was further potential variation on which selection pressure could act. Also, these minor differences began to give decidedly blurred edges to the old concept of a species being immutable and having sharply defined characteristics. It added weight to Darwin's concept of species as always changing and evolving – a blow to Victorian 'closet scientists'. Darwin also intently studied the changes in plants after they were transplanted and started contributing notes to the *Gardener's Chronicle* in 1841 on his various researches (and also, over the years, several evolutionary 'feelers' to gauge public response). After transplanting 'improved varieties of the Heartsease', Darwin saw the notorious effect of sudden change of flower colour and markings. These were themselves equally fickle because the flowers returned to their original colour by the end of the same summer. (Variations in response to local conditions happen in the wild and can make sure identification of the wild *Viola* species extremely difficult.) The other side of the coin was the rapidity with which new violas could be bred.

The pansy was developed early in the nineteenth century by aristocrats cultivating and crossing wild plants such as tricolor pansy (*Viola tricolor*) and mountain pansy (*V. lutea*) (see both in Figure 9.11) and others, all of which

naturally hybridise producing immense variation. Appropriately these wild heartsease were planted in a heart-shaped flower-bed by a Lady Monke who began developing their potential with the help of the estate gardener. In 1814 they converted the dark lines at the flower's centre to a dark eye never seen before and noted by Charles Darwin as the first great change.

He wrote how in 1835, twenty years after the

**Figure 9.11** Pansies, wild to cultivated: 1 tricolor pansy (*Viola tricolor*), wild, highly coloured and variable; 2 mountain pansy (*Viola lutea*), wild, yellow or purple; 3, 4, 5, 6 and 7 Victorian cultivars – Tiger's face, Enterprise, Minerva, John Bull, Anna Maria. Pansies afforded Darwin with evidence of much variability within a species. (From *The Ladies' Flower-Garden* by Jane Loudon, 1840 edition)

175

first selections from 'the small, dull, elongated, irregular flowers of the wild pansy' there were on sale four hundred named varieties of 'more beautiful, flat, symmetrical, velvet-like flowers, more than two inches in diameter, magnificently and variously coloured'. It was developed by textile workers in the 1840s; the varieties illustrated (see Figure 9.11) were featured in Jane Loudon's *The Ladies' Flower-Garden* of 1840. Here was an example of small variations being accumulated to make a significant change. One species could ultimately turn into another.

*Roses.* Nurserymen's roses offered a similar situation to that seen in the *Viola* species. In particular there was the extraordinarily rapid creation of varieties of one rose, the history of which was recent and authentically known. It was the burnet rose (*Rosa spinosissima* also known as *R. pimpinellifolia*, see Plate 5). Some plants of this attractive creamy-white rose were transplanted from the wild by a Perth nurseryman in 1793. One of the plants produced flowers tinged faintly red and from its seeds another plant produced semi-monstrous flowers – tinged red. This flower in turn produced seed from which came semi-double roses. After less than twenty years there were twenty-six distinct varieties, and less than fifty years after the original transplanting three hundred varieties were in existence, varying from crimson to marbled, white, yellow and many more.

The rose was as variable in the wild. In Caithness, northern Scotland, Robert Dick made observations of individual plants over long periods of time. He wrote:

External influences – such as soil, situation, climate, and such like – exercise a powerful effect on wild roses. Take for instance, the *Rosa spinosissima* . . . how very unlike the common dog rose (*R. canina*) it is. Would you believe that one bush of it on the boulder clay here, has put forth flowers hardly distinguishable from dog-roses. The leaves large, the flowers white, the prickles hooked, and so on . . . Some stocks . . . have pink petals; in dry years, red petals and excessively hairy leaves; in wet seasons, white petals and smooth leaves; in short, the leaves and the whole plant vary excessively.

He sent a number of wild roses to Babington,

Professor of Botany at Cambridge, but felt his identification was not quite correct. Dick's comments on the fickle inconsistencies of wild roses warm the heart of anyone who had given up ideas of accurate identification in total despair:

And suppose the plant changed to another soil, and favoured by shelter, its improved appearance is hardly credible . . . I have seen something worth noting. Some plants of *Rosa spinosissima* grew on the face of a brae of blue boulder clay. Drains and improvements on the soil atop of the clay sent a perpetual stream of water over the roots of the plants. In two years they have so altered that I can hardly believe my eyes . . . All the roses growing wild in Caithness may have come from one stock; but from what particular stock I cannot tell.

The difficulty of exactly describing a species when the plants could be so changeable brought Dick close to Darwin's views, although his understanding of the latter was limited to reviews not the original volumes: 'one thing, indeed, I'll grant Mr. Darwin – that hundreds of so-called species may have sprung from one stock . . .' While not wishing 'to meddle with Mr. Darwin's peculiar notions', he independently shared some of Darwin's other conclusions, which was extraordinary in a self-taught man researching alone in one small county, and surrounded by a climate of extremely old-fashioned and dogmatic opinions.

The nature and gravity of Mr. Darwin's 'notions' were such that every field of learning entered the long-awaited and dreaded turmoil. Ideas of evolutionary change by various and devious means had been mooted before but Darwin's observations and experiments were such that his could not be ignored. For he was the epitome of each aspect of serious Victorian natural history study: he had made meticulous and copious observations in the field and he was a collector. He was an ingenious and dedicated experimenter with detailed knowledge of his subjects, painstaking in self-criticism and in technique (such as his practising making consistently sized droplets in feeding sundew (see page 159). Above all he could visualise all this detail in the perspective of the vast whole where things 'most remote in the scale of nature, are bound together by a web of complex relations'. One unexpected topic of controversy following his

*Origin of Species* was the issue of the aesthetic appeal of flowers. In 1871 Darwin again entered the arena with *The Descent of Man* which included comment on that most human of qualities which was so closely associated with flowers: the sense of beauty.

## The Question of Floral Beauty

> Proud man is disposed to think that 'Full many a flower is born to blush unseen,' because he has not deigned to explore it . . . (Edward Bevan, *The Honey Bee*)

Besides the well-aired controversy of species changing and origins there were issues (important at the time) such as the dilemma of the beauty of flowers and thus their *raison d'être* — were they for 'proud man'? After centuries of nature and flowers having oriented around man's perception and the good of his soul, it was a shattering suggestion that the existence of beautiful scented flowers existed merely for insect eyes and tongues. From contemplative gifts from God, or sentimental toys, 'Flora's gems' became a set of cogs in a enormous somewhat unpredictable machinery of natural processes functioning independently of, and in spite of, the protestations of men.

This concept directly contradicted the traditional view put forward by natural theology. William Paley saw the beauty of flowers and their great variety as having been created solely for man's delectation. It was the:

> most interesting and lovely part of the vegetable creation, which appears . . . manifestly pre-ordained for the excitement of delight, of an instinctive emotion especially harmonized to such excitement . . . The profusion of vegetable beauty displayed throughout the year in the warm climates, and during the summer months in the colder regions of the habitable globe, might fail, or cease to excite attention, curiosity, or emotion, were it all of one kind, were all the blossoms, the corollæ, and the anthers, alike in shape or colour; perpetual scarlet might satiate or pall the sense; but the diversity is infinite. (*Natural Theology*)

As has been seen, this idea of flowers being part of the great Design for man's use and edification stemmed from Genesis (see page 47). J.L. Knapp wrote that as few flowers provided food or clothing, 'we can collect them for amusement, in admiration of their beauty . . . and man, who is exclusively sensible of its existence, can alone find pleasure in viewing it'. For it had long been an accepted fact 'that the most highly adorned productions of Flora's kingdom were called into existence' only at the appearance of man and his intellect capable of contemplating floral beauty.

The idea of man's exclusive pleasure went further. As befitted Victorian preoccupations of a master-race, the appreciation of floral beauty (and thus the point of its creation) was further limited to an upper echelon of mankind. Orchids, for instance, had been designed expressly 'to comfort the elect of human beings in this age'. And it was not just these most rare and spectacular flowers which were destined for the few: the colours of the entire landscape were seen as having been carefully selected with delicacy — appropriate, no doubt to the civilised sensitivity of 'weak nerves'. In 1856, Dr M'Cosh commended the 'Adaptations of the Colours of Plants to the Natural Tastes of Man':

> the distribution of colours in the vegetable kingdom is in beautiful accordance with the now established laws of harmonious, and especially of complementary colours [see Figure 9.12] . . . Artists lay it down as a maxim that a large portion of a painting should be of a neutral colour. Our natural tastes would not tolerate a scarlet or purple ground to a historical painting. . . It is the same in the beautiful canvas which is spread out before us in earth and sky. The ground colours of nature, if not all neutral, are at least all soft and retiring.

Dr M'Cosh hastened to make allowances for such artistic licence displayed by God's works. 'How grateful should we be that the sky is not usually dressed in red.' (His horror of perpetual scarlet was shared by William Paley (see this page.)) From amidst the harmonious 'retiring' blue and green background, 'the more regular and elegant forms, and the gayer colours of nature, come forth to arrest the attention, to excite and dazzle us, not only by their own splendour, but by comparison and contrast'. The contrast of violet and yellow of woody nightshade (see Plate 15), and many more in that range of colours appeared to be the perfect illustration

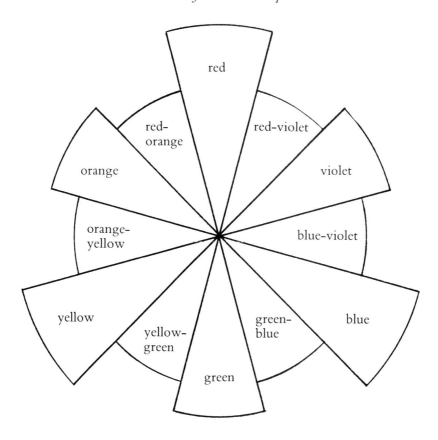

**Figure 9.12** The colour wheel. Complementary colours are opposite each other.

of nature fulfilling the decree of the Victorian Artistic Establishment who had taken such pains 'to shew what colours may be placed in juxtaposition, and what colours may be kept at a distance. . .' Complementary colours such as yellow and violet appear opposite each other on the colour circle (see Figure 9.12) – when placed 'in juxtaposition' each shows the other to best advantage. The woody nightshade's berries also have the dramatic impact of complementary colours – red and green. Yellow and blue are semi-complementary colours and thus have a similar effect in combination. (Today the juxtaposition of yellow, orange-yellows with blues and blue-violets are understood as a perfect contrast for a bee's eye, giving flowers of these combined colours the advantage of efficient advertisement and clear insect directives to pollen and nectar.)

This man-centred view of floral beauty explained by Dr M'Cosh in 1856 still left some difficult questions for the natural theologians. In the remote Amazon jungle at the same time as Dr M'Cosh was putting forward his views on colour schemes for man, Henry Walter Bates was seeking the royal water-lily and musing on the 'brilliant colours and ornamentations' of male birds and insects:

I think it is a childish notion that the beauty of birds, insects, and other creatures is given to please the human eye . . . Surely, rich plumage and song, like all the endowments of species, are given them for their own pleasure and advantage. This, if true, ought to enlarge our ideas of the inner life and mutual relations of our humbler fellow creatures.

He and other explorers brought word of a profusion of orchids and bromeliads of unbelievable beauty blooming high in the jungle tree-tops out of sight of any man. Equally remote were the carpets of bright alpines amidst inhospitable melting ice. The natural theologians replied that God had placed the blooms in high and remote places 'for His own pleasure and delight' (see Plate 7). This was also the reason presumably, for the bewildering fact noted by John Ellor Taylor that: 'The most gorgeous of exotic plants blossom in lands where mankind are little above the brute in intellectual development, and care as little as the animals for the floral loveliness so lavishly surrounding them ' (see Figure 6.6).

Then there was the problem of night-flowering species; their perfume was an undoubted delight for man, but in the dark they could not be seen, which negated the presence of their delicate pale colours. One traditional interpretation was that they carried a lesson – the quietly-coloured evening primrose described by Rebecca Hey had carried a message of humility (see page 54) or a ray of hope in the tomb. The evolutionary view of the evening primroses was that they were rather a fortuitous accident upon which a firm relationship of mutual benefit had become established: the night-flying moth found food and the pale night-flowering bloom found a carrier of pollen. Scent and colour were part of the flower's strategy. White and pale colours reflect every glimmer of light against a background of darkness and moths sense the slightest perfume. (Darwin looked in detail at the incidence of colour and scent and found that 'white flowers are by far the most favoured in nature in the matter of perfume.')

Darwin, far from being the objective scientist unmoved by the simple appeal of colour and form, was an avid admirer of nature's art. He delighted in scenery and appreciated the sublime beauty of bare rock but, for his lasting pleasure, plants were the vital ingredient. It was the brilliant rich colours and flowing shapes of tropical flowers which struck him first as he set foot in the tropics. He saw it all as a picture from the *Arabian Nights*, but a real one. Surrounded by the quieter colours of home he was still a passionate enthusiast and he had made a study of

the different colours of flowers from his early student days with John Stevens Henslow. The pure blue of lobelia was a particular inspiration to him, but appreciation of such beauty in no way clouded his view as to its origin: 'Flowers rank amongst the most beautiful productions of nature; and they have become through natural selection beautiful, or rather conspicuous in contrast with the greenness of the leaves, that they might be easily observed and visited by insects, so that their fertilisation may be favoured.' He replied to the natural theologian's view in *The Descent of Man*:

With respect to the view that organic beings have been created beautiful for the delight of man, – a view which it has lately been pronounced may safely be accepted as true, and as subversive of my whole theory, – I may first remark that the idea of the beauty of any particular object obviously depends on the mind of man . . . and that the idea is not an innate and unalterable element in the mind. We see this in men of different races admiring an entirely different standard of beauty in their women. With the great majority of animals, however, the taste for the beautiful is confined, as far as we can judge, to the attraction of the opposite sex. . . When, however, it is said that the lower animals have a sense of beauty, it must not be supposed that such sense is comparable with that of a cultivated man. . . I refer here only to the pleasure given by certain colours, forms, and sounds, and which may fairly be called a sense of the beautiful; with cultivated men such sensations are however, intimately associated with complex ideas and trains of thought. . . A more just comparison would be between the taste for the beautiful in animals, and that in the lowest savages, who admire and deck themselves with any brilliant, glittering, or curious object. . . When we behold a male bird elaborately displaying his graceful plumes or splendid colours before the female, whilst other birds, not thus decorated, make no such display, it is impossible to doubt that she admires the beauty of her male partner. As women everywhere deck themselves with these plumes, the beauty of such ornaments cannot be disputed.

Just as man can give beauty, according to his standard of taste, to his male poultry, or more strictly can modify the beauty originally acquired by the parent species . . . so it appears that female birds in a state of nature, have by a long selection of the more attractive males, added to their beauty or other attractive qualities.

These views on the uses and origins of beauty and colour elicited a predictable response in *Proserpina* from John Ruskin, another avid admirer of nature and flowers, who ironically felt a similar child-like gratitude and aesthetic depth to Darwin's; but there their common ground ended:

His [Darwin's] ignorance of good art is no excuse for the acutely illogical simplicity of . . . his talk of colour in the *Descent of Man*. Peacocks' tails he thinks, are the result of the admiration of blue tails in the minds of well-bred peahens, – and similarly, mandrills' noses the result of the admiration of blue noses in well-bred baboons. But it never occurs to him to ask why the admiration of blue noses is healthy in baboons, so that it develops their race properly, while similar maidenly admiration either of blue noses or red noses in men would be improper, and develop the race improperly. . . And when he imagined the gradation of the cloudings in feathers to represent successive generation, it never occurred to him to look at the much finer cloudy gradations in the clouds of dawn themselves; and explain the modes of sexual preference and selective development which had brought *them* to their scarlet glory, before the cock could crow thrice.

Like Dr M'Cosh, Ruskin saw floral beauty as lost to the ignoble of the human race.

Putting all these vespertilian speculations out of our way, the human facts concerning colour are briefly these. Wherever men are noble, they love bright colour;[1] and wherever they can live healthily, bright colour is given them

– in sky, sea, flowers, and living creatures. On the other hand, wherever men are ignoble and sensual, they endure without pain, and at last even come to like (especially if artists) mud-colour and black, and to dislike rose-colour and white. And wherever it is unhealthy for them to live, the poisonousness of the place is marked by some ghastly colour in air, earth, or flowers.

However, even Ruskin had to admit that there were exceptions to 'such widely founded laws' in the 'poisonous berries of scarlet, and pestilent skies that are fair'.

It was only after all the brouhaha over evolution had died down that the true significance of flower colour to insects began to emerge. At the time that Darwin was first investigating the inter-dependence of flowers and insects little was known of the perception of insects, particularly their ability to see colour. For much of the nineteenth century it was thought that bees, butterflies and their kin could only see in shades of grey, making patterns far more significant than plain bright colours. It was Darwin's neighbour and protégé, Sir John Lubbock (Lord Avebury) who began experiments on insect vision. As an eleven-year-old boy he had an interest in natural history which was fostered and directed by Darwin (who imbued all of his own children with his own great love and respect for the natural world). Destined for the family bank, he later achieved eminence in the fields of anthropology, entomology and botany. He began his ingenious experiments on insect behaviour in the 1870s, involving puzzles and mazes for ants and colour tests for bees. He concluded that bees were not only attracted by bright colours, but they also could tell one colour from another. But, as John Ellor Taylor pointed out, 'every cottager in England' had known of insect attraction to colours long since, and had turned his knowledge of it to practical account by hanging:

brilliantly-coloured paper 'fly-cages' . . . from the roof of his cottage, to save its clean whitewash from soiling. . . The cottager's experiments have further had the disadvantage over those of the indefatigable baronet, inasmuch as they were practised upon a less specialized order of insects than his! . . . the cottager has confined his to the . . . house-

---

1. It is interesting that in his painting Ruskin adhered closely to his preaching on the pure bright colours of nature: his kingfisher's wing vibrates unbelievably with jewelled turquoise and his (rather pink) wild roses have a clarity and vigour which one would imagine incompatible with watercolour. (Paintings in the Ashmolean Museum, Oxford, not on public view.)

flies! (*Flowers, their origin, shapes, perfumes and colours*)

Be that as it may, the cottage tradition had not been recognised in the context of insects being attracted to particular flowers. Unfortunately, Lubbock failed to carry out a definitive control experiment to eliminate the possibility of bees discriminating only the degrees of brightness of the different colours. It was not until 1913 that Karl von Frisch's famous experiments proved without a doubt that the bees were really responding to different colours and it could be said that the glorious flower colours were all a magnificent show for insects.

## The New World of Flowers

### The Birth of Twentieth-century Conflicts

Darwin, Müller and others had opened up a 'New World' of flowers – with intricate relationships, variability, structural complexity and microscopic detail all awaiting impassioned investigation. A new type of botanist emerged to study them, eager to analyse in test-tubes and scrutinise behind compound lenses, but never venturing outside the laboratory. There was a sense of urgency and ridiculing of the tradition of dedicated amateurs carefully noting observations in the field and compiling Floras.

How plants should be studied became an inseparable part of a split of generations and attitudes which has lingered into our own times. Fieldwork became the domain of amateurs and bumbling old men (epitomised by the ageing Professor Babington, see page 79) in the eyes of the new thrusting style of biologist. Real botanists and biologists concerned themselves with how vegetable structures functioned and interacted, disregarding the name or appearance of the whole plant. Thus, sadly, in the 1880s the everyday study of plants growing close at hand in garden, greenhouse, field and wayside became divorced from botany and remained thus well into the twentieth century. It became possible for a professional botanist to know the internal anatomy of an oak tree without knowing how it differed from an ash. The enthusiastic amateur was thus largely alienated by virtue of the shift in subject-matter.

New facts and interpretations of plants were further excluded from the non-specialist reader because the emerging professionals wrote their results and observations for each other, not the laity. A specialised basic knowledge was assumed, jargon evolved and language was precise and clinical without personality, affection or soul (although the latter two were, and still are, very much in existence). Floral description and interpretation no longer reflected the individual or the philosophical, moral and fashionable preoccupations of the time. With the passing of the subjective approach in writing the delightful vignettes (see Figures 6.6 and 8.14) of the mid-nineteenth century were also superseded by instructive diagrams. The charm and the artistry now lay only with the inherent qualities of the plants themselves.

Understandably the amateurs felt immense resentment against the new jargon which so inconsiderately and effectively excluded them. One amateur botanist, John Ruskin, who held the Chair of Fine Arts at Oxford, refused to remain silent and accused science of having become hostile to art. His impact was such that a public reply came from the Chair of Botany. Another familiar twentieth-century conflict was emerging: the concept of science versus art. Previously science had been a magic looking-glass through which men marvelled at the order and harmony of the natural world, uncovering the delightful complexity of a Design centred on 'good', man's in particular. This sense of comfort and security had been a consistent source of emotional benefit – 'nature's balm'. Now spiritual consolation in studying nature was gone. Botany and all the natural sciences presented instead a terrifying mirror of a world of chance, competition and change. The study of this world of unknowns and uncertainty was positively subversive to joyful contemplation. Curiosity concerning the nature of things was no longer respectable, it had become presumptuous and meddling.

The quest for nature's healing salve reappeared as one of the many motivations behind the amenity movement. This was gathering momentum in the 1880s with land being acquired expressly for nature reserves. (Queen Victoria opened Epping Forest as a public park in 1882.) John Ruskin's thoughts on the 'practical lesson' of flowers and trees with which he ended *Proserpina* are particularly apt:

Nor is the world so small but that we may yet

leave in it also unconquered spaces of beautiful solitude; where the chamois and red deer may wander fearless, – nor any fire of avarice scorch from the Highlands of Alp, or Grampian, the rapture of the heath, and the rose.

A similar attitude of preserving the living world rather than destroying it through wanton exploitation stemmed from a very different source. This was a new philosophy called Vitalism which sprang from the ashes of traditional thought after the impact of Darwinism. In contrast to the bleak desolation of Nature 'red in tooth and claw', the Vitalists centred upon the facility to survive and surmount all the pressures of chance and change – a creative Vital Spirit inherent in all life. Darwin had put man in his biological context: co-existing, subject to the same pressures and changes as other species, and above all a mere part of a living world. Man was no longer set above nature nor the focal point of its existence. The Vital Spirit common to all species carried an inherent reverence towards all living things. The wanton taking of life was ethically wrong. Subscribers to this view (John Ruskin and William Morris amongst them), saw co-operation as the key of life rather than competition. Vitalism influenced social and educational reform and thus brought the teaching of biology in schools into the limelight. The new approach of studying nature's processes was far more at one with the Vitalist philosophy than the traditional instruction of making a herbarium or a museum, and thus with alterations suited to the very young, 'Nature Study' was born. Sir John Lubbock became a champion of the new subject, bringing to it his own studies of the social life of ants and the interdependence of flowers and colour-conscious insects: topics bound to delight children and rouse interest in natural history (or biology as it was now called), just as Charles Darwin had influenced Lubbock in his boyhood at Downe. Thus, in a roundabout way Darwin influenced the teaching of Nature Study in schools twice over.

Unfortunately, the philosophy and idealism which were part of its birth brought sentimentalism too, and the anthropomorphic approach so typical of the Victorian sentimentalists of fifty years before returned with disastrous effect. Nature study acquired the image of the inconsequential, the feminine and the juvenile, dragging down with it natural history (which was already

suffering badly). The image of both is familiar enough: some scientists of the old generation still deride both subjects and it is only relatively recently that field study and the natural history approach have emerged from being considered outmoded and useless. The idea of studying the interaction of plants and creatures living together had been Darwin's. His emphasis on the fragile inter-relationships between animals and plants and the physical environment in the *Origin of Species* effectively launched the science of ecology and with it a more level-headed view of nature. Time and again Darwin drew attention to the delicate balance of relationships between things which were apparently unconnected with each other. In fact, it is only now that we are beginning to conceive of the fragility of the balance affecting a plant, an animal or a whole habitat, and to realise the far-reaching effects of changing one aspect of the physical environment or of destroying a small cog in the immense machinery of plant-animal interdependence.

Part of the interest of tracing through the attitudes from another age is to compare them with our own. In some aspects we still view flowers and nature in very much the same way as the Victorians: we thrill at the exotic, the macabre and the concept of wilderness (still in the comfort of an armchair, albeit via a different medium). Sentimental renderings of rustic cottage gardens, 'laughing streams, and flower-bedecked fields', harvest mice and pastel-tinted, honeysuckle hedgerows still abound, together with nostalgia for a pre-Industrial lifestyle. Among the cultivated flowers there are still fanatical favourites and status plants striving to be better than their neighbour and fashionably styled greenhouses – merely different ones. As in the romantic decades of the nineteenth century there are still those who seek the solitude of wild habitats. There has been a great change in the desire to encapsulate it in glass in the home: nature has been ushered into the garden, with plants chosen to attract bees, butterflies and birds. Some of the old desire to possess wild things remains: regardless of their prospect of survival or rarity, coveted plants of the wild are still uprooted, although more casually by ordinary people, and less efficiently on a commercial basis. And, alas, plants and their habitats remain for many mere chattels for use, occasional dilettante enjoyment without responsibility, or destruction for gain, but worse than the Victorians – without the mitigation of divine intention – coldly and unmoved. More optimistically, there are still some extra-ordinary people who, with or without recompense, devote their energies and much of their lives to the understanding, discovery and portrayal of plants and their world – Honour to them, as Charlotte Yonge would have said. For ultimately the attitude to flowers and nature in any age reflects man's attitude to fellow man – and ultimately to his idea of his creator.

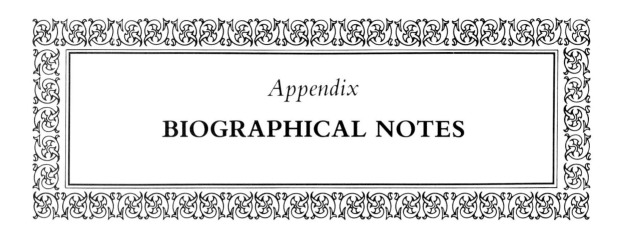

*Appendix*

# BIOGRAPHICAL NOTES

AITON William 1731–1793 Scottish pupil at Chelsea Physic Garden. Director of Kew.

AITON William Townsend 1766–1849 Son of William Aiton, succeeded his father to Directorship of Kew, resigned 1841.

ANDREWS James c. 1801–1876.

BABINGTON Charles Cardale 1808–1895 Father a physician and keen amateur botanist. As a pupil of John Stevens Henslow, he became devoted to botany; his herbarium contained 55,000 sheets. In 1861 succeeded Henslow to Chair of Botany at Cambridge adding John Lindley's collection to the Herbarium there.

BANKS Sir Joseph 1743–1820 Inherited wealth enabling him to indulge his scientific passions.

BATES Henry Walter 1825–1892 He met Alfred Russel Wallace in 1844: Bates's particular interest was beetles, Wallace's was botany and making a herbarium but Bates soon influenced him to become an ardent beetle collector. Bates hated his work as a clerk in a hosiery factory and the two friends decided to make a joint expedition to the Amazon: 'to make . . . collection[s] of objects . . . and gather facts', as Wallace expressed it in one of his letters, 'towards solving the problem of the origin of species' – 'a subject on which we had conversed and corresponded much together'. Two years after his return to England Bates met Charles Darwin who 'strongly urged' him to write a book: Bates had made important observations and interpretations of insect colouring which provided valuable evidence for Darwin's ideas. He married in 1863. His financial worries did not disappear until 1864 when he was appointed assistant secretary to the Royal Geographic Society.

BAUER Ferdinand 1760–1826 Artist and adventurer – went to Greece as illustrator for *Flora Græca* (spanned 1806–40 as author died, replaced by Sir James Edward Smith (see page 6), who was re-placed on his death by John Lindley); accompanied Flinders on Australian expedition, illustrating plants.

BAUER Francis 1758–1840 Adopted Britain, like his brother.

BENTHAM George 1800–1884 1831: called to the Bar; 1833: inheritance freed him to devote himself to his herbarium and library but these began to outstrip his means; gave his 100,000 specimens to Kew, 1854.

BEVAN Edward 1770–1860 Physician and eminent apiarian.

BLAKE William 1757–1827.

BRIDGES Thomas 1807–1865 Solicited advances to collect on his own account; 1828: arrived South America – set up as small time brewer to finance plant-collecting. In the 1850s settled in California collecting and exploring. Died of malaria at sea, returning from Nicaragua.

BROWN Lancelot 'Capability' 1715–1783

BUCKLAND William 1784–1856 1840: President of the Geological Society.

BUCKLEY Arabella Secretary to Sir Charles Lyell. The first popular writer to convey Darwinian evolution into children's language.

BUFFON Count (Georges Louis Leclerq) 1707–1788 Director of the Jardin du Roi.

BYRON George Gordon (Lord Byron) 1788–1824.

CHAMBERS Sir William 1726–1796.

CLARE John 1793–1864.

COBBETT William 1763–1835.

COLERIDGE Samuel Taylor 1772–1834.

COLES William 1626–1662.

COLLINS Charles 1828–1873 Pre-Raphaelite.

CONSTABLE John 1776–1837.

CRANE Walter 1845–1915 Influenced by Pre-Raphaelites and Japanese art and a student of John Ruskin.

CULPEPER Nicholas 1616–1654.

CUNNINGHAM Allan 1791–1839 Worked in conveyancing office in Lincoln's Inn, became Aiton's clerk involved in cataloguing Kew's plants. 1816: explored under Oxley, discovering Wellington Valley in 1817 (town founded 1825); 1824: investigated settlement possibilities for Brisbane; 1831: returned to Kew; 1837: unexpectedly returned to Australia following deaths of two replacement Colonial Botanists (one of whom was his young brother, Richard, d. 1835). Unhappy as a gardener rather than an explorer botanist, he tried to search out more plants; 1838: rapidly failing health, no doubt accelerated by early exploring privations.

CURTIS William 1746–1799 Founded the *Botanical Magazine* in 1787.

DARWIN Charles Robert 1809–1882 Brought up amidst discussions of his grandfather's ideas on evolution. While studying medicine at Edinburgh University he went on geological excursions: met personalities in geological controversies of 1820s and 1830s. At Cambridge John Stevens Henslow opened his eyes to first-hand botanical investigation and later recommended him as naturalist on board HMS *Beagle*. Darwin's illness on his return (see page 128) can never be positively identified. One very plausible theory was that it was chronic arsenical poisoning as his father prescribed arsenic for his eczema. Other theories included the suggestion of psychosomatic symptoms as a means of avoiding society. However, as well as curtailing social commitments, it severely limited his time spent working: four hours' work, walks in the garden, pony rides, all carefully sandwiched between rests and retiring to bed early, was exceedingly frustrating for a mind with such far-reaching horizons. *How* he managed to produce his extraordinary output in only four hours a day seems to present far more food for thought than why he was so limited.

DARWIN Erasmus 1731–1802 Doctor, inventor, poet. An inscription to Erasmus Darwin in Lichfield Cathedral reads: 'A skillfull observer of Nature, Vivid in imagination, indefatigable in research, Original and far-sighted in his views. His speculations were mainly directed to problems which were afterwards more successfully solved by his Grandson CHARLES DARWIN, An inheritor of many of his characteristics.'

In *Zoonomia; or the Laws of Organic Life*, 1794–6 he envisaged filamentous origins of life which were an important talking point as the nineteenth century dawned.

DICK Robert 1811–1866 Son of an excise officer; early ideas of college education and a learned profession thwarted by mother's death. Victimisation by stepmother of the four children significant in his later life as a scientific recluse: he escaped from everyday traumas at home to the peace of nature and its study, even when deprived of shoes to deter him; later wrote: 'All my naturally buoyant, youthful spirits were broken. To this day I feel the effects . . . . It is this that still makes me shrink from the world.'

In Thurso his solitary habits and outmoded clothes gave him an eccentric image; his geologist's hammer was imagined to be for seeking silver. His few friends were children bringing specimens or begging, and between 1853-64 the geologist, Charles Peach, Wick's Coastguard Officer.

DILLWYN Lewis Weston (see Table 5.1).

DOUGLAS David 1799–1834 Epitomised the Victorian attribute of devotion to duty in the face of adversity; a devotee of natural history. 1810 or 1811-18: apprentice gardener; 1820: at Botanical Garden, Glasgow. Sir Willian Jackson Hooker, his teacher and friend, took him on botanical field excursions. 1823: started travels in North America and Upper Canada.

EDWARD Thomas 1814–1886.

EHRET Georg Dionysius 1708–1770 Like the Bauer brothers, adopted Britain as his home.

ELLACOMBE Henry Nicholson 1822–1916 Canon H.N. Ellacombe was the son of the Rev. Henry Thomas Ellacombe (1790–1885), a skilful florist and a prominent writer in William Robinson's journal, *The Garden*. Canon H.N. Ellacombe carried on his father's parish (for 68 years), botanical interests and fine garden which remained unchanged by Victorian fashions. He corresponded with Kew and some of his plants were featured in *Curtis's Botanical Magazine*.

FITCH Walter Hood 1817–1892 Most outstanding and prolific botanical artist of the time. Apprentice pattern-drawer in a firm of Glasgow calico designers. He met Sir William Jackson Hooker through helping with herbarium specimens on his free evenings and Hooker, noticing Fitch's talent, trained him in botanical draughtsmanship. Illustrator of George Bentham and Hooker's *Flora* and many more, also *Curtis's Botanical Magazine* 1834-77, being his own lithographer from 1845 (see Plates 11 and 13). 1879: granted a Civil List pension of £100 p.a. on the strength of his lithographs for *Victoria regia* (1851), which appealed to Disraeli's imperialist views.

FORTUNE Robert 1812–1880 Educated parish school; apprenticed at local gardens; worked at Edinburgh Botanic Garden; Superintendent of hothouse at Horticultural Society gardens at Chiswick. 1843: Horticultural Society offered him opportunity to collect in China; after a short spell as Curator of Chelsea Physic Garden returned to China several times taking in Japan on his last voyage, 1860-2.

FRANCIS George William 1800–1865 Wrote *An Analysis of the British Ferns and their allies* (1837) – the official launch of the fern craze. 1849: emigrated with large family to Australia, rented an old botanic garden; later appointed Director of Adelaide

Botanic Garden; wrote on various topics including *Chemistry for Students, Manual of Practical Levelling for Railways and Canals, The Art of Modelling Wax Flowers, Electrical Experiments.*

FRITH William Powell 1819–1909.

GATTY Margaret (née Scott) 1809–1873 Great in the belief that joy is to be found in work – the theme of her first tale. Father was Nelson's chaplain on *Victory.* Aged ten, studied, drew and etched on copper in print room of British Museum. 1839: married Yorkshire clergyman, had seven children; took up natural history while convalescing aged 39 (1848), publishing authoritative book on British seaweeds (1862) as well as moral tales for children, such as an earwig's experiences inside an orchid and *Aunt Judy's Magazine* (1866) – the latter being a labour of love, the subscriptions supporting three cots at Great Ormond Street Hospital. During her last years, developed paralysis of right arm, went on working with left; then a paralysis of left, went on working by dictation until speech affected.

GOETHE Johann Wolfgang von 1749–1832.

GOSSE Philip Henry 1810–1888 Born into poor-genteel family in reduced circumstances, father a skilled miniature painter and unsuccessful writer. 'Discovered' sea-shore life encouraged by scientifically-inclined aunt recognising his talent. 1827: clerk in whaler's office in Newfoundland; farmer and schoolmaster in America; 1844: collector in Jamaica for British Museum. Finished his career as author, 1865; much of his last 20 years spent cultivating orchids; at 76 re-entered scientific world with book in which he drew all the microscopic illustrations.

GRAY Thomas 1716–1771.

GREENAWAY Kate 1846–1901 John Ruskin praised her illustrations.

GREW Nehemiah 1641–1712.

GUTTERIDGE Joseph 1816–1899 Childhood natural history interests opposed by stepmother; 1829: apprenticed as ribbon weaver, 1831: witnessed riots against first steam looms; married. 1840s – known as a 'Free Thinker' – increasingly plagued by questions about nature of life and its origins (finally turned to Spiritualism for the answers); intellectual honesty prevented him stating required religious beliefs to obtain freeman of the city's dole – unable to pay burial costs in a hard winter, they shared their one bare room for a week with the corpse of their child killed by smallpox. Permanent injury after fall from loom. 1855–65: his wife died, he remarried and there was a decline in silk ribbon trade leading to severe privations. 1891: made his diary available for newspaper's local Coventry history – published in weekly extracts – later became a book by popular demand.

HENSLOW John Stevens 1796–1861 Father a solicitor: both parents interested in natural history.

Cleric, all-round naturalist, became Professor of Botany at Cambridge knowing little botany – unorthodox approach of personal discovery and field excursions. Created Botanic Gardens at Cambridge, important today for its species collections, e.g. tulips (see Plate 15) and others.

HIBBERD Shirley 1825–1890 Son of a retired sea captain; planned medical study curtailed by father's death, thus apprenticed to bookseller; soon entered horticultural journalism. Married twice; nature an integral part of his lifestyle – was vegetarian and kept moving house further out of London in order to experiment on fruit and potato growing.

HOOKE Robert 1635–1703.

HOOKER Sir Joseph Dalton 1817–1911 Tibetan travel was boyhood inspiration from an old book. Educated Glasgow University; 1839–43 assistant surgeon of Ross's Antarctic expedition; talented surveyor; pioneer of study of plant distribution.

HOOKER Sir William Jackson 1785–1865 A true Victorian who worked 18 hours a day without hesitation. Son of a merchant's clerk who collected rare succulents and read travel books. Due to inherit from godfather, was educated as a gentleman at Norwich high school; after inheritance decided on life of travel and natural history. 1804: discovered an unrecorded moss, identified by Sir James Edward Smith (also living in Norwich) who introduced him to Dawson Turner who in turn introduced him to Sir Joseph Banks. 1809: Hooker went on the first botanical expedition to Iceland, specimens (and nearly his life) lost in ship fire; 1814: botanised on Continent – met Lamarck and Humboldt; 1820: without paper qualifications and never having even attended a lecture became Professor of Botany at Glasgow (due to Banks). His lectures were so popular that private citizens attended. At that time botany was identification of dried herbaria for *materia medica*: having no textbook, he wrote one; began field excursions for students to study plants. With impracticalities of field-collecting in mind, specifically in the Scottish Highlands, he wrote his *British Flora* which later merged with another into the famous 'Bentham and Hooker' *Flora.*

JEKYLL Gertrude 1843–1932.

KEATS John 1795–1821.

KERNER von Marilaun Anton (Marilonn) 1831–1898 Viennese; Professor of Botany and Director of Botanical Gardens.

KERR William d. 1814.

KINGSLEY Charles 1819–1875 Clergyman, poet, naturalist; for many years considered extreme Radical. 1859: Chaplain to Queen Victoria.

KNAPP John Leonard 1767–1845 Father a rector; joined the Navy, resigned through ill-health; captain in Northamptonshire militia. Made long summer botanical excursions; two species of grasses named after him, wrote and illustrated book on

British grasses.

LANKESTER Edwin 1814–1874 Self-taught from the age of twelve. When he was 20, local natural history Society (Saffron Walden, Essex) lent him £300 to enable him to study botany at London University under John Lindley. He became a Professor of Natural History.

LANKESTER Phoebe (née Pope) 1825–1900 1845: married Edwin Lankester who gave her botanical inspiration. Eight children: eldest son, Edwin Ray Lankester, also became a professor, involved in early biology teaching in schools.

LEE(I) James 1715–1795 First of several generations who in partnership with Kennedys started the famous nursery at Hammersmith; it was a second-generation Kennedy who officially crossed Napoleon's lines (see page 3).

LEEUWENHOEK Antoni van 1632–1723.

LINDLEY John 1799–1865 First holiday at 52; never felt fatigue until 50. 1829: Professor of Botany at University College, London; supported an alternative plant classification to that of Linnaeus. 1835: Director of Chelsea Physic Garden; editor of *Gardener's Chronicle*.

LINNAEUS Carl 1707–1778 Professor of Medicine and Botany at University of Uppsala from 1741.

LLEWELYN John Dillwyn (see Table 5.1).

LOUDON Jane (née Webb) 1807–1858 At 17 forced to earn livelihood by father's death: wrote *The Mummy, a Tale of the Twenty-second Century*, a romance of the future – reviewed in one of John Claudius Loudon's journals, after which he sought acquaintance of its (supposedly male) author; they met and married. She was his accompanying secretary on his landscape garden journeys and began writing ladies' botany books to pay his debts on his grander volumes; on his death she received Civil List pension.

LOUDON John Claudius 1783–1843 The ideal of intense work and determination. Son of a Lanarkshire farmer; childhood gardening interest; good education in Edinburgh and continued at night classes while apprenticed to nurseryman and landscape gardener. Kept journal in French to familiarise himself with language. Set up school of farming in horrified response to inefficient English farming. Usually fasted between seven o'clock breakfast and eight o'clock dinner, working by day, writing by night; at one stage editing five monthly publications.

LUBBOCK Sir John William 1834–1913 Father an eminent mathematician as well as banker. Sponsored Bank Holidays Act (1871) (nick-named St Lubbock's Days), Wild Birds Protection Act (1880), Open Spaces Act (1880) and others. Regardless of fashion, wore elastic-sided boots to allow him to reach his work-table in minimum time.

LYELL Sir Charles 1797–1875 Father a botanist and friend of Sir William Jackson Hooker; 1816: attracted to Geology by William Buckland's lectures, made geological tour of Scotland with him; wrote joint papers with Sir Roderick Murchison.

MAETERLINCK Count Maurice 1862–1949.

MARCET Mrs Jane 1769–1858 Daughter of a rich Swiss merchant in London.

MASSON Francis 1741–1805 Selected by William Townsend Aiton to go to the Cape.

MILLER Philip 1692–1771 A fanatical Scottish gardener. 1722: Curator of Chelsea Physic Garden – introduced many foreign plants but was extremely secretive and possessive about them; would only employ Scottish gardeners at Chelsea; trained William Aiton; dismissed his charge in his last year for obstinacy. Linnaeus visited him and persuaded him to alter plant classification in his classic *Dictionary of Gardening*.

MONTAGUE Lady Mary Wortley 1689–1762.

MORRIS William 1834–1896 Inspired by a passion for beauty and stood for natural decoration and pure colour. Rossetti persuaded him to concentrate on painting rather than poetry. With fellow Pre-Raphaelites started a decorative art business 1862. In 1884 he and others formed the Socialist League.

MÜLLER Fritz 1822–1897.

MÜLLER Hermann 1829–1883 Taught in Realschule in Lippstadt and quite late in life was inspired by Charles Darwin's book on orchids.

MURCHISON Sir Roderick Impey 1792–1871.

NESFIELD William Andrews 1793–1881 Engineer and landscape gardener at Harewood, Castle Howard; laid out Regent's Park, St James's Park. His son, William Eden, was a leader of the Gothic revival designing lodges at Regent's Park and at Kew.

OWEN Richard 1804–1892.

PALEY William 1743–1805.

PAXTON Sir Joseph 1803–1865 Once dismissed by Queen Victoria as 'a common Gardener's boy', one of the most remarkable and versatile of Victorians: quintessence of the self-made man. Son of a small farmer; Grammar School education. 1854–65: Liberal MP for Coventry. Designer of mansions, landscaped public parks, involved in town-planning projects; hydraulic engineer; a Director of railways; edited gardening magazines, wrote several books.

POPE Alexander 1688–1744.

POPE Clara Maria d. 1838 Modelled for some of the prettier figures in the famous 'Cries of London' painted by her first husband, Francis Wheatly.

PRATT Anne 1806–1893 (later Mrs Pearless) Wrote on many very Victorian topics: e.g. wrote *The Excellent Woman, as described in the Book of Proverbs*. Father a wholesale grocer; married 1866. Her contribution to encouraging interest in wild flowers recognised by grant from Civil List.

REDOUTÉ Pierre-Joseph 1759–1840.

REPTON Humphry 1752–1818.

ROBINSON William 1838–1900 Attacked formalised garden style as at Kew; like John Ruskin, refused to use Latin names for plants.

ROUSSEAU Jean-Jacques 1712–78.

RUSKIN John 1819–1900 Brought up in strictly Puritan manner – without toys, under scrutiny, long Bible readings, but an immensely cultured background: as infant trained in drawing, music, literature, reading aloud, observing nature; as soon as he could read and write, creating his own verse and prose. Aged 14, introduced to Alps: family travelling to methodically observe beauties of nature and art. To him, hothouses were as suspect as botanical Latin: he apologised to visitors for having one – it was for growing grapes for his friends. He had immense concern for social and industrial problems.

SCHOMBURGK Sir Robert Hermann 1804–1865.

SCOTT Sir Walter 1771–1832

SHELLEY Percy Bysshe 1792–1822.

SMITH Charlotte 1749–1806 Some of her poems featured in *The Temple of Flora*.

SMITH Sir James Edward 1759–1828 Son of a wealthy wool merchant; first educated by mother (an ardent flower lover); read medicine at Edinburgh; wrote large *English Flora* (1824–8). Founder Linnaean (later Linnean) Society: his botanical correspondent, Samuel Goodenough (1743–1827, Bishop of Carlisle from 1808 see page 5), became its first treasurer. (J.S. Duncan's *Botano-Theology* was largely compiled from Smith.)

SMITH William 1769–1839 Father of English Geology.

SOWERBY James 1757–1822.

SPRENGEL Christian Konrad 1750–1816.

STILLINGFLEET Benjamin 1702–1771.

STURTEVANT Edward Lewis 1842–1898 farmer botanist, physician, agricultural experimenter at 'Waushakum Farm', Massachusetts.

TALBOT William Henry Fox (see Table 5.1).

TAYLOR John Ellor 1837–1895 Eldest son of a foreman in Manchester cotton factory. No formal education beyond vague instruction at local school held in a chapel. Became editor of the 'Norwich People's Journal', founded a Science Gossip Club and Norwich Geological Society; 1872: Curator of Museum at Ipswich. Married a headmaster's daughter.

TENNYSON Alfred, Lord 1809–1892.

THOMSON James 1700–1748.

THORNTON Robert John 1768–1837.

TURNER Dawson 1775–1858.

TURNER Joseph Mallord (or Mallad) William 1775–1851.

TURPIN Pierre Jean François 1775–1840.

TWAMLEY Louisa Anne (later Mrs Meredith 1812–1895 Educated by her mother; 1839: married her cousin, Charles, and sailed for Australian life on a sheep station; 1842: in debt. After six years as a police magistrate, Charles later became noted politician. For her literary and artistic services to colony, Tasmanian government granted her a pension much of which was lost in bank failures; her last years also marred by lameness, blindness in one eye and regrets of the past in spite of a previous image of vivacity and cheerfulness.

VEITCH John Gould 1839–1870 Great grandson of John Veitch (1752–1839), founder of nursery.

VEITCH James Harry 1868–1907 Eldest son of John Gould Veitch.

WALLACE Alfred Russel 1823–1913 His father, a dabbler, had lost most of his money. At 13 years old spent a year as pupil–teacher at Grammar School; at 17, was making a herbarium; went as an English master to Leicester where he met Henry Walter Bates. They left for South America 1848, in 1849 were joined by Wallace's younger brother who died of yellow fever, 1851; Alfred returned to England, 1852, then going on historic expedition to Far East. Wallace's ideas on evolution differed in some major points from Darwin due to his strong Spiritualist convictions. He wrote on his beliefs, land nationalisation, vaccination and had done experiments on hypnotism while teaching. Married 1866; created a garden of nearly 1,000 species.

WALLICH Nathaniel 1786–1854 Born Copenhagen; surgeon to Danish settlement near Calcutta. A Briton by adoption: introduced great numbers of plants.

WARD Nathaniel Bagshaw 1791–1868 Son of doctor. Chilhood collecting of plants and insects; at 13 years old the sight of tropical vegetation of Jamaica's interior inspired him to become ardent botanist. Succeeded to father's practice; habitually rose at 5 a.m. to allow time for plant-collecting round London, visiting botanic gardens and nurseries. His herbarium contained 25,000 species.

WARNER Richard 1763–1857.

WHITE Gilbert 1720–1793.

WITHERS Mrs A.I. Active 1827–64 One of the botanical art teachers.

WOOD John George 1827–1889 Wrote twelve hours a day, starting 4.30 a.m. followed at 8 a.m. by a three-mile fast run across hilly country, a cold bath, then breakfast. Also natural history lecturer in Britain and in 1883, in America.

WORDSWORTH Dorothy 1771–1855.

WORDSWORTH William 1770–1850.

# SELECT BIBLIOGRAPHY

Allan, M. *Darwin and his Flowers*, 1977

Allen, D.E. *The Naturalist in Britain*, 1976

Arnold, H.J.P. *William Henry Fox Talbot, Pioneer of photography and man of science*, 1977

Barber, L. *The Heyday of Natural History*, 1980

Barlow, N. (ed. from MS.) *Charles Darwin's Diary of the Voyage of HMS 'Beagle'*, 1933

Bartholomaeus Anglicus, *De Proprietatibus Rerum*, Thomas Berthelet 1535 edn

Bateman, J. *Orchidaceae of Mexico and Guatemala*, 1837–43

Bates, H.W. *The Naturalist on the Amazons*, 1863

Bath Natural History and Antiquarian Field Club, *Proceedings*

Bath Microscopical Society, *Soirée Programmes*

Bayne, P. *Life and Letters of Hugh Miller*, 1871 via Barber, L. *The Heyday of Natural History*, 1980

Mrs Beeton's *Cookery Book and Household Guide*, 1890 and 1899 edns

Bevan, E. *The Honey Bee: its natural history, physiology and management*, 2nd edn, 1838

Blunt, W. *The Art of Botanical Illustration*, 1950

—— *Tulipomania*, 1950

—— *The Compleat Naturalist*, 1971

Buckley, A.B. *The Fairy-land of Science*, 1879

Buday, G. *The History of the Christmas Card*, 1954

Caddy, F. *Through the Fields with Linnaeus. A Chapter in Swedish History*, Vols 1 and 2, 1887

*Cassell's Household Guide*, 1875 via Henderson, M. and Wilkinson, E. *Cassell's Compendium of Victorian Crafts*, 1978

Clare, J. *Natural History Letters*, 1825 via Johnson E.D.H. *The Poetry of Earth*, 1966

Coats, A.M. *Garden Shrubs and their Histories*, 1963

—— *The Quest for Plants*, 1969

Cobbett, W. *The English Gardener*, 1833

Coles, W. *Adam in Eden*, 1657

Collingwood, W.G. *Ruskin Relics*, 1903

Crane, W. *A Floral Fantasy in an Old English Garden,*

*set forth in verses and coloured designs*, 1899

Culpeper, N. *The English Physician Enlarg'd*, 1788 edn

Cunningham, A. see Lee

*Curtis's Botanical Magazine*

Darwin, C. *Diary of the Voyage of H.M.S. 'Beagle'* see Barlow, N.

—— 'On the Agency of Bees in the Fertilisation of Papilionaceous Flowers', *Gardener's Chronicle*, p. 725, 1857 and pp. 824, 844, 1858

—— *On the Origin of Species by means of natural selection, or the preservation of favoured races in the struggle for life*, 4th edn, 1866

—— *On the Various Contrivances by which British and Foreign Orchids are Fertilised by Insects and on the good effects of intercrossing*, 1st edn, 1862; 2nd edn, 1877

—— *The Variation of Animals and Plants under domestication*, popular edn, 1905

—— *Insectivorous Plants*, 1st edn, 1875; 2nd edn, 1888

—— *The Effects of Cross- and Self-Fertilisation in the Vegetable Kingdom*, 1876

—— *The Power of Movement in Plants*, 1880

—— *The Descent of Man*, 2nd edn, 1883

Darwin, E. *The Botanic Garden. A Poem in Two Parts Part I: The Economy of Vegetation, Part II: The Loves of the Plants*, 4th edn, 1799

—— *Phytologia, or the Philosophy of Agriculture and Gardening*, 1800

Darwin, F. (ed.) *Life and Letters of Charles Darwin*, 1887

Douglas, D. *his journal* via Harvey,, A.G., *Douglas of the Fir, a biography of David Douglas, botanist*, 1947

Dick, R. private letters in Smiles, S.

Duncan, J.S. *Botano-theology. An arranged compendium chiefly from Smith, Keith and Thomson*, 1825

Ellacombe, H.N. *The Daisy: its history, poetry, and botany* (reprinted from *The Garden*), 1874

*English Cyclopaedia* Updated version of *Penny Cyclopaedia*, 26 vols, 1856–72

Francis, G.W. *The Little English Flora, or a botanical*

*and popular account of all our common field flowers*, 3rd edn, 1849

*Gardener's Chronicle*, 1858

Gatty, M. *Parables from Nature*, 1879 edn

Genders, R. *Collecting Antique Plants. The History and Culture of the Old Florists' Flowers*, 1971

Gosse, E. *Father and Son. A Study of two Temperaments*, 1925

Gosse, P.H. *A Naturalist's Sojourn in Jamaica*, 1851

—— *Wanderings through the Conservatories at Kew*, 1857

—— *The Romance of Natural History*, 1861

Greenaway, K. *The Language of Flowers*, 1884

Grew, N. *The Anatomy of Plants*, 1682

Gutteridge, J. in *Master and Artisan in Victorian England, The Diary of William Andrews and the Autobiography of Joseph Gutteridge*, 1969

Hey, R. *The Moral of Flowers*, 1833

Hedrick, U.P. (ed.) *Sturtevant's Edible Plants of the World*, 1972

Hibberd, S. *Brambles and Bay Leaves; Essays on the Homely and the Beautiful*, 1855

—— *Rustic Adornments for Homes of Taste, and Recreations for Town Folk in the Study and Imitation of Nature*, 1856; enlarged edn, 1870

—— *Garden Favourites*, 1858

—— *The Amateur's Greenhouse and Conservatory*, 1873

Hooke, R. *Micrographia*, 1665

Hooker, J.D. *Himalayan Journals*, Vols 1 and 2, 1854

Hooker, W.J. *Victoria regia or illustrations of the Royal Water Lily*, 1851

—— *A century of ferns; being figures with brief descriptions of one hundred species of ferns*, 1854

*Illustrated London News*

Jackson, M.E. *Botanical Dialogues, between Hortensia and her four children. By a Lady*, 1797

Kerner von Maurilaun, A. *Flowers and their Unbidden Guests* (trans. and ed. by W. Ogle), 1878

King, R. *The World of Kew*. 1977

Kingsley, C. *Glaucus; or Wonders of the Shore*, Camb. edn, 1855

Knapp, J.L. *The Journal of a Naturalist*, 1829

Lankester, E. *Half-Hours with the Microscope, being a popular guide to the use of the Microscope as a means of amusement and instruction*, 1859

Lankester, P. *Wild Flowers Worth Notice*, 1861

Lee, I. *Early Explorers in Australia, from the log-books and journals, including the diary of Allan Cunningham, botanist from March 1, 1817 to November 19, 1818*, 1925

Lee, J. *An Introduction to the Science of Botany, chiefly extracted from the Works of Linnaeus*, 4th edn, 1810

Lee, R.W. *A History of Valentines*, 1953

Lemmon, K. *The Covered Garden*, 1962

Lindley, J. *Ladies' Botany: or A Familiar Introduction To the Study of the Natural System of Botany*, Vol 2, 1834–37, 2nd edn

Linnaeus, C. *Reflections on the Study of Nature* (trans. by J.E. Smith), 1785

—— *Amoenitates Academicae* in *Stillingfleet's Tracts*, 1759

—— *Philosophia Botanica and other treatises* trans. in Rose, H. *The Elements of Botany*, 1775

—— *Praeludia Sponsaliarum Plantarum* in Blunt, W. *The Compleat Naturalist*, 1971

Loudon, J. *The Ladies' Flower-Garden of Ornamental Annuals*, 1840

—— *Facts from the World of Nature*, 1848

Loudon, J.C. *Encyclopaedia of Gardening*, 1822

—— *The Suburban Gardener and Villa Companion*, 1838

—— *Encyclopaedia of Cottage, farm and villa architecture and furniture*, 1842

Lyell, C. *The Antiquity of Man*, 1863

Maeterlinck, M. *Life and Flowers*, 1907

Marcet, J. *Conversations on Botany*, 3rd edn, 1820

—— *Lessons on Animals, Vegetables and Minerals*, 3rd edn, 1859

Markham, V. *Paxton and the Bachelor Duke*, 1935

Masson, F. *Stapeliae Novae*, 1796

M'Cosh, J. and Dickie, G. *Typical Forms and Special Ends in Creation*, 1856

Miller, H. *The Old Red Standstone*, 1865 edn

Miller, P. *The Gardener's Dictionary*, 1731

Millican, A. *The Travels and Adventures of an Orchid Hunter*, 1891

Montague, Lady M. Wortley *Complete Letters*, 1763 edn

Moriarty, H.M. *Viridarium; or Green House Plants*, 1806, via Blunt, W. *The Art of Botanical Illustration*, 1950

Müller, H. *The Fertilisation of Flowers* (trans. and ed. by D'Arcy Thompson, W.), 1883

Müller, F. via Müller, H. *The Fertilisation of Flowers*, 1883

Neumann, M. *Grundsätze und Erfahrungen über die Anlage, Erhaltung und Pflege von Glashäusern aller Art*, 1852

Paley, W. *Natural Theology, or Evidences of the Existence and Attributes of the Deity collected from the Appearances of Nature*, 1802 in *Complete Works*, 1825

*Penny Cyclopaedia* see *English Cyclopaedia*

Pratt, A. *The Flowering Plants of Great Britain*, 5 vols, 1855

Ruskin, J. *Proserpina*, 1874–1886

Salisbury, E.J. *The Living Garden*, 1945

Smiles, S. *Life of a Scotch Naturalist*, 1876

—— *Robert Dick. Baker, of Thurso Geologist and Botanist*, 1878

Smith, Lady (ed.) *Smith's Memoirs and Correspondence* Vols 1 and 2, 1832

Smith, J.E. and Sowerby, J. *English Botany*, 1790–1814

Sturtevant, E.L. see Hendrick, U.P.

Taylor, J.E. *Flowers, their origin, shapes, perfumes and colours*, 2nd edn, 1878

—— *The Sagacity and Morality of Plants. A sketch of the life and conduct of the vegetable kingdom*, 1891 edn

Tergit, G. *Flowers through the Ages*, 1961

Thornton, R.J. *The Temple of Flora*, 1799, 1807 edns

Twamley, L.A. (later Mrs Meredith) *The Romance of Nature; or, the flower seasons illustrated*, 1836 edn

—— *Flora's Gems; or, the treasures of the parterre*, c. 1837

Wallace, A.R. *A Narrative of Travels on the Amazon and Rio Negro*, 1853

Warner, R. 'Floral Decay: emblematical of men's mortal condition', in *Poetical Trifles*, c. 1850

Wood,, J.G. *Common Objects of the Country*, 1858

Yonge, C.M. *The Herb of the Field*, 1853, reprinted from 'Chapters on Flowers' in the *Magazine for the Young*

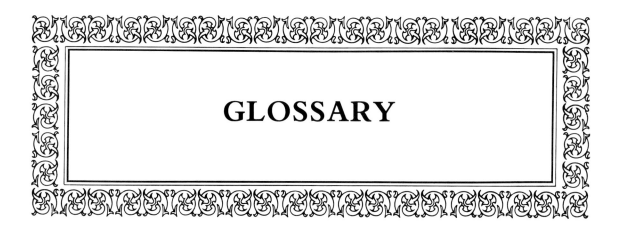

# GLOSSARY

*epiphyte* – plant attached to another merely for support, not extracting nourishment, e.g. lichens, mosses, some orchids; in contrast to a *parasite* living on another from which it obtains nourishment and without which it cannot live, e.g. broomrape.

*Flora* – list of plant species of a particular area, with a key to aid identification and description of each species.

*flower parts*

*carpel* – at the centre of the flower; female reproductive organ of the flowering plant. Consisting of the *ovary* at the base, containing *ovules* (which after fertilisation will become the *seeds*); *stigma*, the surface receptive to pollen grains and which is sometimes held aloft on a *style* or stalk.

Some flowers have several carpels which are collectively called the *pistil*.

*stamen* – arranged around the carpel or pistil; male reproductive organ producing *pollen grains* within pollen sacs inside the *anther* which is at the tip of a stalk or *filament*.

*herbarium* – collection of preserved plant specimens, for reference and identification purposes.

*species* – plants (or animals) having the greatest mutual resemblance: the smallest unit of classification in common usage. A number of similar species are grouped in a *genus*, similar *genera* are grouped in a *family*.

# INDEXES

## GENERAL INDEX

Adam in Eden 47, 85-6
Africa 2, 108
Aiton, William 2, 5, 184, 187
Aiton, William Townsend 2, 184, 185, Fig. 7.1
album 32, 35, Pl. 5
Amazon 111, 128, 178-9; *see also* rain forest
anther 49, 64, 195, Figs. 8.5, 9.10
aquarium 86, 91-3, 137, Figs. 5.17, 8.4
artisan 20, 23, 25, 53, 89
*Aunt Judy's Magazine* 73, 186
Australia 23, 25, 36, 89, 185, 188; collecting in 2, 122-5, 129-30, 132; plants of 103-4, 106, 108, 114, 130, 184, Fig. 7.1

Babington, Charles Cardale 79, 176, 181, 184
Banks, Sir Joseph 2, 6, 13, 184, 186
Bateman, James 115-16, 152-3, Fig. 6.6, Pl. 10
Bates, Henry Walter: life 25, 123, 128-9, 130-2, 184; quotes on plants 60, 102-3, 111
Bath Natural History and Antiquarian Field Club 52-3, 80, Fig. 5.8
Bauer, Ferdinand 2, 184
Bauer, Francis 2, 184
Beauharnais, Josephine 3
beauty 49, 142-3, 177-80, Fig. 9.12
Bedford, Duke of 115
bee: and pollination 64, 146-7, 151, Figs. 4.8, 8.11, 9.10, Pl. 17; and Victorian society 9, 39-42, Fig. 3.10
Beeton, Mrs 30, Fig. 3.2
Bentham, George 77, 184
Bevan, Edward 9, 64, 184
Blake, William 10, 184
botanical excursion 19-20, 79, 81, 186
botano-theology *see* natural theology
botany 3-5, 32, 47, 69-72; in schools 139, 182, 187
Bridges, Thomas 109-10, 184
Brown, Lancelot 'Capability' 2, 13, 184
Buckland, William 169, 184, 187
Buckley, Arabella 43-4, 64, 141-2, 151, 184, Fig. 8.11

Buffon, Comte de 4, 74, 145, 166-7, 184, Fig. 5.5
Byron, Lord 10, 184

Calcutta Botanical Garden 98, 107
calyx 43, 49, 58, 72
Campbell, Dr 126
Canada 130
Carboniferous era 169-70, Figs. 9.8, 9.9
Carlisle, Bishop of 5-6, 188
carpel 64, 70
carpet bedding 13, 95, Fig. 6.1
Catastrophism 168-9
Chambers, Sir William 184
Chatsworth 10, 19, 110, 112, 121; *see also* Great Conservatory, Chatsworth
Chelsea Physic Garden 117-18, 184, 185, 187
China 106, 114, 123, 163; *see also* Fortune, Robert, life
Clare, John 10, 23, 42, 93, 184, Fig. 4.3
coal 37, 44-5, 137, 167, 169, Fig. 9.7
Cobbett, William 96-7, 184
Coles, William 164, 184
colour 49, 142, 177-8, Fig. 9.12
compound microscope *see* microscope
conservation 117, 181-2, Fig. 6.12
conservatory 95-7, 103-4; illustrations of Figs. 2.2, 2.3, 2.4, 6.3, Pl. 8; *see also* Great Conservatory, Chatsworth, Palm House, Kew
conversations botanical 5, 70, 72
conversazione 3-4, 137
Cook, Captain 2, 121
cottage flowers 39-42, 53
Crane, Walter 32, 184, Figs. 3.5, 5.15
cross-pollination 24, 139, 147
Crystal Palace 89, 107, 110, 112-13
Culpeper, Nicholas 81, 164
Cunningham, Allan 104, 114-15, 132, 185, Fig. 7.1; collecting hazards 122-5, 129-30
Cunningham, Richard 130
*Curtis's Botanical Magazine* 6, 79, 155, 185; illustrations Figs. 6.10, 7.1, 7.2, 9.1, Pls. 11, 13

Dalhousie, Lady 127
Dalton, James 77
Darwin, Charles: life and work 128-9, 145-

7, 185, 187; quotes: beauty 179-80, evolution 171-2, 182, Fig. 9.4, other plant investigations 153-7, 173-7, Fig. 8.15, pollen mechanisms 63, 139, 141-2, 147-53, Figs. 4.9, 8.9, 8.11, sundew 89, 157-60, Figs. 8.17, 8.18
Darwin, Erasmus 5, 38-9, 140-1, 146, 154, 157, 185, Fig. 3.7
Darwin, Sir Francis 145, 155, 160
decay 44, 47, 58, 91
Devonshire, Duke of 22, 107, 112, 115, 130
Dick, Robert: life and work 25-6, 170-1, 185, Figs. 2.14, 2.15, collecting 81-4, Figs. 5.12, 5.13, 5.14, herbarium specimens Figs. 5.9, 5.10, 5.11, 5.12, 5.13, 5.14, 9.9, quotes 86-7, 176-7
Dillwyn, Lewis Weston 77, Fig. 5.7
dinosaurs 168-9
Douglas, David: life 125, 127-32, 185; plant introductions 100, 121, 123, Fig. 7.3
Drake, Miss 115-16

ecology 182
Edward, Thomas 25, 53, 185
Ehret, George Dionysius 2, 3, 185
elephant hawkmoth 144, Fig. 8.8
Ellacombe, Henry Nicholson 52-3, 79, 185
epiphyte 60, 114, 117, 118, 195, Fig. 6.6
evolution *see* Darwin, Charles
extinction 117-19, Figs. 5.15, 6.13

fashion flowers 12, 30-1, 110, 114
fern craze 87-9, 93
fernery 26, 85-6, 93, 95, Figs. 5.17, 5.18
field club 19-20, 52-3, 79-81, Fig. 5.8
field excursion *see* botanical excursion
filament Fig. 9.10
Fitch, Walter Hood 21, 32, 79, 110, 185; illustrations Fig. 7.2, Pls. 7, 11, 13
Flora 79, 83, 181, 184, 186, 188, 195
floral clock 54, 67-9
floral symbols 37, 49
florist's clubs and floricultural societies 23
florist's flowers 22-3
flower arranging 29-30, Figs. 3.1, 3.2
flower identification 3, 10, 15; *see also* Flora, Language of Flowers, Linnaean classification
flower painting 2, 3, 6, 9, 14, 32, 81

flower pressing 3, 14, 37, 83, Figs. 5.7; *see also* Dick, Robert, herbarium specimens
Fortune, Robert: life 98, 122, 123, 127, 185; plant introductions 98, 132, Fig. 7.2
fossil 44–5, 167–8, 169–70, Figs. 9.5, 9.6
Fox-Strangways family 74–77, Table 5.1
France 2–5, 10, 12
Francis, George William 70, 164, 185–6, Fig. 5.3

Gardener's Chronicle 32, 147, 152, 174, 187
Gatty, Margaret 157–8, 186
George III 2, 6, 22
Gibson, John 107, 115
glass-house 11–12, 13, 17, 95–7, Figs. 6.2, 6.4; *see also* conservatory
glass: manufacture 93, 97; tax 97
Gosse, Philip Henry: life 91, 121, 172, 186; quotes 20–1, 103, 108–9, 114, 118–19, 132
Great Conservatory, Chatsworth 97, 104–7, 115, Fig. 6.7
Greenaway, Kate 186, Figs. 4.2, 4.4, Pl. 3
greenhouse *see* glass-house
Grew, Nehemiah 135, 186
Gutteridge, Joseph: life 23–5, 81–3, 186; plant study and collecting 23, 81, 84, 139; quotes on plants and botanists 53–4, 112–13, 143

Hardy, Thomas 85, 170
healing herbs 164, 186, Fig. 9.3
Henslow, John Stevens 77, 139, 169, 179, 185, 186
herbaceous border 42
herbarium 3–5, 74–5, 83–4, 182; important herbaria 5, 77–9, 114, 145–6, 184, 188; illustrations of *see* Dick, Robert, herbarium specimens
Hey, Rebecca 10, 30, 47, 54–7
Hibberd, Shirley: life 186; on nature's processes 74–5, 91–3, illustrations Figs. 2.7, 3.9, 3.10, 5.17, 5.18, 6.2, 6.3, quotes 15–16, 18, 39–40, 62, 84–6, 90–1
Himalayas 98–101, 123–4, Pl. 7
honey-guide 141
Hooke, Robert 135, 186, Fig. 8.4
Hooker, Sir Joseph Dalton: and Darwin 145, 155, 172; Himalayan expedition 122–8; life 77–9, 186; on mountains and rhododendrons 98–101, 116–17, 132, Fig. 4.7, Pl. 7
Hooker, Sir William Jackson: life and influence 6, 77–9, 185–7; plants 84–5, 98, 110, 112, 161, Figs. 6.10, 9.1
Horticultural Society *see* Royal Horticultural Society
hothouse *see* glass-house
hot water piping 108–9, 115
hybrid 24, 116, 139, Fig. 8.10

India, plants of 62, 116–17, 132, 163
industrialisation 10–11, 14, 15, 18–20, 23
insect: pollinators 62, 141, 148–53, Fig. 4.8, *see also* bees, moths; suffering via plants 61–3, 89, 158, 161; vision 177, 179, 180–1

Japan 97–8, 122–3, 125, 127, 185; plant from Fig. 7.2
Jekyll, Gertrude 30, 42, 101, 186, Fig. 3.6
jungle *see* rain forest

Keats, John 91, 186
Kerner von Marilaun, Anton 62–3, 186

Kerr, William 122–3
Kew: cultivation of plants 99, 106, 110–11, 114–15, 121; history of 2, 6–7, 20–1, 77–9, 184, 187; *see also* herbarium, important herbaria, Palm House
Kingsley, Charles 59, 81, 88, 186
Knapp, John Leonard: life 79, 186; quotes 49, 53, 62, 177

Language of Flowers 10, 37–8, 49, 56, Pls. 3, 4
Lankester, Edwin 135, 187
Lankester, Phoebe 19–20, 23, 33, 53, 64–5, 187
Lee (I), James and Lee Nursery 12, 104, 116–18, 187
Leeuwenhoek Antoni van 135, 187
Lindley, John: life 61, 77, 114, 184, 187; quotes 49, 51, 104, 156–8, Figs. 8.3, 8.16, 9.1
Linnaean classification 3, 5, 15, 69–70, 116, Fig. 5.3
Linnaean (Linnean) Society 5, 6, 77, 172, 188
Linnaeus, Carl: life 3, 69–74, 187, Figs. 1.1, 5.5; quotes 3, 47, 54, 72, 74; *see also* floral clock, Linnaean classification, Linnaean Society
Llewelyn, Emma Thomasina Table 5.1, Pl. 5
Llewelyn, John Dillwyn 77, 115, Fig. 5.7, Table 5.1, Pl. 5
Llewelyn, Thereza Mary Dillwyn 77, Fig. 5.7, Table 5.1
Loudon, Jane: life 18, 187; quotes 99, Figs. 6.5, 9.11
Loudon, John Claudius: life 187; quotes 22, 67–8
Lubbock, Sir John William 180–2, 187
Lyell, Sir Charles 168, 172–3, 184, 187

M'Cosh, J. 166, 177–8
Maeterlinck, Count Maurice 69, 187
Marcet, Jane 72, 187
Masson, Francis 2, 22, 95, 122
microorganisms 137, Fig. 8.4
microscope 135, 139, 145, Fig. 8.4; microscopic subjects 135–9, 145, 159–60, 165, illustrations of Figs. 8.1, 8.2, 8.3, 8.4
Miller, Hugh 25, 26, 74, 169–71
Miller, Philip 47, 117–18, 187
Millican, Albert 117, Fig. 6.13
Montague, Lady Mary Wortley 37, 187
Moriarty, Henrietta Maria 63
Morris, William 30, 182, 187, Fig. 4.1
moth pollinators 144, 147–8, 152–3, 174, 179, Fig. 8.8
Müller, Fritz 143, 145, 152–3, 155, 187
Müller, Hermann 143–4, 187, 275
Murchison, Sir Roderick Impey 25, 168, 170, 172, 187
museums 6, 139

Natural History Museum 139, 169
natural selection 172, 173–4, 179
natural theology 49–51, 53; viewpoint on specific topics 54, 58, 142, 161–6, 177–9, *see also* Paley, William
nature reserves 181
nature study *see* botany in schools
nectar 63, 64, 140–1, 144–5, 147n1, 161; of orchids 147–51
nectary 55, 152–3, 174; illustrations Figs. 8.7, 8.9, 8.13

Nesfield, William Andrews 21, 187, Figs. 2.4, 2.5
night flowers 54, 144, 179, Figs. 8.7, 8.8
Noah's flood 167–8
North America 29, 170, 186, 188; collecting in 127–30, 185; plants of 62, 100, 104, 121, 127, 129, 156, Fig. 8.16
Northumberland, Duke of 110, 115
nurserymen 12, 14, 117–18; *see also* Lee, Veitch

Oldham, Richard 122
orchid craze 114–16
Osborne 99, 121
ovules 64, 140, 192
Owen, Sir Richard 169, 172, 187
Oxley 124

Paley, William 163, 172–3, 187 *see also* natural theology
Palm House, Kew 21, 107–9, Fig. 6.8
paper flowers 3, 29
parasite 60, 114, 192, Figs. 4.7, 6.6
parterres 13, Fig. 2.5
Paxton, Sir Joseph 10, 97, 110, 112–13; life 22, 187, Fig. 6.11; *see also* Crystal Palace, Duke of Devonshire, Great Conservatory, Chatsworth
Penny Magazine 25
perfume 179
petrified trees 167, 172, Fig. 9.5
pinetum 121
pistil 64, 192; *see also* stigma
plant: dyes 163, Fig. 9.2; naming 5–6, 73–4, 109, Fig. 5.5; sleep 69, 153–5, 157; use 47, 161–4, Figs. 9.2, 9.3
pollen 135–7, 139–40, 144–5; illustrations Figs. 8.2, 8.5; of orchids *see* pollinia
pollination 139–41, 146–7; *see also* orchids, Plant Index
pollinia 148–52, Figs. 8.10, 8.11
poisonous plants 56, 166, Pl. 15
Pope, Alexander 50, 187
Pope, Clara Maria 187, Fig. 3.4
Portland Duchess of 3–5, 11
Pratt, Anne 20, 37, 53, 73, 187
Pre-Raphaelites 30, 184, 187, Pl. 1
Prince Albert 37, 104

Queen Adelaide 9, 115
Queen Charlotte 2–3, 5
Queen Victoria 9–10, 26, 37, 99, 104, 109, 115, 186, 187

railways 18–20, 80, 104, 167–8, 187, Fig. 2.10
rain forest 60, 99, 101–3, 111, 117–19, Fig. 6.6
Redouté, Pierre-Joseph 2–3, 187
Repton, Humphry 13, 188
Robinson, William 42, 100–1, 185, 188
Romanticism 10–11, 13, 39, 49, 85
Rousseau, Jean-Jacques 10, 49, 53, 188
Royal Horticultural Society 13, 106, 114, 118, 122, 123
Ruskin, John: attacks on science 6, 70–1, 143, 180, 181; life and thoughts 50, 181–2, 184, 186, 188

Schomburgk, Sir Robert Hermann 109, 115, 153, 188
seedling 142, 153
seeds 64, 135–7, Fig. 8.2

self-pollination 140
sentimental flower book 3, 6, 10-11, 32, Pls. 2, 3
Shakespeare, William 10, 32, Fig. 3.4
Shelley, Percy Bysshe 188, Fig. 8.15
Siegesbeck, Johann 73-4
Sikkim Himalaya *see* Himalayas
Smith, Charlotte 68, 188
Smith, Sir James Edward 5-6, 64, 77, 184, 186, 188
Smith, William 167-8, 188, Fig. 9.6
South America 49, 60, 109, 145, 153; *see also* rain forest
Sowerby, James 32, 79, 188, Figs. 5.1, 5.5
Sprengel, Christian Konrad 141, 147, 173, 188
stamen 54, 70, 144, 192, Pl. 16, Figs. 8.5, 9.10
stigma 70, 140, 192, Figs. 8.5, 9.10
Stillingfleet, Benjamin 3-4, 188
Stourhead 19, fig. 3.8
stove house *see* glass-house
Sturtevant, Edward Lewis 163, 188
style 49, Pls. 16, 17

Talbot family 74-7, Table 5.1
Talbot, William Henry Fox 74-7, Figs. 5.6, 8.1, Table 5.1
Taylor, John Ellor: life 25, 172, 188; quotes: general 26, 64-5, 142, 147, 180-1, moral 58-60, Fig. 4.6
*Temple of Flora* 6, 39, 188, Figs. 1.1, 1.2, 2.13
Thiselton-Dyer, Lady Harriet Ann 79
Thiselton-Dyer, Sir William 79
thorns 47, 166
Thornton, Robert John 6, 72, 188
timescale 166-72, Figs. 9.4, 9.5
Turner, Dawson 77, 186, 188
Turpin, Pierre Jean François 2, 32, 188
Twamley, Louisa Anne (Mrs Meredith): life 23, 36, 188; thoughts 10, 23, 31-2, 49

Valentine cards 35, 38-9, 45, Pl. 4.
Veitch, James Harry 125
Veitch, John Gould 98, 127
Veitch Nursery 115-17, 153, 161, 188
verses Pl. 2; moral 55-7; sentimental 9, 32-3, 35-8, 42-3

Vitalism 182

Wallace, Alfred Russel 102-3, 119, 161, 188
Wallich, Nathaniel, 98, 106-7, 188
Wardian cases: decorative 15, 88-91, Figs. 2.7, 5.16; travelling 13, 89, 98, 107, 110
Ward, Nathaniel Bagshaw 89, 137, 188
Warner, Richard 58, 188
Wedgwood, John 13, 146
weeds 47, 51, 166, Fig. 4.3
White, Gilbert 79, 146, 188, Fig. 4.6
Withers, Mrs 115-16, 188, Pl. 10
Wood, John George 17, 54, 135-6, 188
woodland garden 42, 93, 100-1, 121
Wordsworth, Dorothy 49, 85, 188
Wordsworth, William 10, 42, 49, 85, 188, Fig. 2.1

Yonge, Charlotte M.: moral quotes, general 47, 50-1, 62, 142, specific plants 57, 59, 162-3, 166; sentimental quotes 30-1, 43-4, 87-8, 113-14

## PLANT INDEX

abutilon 112, 145; *Abutilon darwinii* 155, Pl. 13
acacia 103-4, 130, 154-5, Fig. 7.1
*Aesculus hippocastanum* 59, 158, Fig. 2.10
American fly-trap 62
*Anagallis arvensis* 54, 68, Fig. 4.3
anemone 23, 59
*Angraecum sesquipedale* 152-3, 174, Fig. 8.13
*Apocynum androsaemifolium* 62
aquilegia 42, 48, 55, Fig. 4.5

banana 95, 103, 106-7, Pl. 6
burnet rose 176, Pl. 5
butterfly orchid 148, 151, Fig. 4.4, 8.9

carnation 38, 79, 95
carnivorous plants *see* sundew, Venus' fly-trap
*Cattleya skinneri* 114-15, Pl. 10
columbine 42, 48, 55, Fig. 4.5

*Dactylorhiza praetermissa, D. fuchsii* 147, Fig. 8.10
daisy 38, 52-3, 69
*Dendrobium devonianum* 107, Pl. 11
dogsbane 62
*Drosera rotundifolia* 87, 89, 137, 157-60, Figs. 8-17, 8.18
'dwarf Cavendish' banana 106-7, Pl. 11

*Equisetum* spp. 170, Figs. 9.8, 9.9
evening primrose 54, 121, 155, 179

ferns 44, 137, 169-70; fascination and use of 15, 26, 84-8, 166, 185; illustrations Figs. 5.12, 5.13, 5.14, 9.7; *see also* fernery, General Index
forget-me-not 33-36, 38, 39, Fig. 4.3, Pl. 14

geranium *see* pelargonium
goat's-beard 67-8, Fig. 5.2
golden-rayed lily of Japan 98, Fig. 7.2
gorse 73, 164

hawkweeds 67-8
heartsease 30, 174-5, Pl. 4
*Hedera helix* 49, 56, 60, 164
hibiscus 103, 155, 163, *Hibiscus rosa-sinensis* 103, Pl. 12
*Hieracium* sp. 67-8
hollyhock 32-3, 42-3, Fig. 3.6
honeysuckle 42, 144, Figs. 8.7, 8.8
hop 20, 65, 153, Fig. 2.11
horse chestnut 59, 158, Fig. 2.10
*Humulus lupulus* 20, 65, 153, Fig. 2.11

insectivorous plants *see* sundew, Venus' fly-trap
ivy 49, 56, 60, 164

lilies, *Lilium auratum* 98, Fig. 7.2
*Listera ovata* 63, Fig. 4.9

mallow, *Malva sylvestris* 68, 135, 155, Figs. 8.2, 8.5
mimosa, *Mimosa pudica* 154-5, Fig. 8.15
*Musa acuminata, M. Cavendishii* 106-7, Pl. 6

*Nepenthes distillatoria* 106, 161, Fig. 9.1
North American pines 18, 29, 100, 104, 121, 127-8
*Nymphaea alba* 65, 68

*Odontoglossum crispum* 117
oenethera 54, 121, 155, 179
orange fruit 103, 104, 162-3
orchids: collecting 116-19, Fig. 6.13, (Pl. 11); cultivation 95, 114-15, 116, 186; fascination and use of 113-16, 163, 177, Figs. 6.12, 8.14, Pl. 10; pollination 147-53, 174, Figs. 8.9, 8.10, 8.13
*Osmunda regalis* 86, 112, Figs. 5.14, 5.15

pansy 30, 38, 42, 174-5, Fig. 9.11, Pl. 4
passion flower 49, 102, 103, 135-7, 145, 155
pelargonium 2, (12), 95, 137, 139, 160, 174
*Phyllitis scolopendrium* 86, Fig. 5.13

*Picris hieracloides* Fig. 5.1
pink 12, 22-23, 30, 38, Fig. 2.12
*Pinus lambertiana* 121, 127-8, Fig. 7.3
pitcher plant 62, 106, 161, Fig. 9.1
*Platanthera chlorantha* 148, 151, Figs. 4.4, 8.9

rhododendron 99-101, 121, 126-7, Pl. 9; *Rhododendron dalhousiae* 99, 127, 132, Pl. 7
*Rosa pimpinellifolia* (*R. spinosissima*) 176, Pl. 5
rose 3, 37-8, Figs. 1.2, 4.1; quotes 9, 30-1, 39, 47, 55, 59; *see also* burnet rose
royal fern 86, 112, Figs. 5.14, 5.15
royal water-lily 2, 109-12, 121, Fig. 6.10

scarlet pimpernel 54, 68, Fig. 4.3
scarlet runner (kidney) bean 146-7
snowdrop 42, 44, 59, Fig. 5.4
*Solanum dulcamara* 55-6, 177-8, Pl. 15
spotted orchid 147, Fig. 8.10
sugar pine 121, 127-8, Fig. 7.3
sundew 87, 89, 137, 157-60, Figs. 8.17, 8.18
sweet briar 29, 42, Fig. 5.10

toad-grass 74, Fig.5.5
*Tragopogon pratensis* 67-8, Fig. 5.2
tree fern 93, 103, 106, 113
tulip 23, 56-7, 58, Fig. 2.13; (*Tulipa greigii* Pl. 14)

*Ulex europaeus* 73, 164

*Vanda coerulea* 116-17, Fig. 6.12
Venus' fly-trap 89, 156-7, Figs. 8.3, 8.16
*Victoria (regia) amazonica*, Victoria water-lily 2, 109-12, 121, Fig. 6.10
*Viola (V. tricolor)* 175, Fig. 9.11

water-lily 43, 65, 68, 106, Fig. 6.9; *see also* Victoria water-lily
woody nightshade 55-6, 177-8, Pl. 15